When Pigs Could Fly and
Bears Could Dance

When Pigs Could Fly and Bears Could Dance

A History of the Soviet Circus

Miriam Neirick

THE UNIVERSITY OF WISCONSIN PRESS

Publication of this volume has been made possible, in part, through support from the Andrew W. Mellon Foundation.

The University of Wisconsin Press
1930 Monroe Street, 3rd Floor
Madison, Wisconsin 53711-2059
uwpress.wisc.edu

3 Henrietta Street
London WC2E 8LU, England
eurospanbookstore.com

Printed in the United States of America

Library of Congress Cataloging-in-Publication Data

Neirick, Miriam.
When pigs could fly and bears could dance: a history of the Soviet circus /
Miriam Neirick.
    p.   cm.
    Includes bibliographical references and index.
    ISBN 978-0-299-28764-1 (pbk.: alk. paper)
    ISBN 978-0-299-28763-4 (e-book)
1. Circus—Soviet Union—History.   2. Circus—Political aspects—Soviet Union.
I. Title.
GV1805.S65N45   2012
791.30947—dc23
2011043507

For my parents

Contents

I decided to make an aviatrix of my pig Chuska. At that time there was a great deal of talk about the aviator, Charles Leroux, who had just lost his life in a balloon accident, and about his successor Gordon, who took balloon flights in several large Russian cities. So I wanted to make worthy aviators of some of my animals, and my first choice fell on Chuska.

I ordered an air balloon of white, paper-like cotton cloth and a parachute of silk.

The balloon rose by means of warmed air, so before the performance I built an oven out of bricks. Straw was burned in this while the balloon, attached to two posts, hung over it. It took thirty soldiers to hold it as it expanded. When the balloon was blown up enough, the soldiers let go the ropes and it rose into the air.

But first it was necessary to teach Chuska to fly. I was living then in a villa in St. Petersburg, on Krestovsky Island. I arranged on my balcony a pulley and some leather straps covered with felt. The pig was brought to the balcony, and I began my first lessons with her. I put the straps around her and by means of the pulley began to draw her upward. Chuska's legs dangled helplessly in the air. Struggling with them and not finding solid ground under them, she gave vent to a terrible squeal. Then I raised toward her as she wriggled in the air a cupful of her favorite food. Smelling the familiar odor, she began to reach toward the cup and, busy with eating, grew calm again. . . .

Afterward I arranged a small landing-place, on which I placed an alarm clock.

Then began the lessons in real flight. As usual, I held a cup of food toward Chuska, but when her nose was about to touch the edge, my hand drew the cup away. Chuska stretched forward to reach the food, a little farther and a little farther, until she jumped from the landing-platform and swung in the straps. At the same moment the alarm clock rang. I repeated this procedure several times, and every time the alarm clock rang, Chuska knew that her cup of food would be given to her, and in her eagerness for the desired cup, she jumped off and swung in the air of her own accord. In this way, she learned that at the ring of the alarm clock it was necessary to jump from the platform into the air. . . . .

At last the performance began. The balloon was filled with warm air. On a little platform in the balloon stood the pig. To her was tied the lower end of the parachute, while the upper end was fastened to the top of the balloon with ropes strong enough to support the weight of the parachute, but no more.

An alarm clock was placed on the little platform beside Chuska, and was timed to ring within a few minutes.

The balloon began to rise, and, when it was quite high, the alarm clock rang. The pig, accustomed to jumping from the platform at this sound, leaped from the balloon and fell like a stone, but at once the parachute began to open, and Chuska, evenly and glidingly swinging, safely descended to earth before the eyes of the astonished spectators, who madly applauded.

After this first flight, the daring Chuska took thirteen other aerial journeys. She traveled all over Russia and exhibited her art in many places. . . . Such is the history of the first four-legged aviators.

V. L. Durov, *My Circus Animals*

Illustrations

Acknowledgments

I am so very grateful to the institutions, organizations, and, most especially, to the people who have given me so much help over the past ten years. Their generosity, patience, smarts, and pure plain goodness have been the making of this book.

I owe a great debt of gratitude to the many institutions that provided funding for the project, including the United States Department of Education and the Mellon Foundation, which sponsored several research trips to Russia. At the University of California, Berkeley, the History Department, the Graduate Division, and the Institute for Slavic, Eastern European, and Eurasian Studies provided significant support for the research and writing of the dissertation on which this book is based. I am also extremely grateful to the administrators of the College of Social and Behavioral Sciences and the History Department at California State University, Northridge (CSUN) who found funds among very scarce resources that allowed me to complete the additional research and revisions that were needed to prepare the manuscript for publication. Finally, I owe great thanks to the librarians and archivists at the Library of Congress European Reading Room, the Robert L. Parkinson Library and Research Center, the Los Angeles Public Library, the Russian State Archive of Literature and Art, and the State Archive of the Russian

Federation whose breathtaking knowledge and patient help were essential to completing my research.

This book was first a dissertation at Berkeley, and working with my advisors there was an uncommon delight. It was a true privilege to study with Yuri Slezkine, whose big brain and good humor made the process and, I hope, the product both intellectually rigorous and fun. His advice and encouragement also propelled this project forward over the past four years, for which I am so thankful. I am extremely grateful to James Vernon, who agreed, so generously, to serve as my advisor after Reggie Zelnik's death. He was a close and thoughtful reader whose advice was always pragmatic and affably offered. I owe many thanks, too, to Eric Naiman, whose enthusiastic and careful comments improved the dissertation significantly. Finally, I will always be so grateful to have studied with Reggie Zelnik, who helped shape the project at its inception and whose commitment to serious and humane scholarship remained its lasting inspiration. I hope that this book will stand as a worthy tribute to him, as to all of my teachers.

This project was very lucky to have lived its second life among my colleagues at CSUN. Many of them have read and commented on more of this book than I should ever have asked them to, most have offered constant support, both emotional and institutional, and all of them have participated in creating a department where teaching, learning, talking, reading, and writing about ideas are pursued and promoted in un-embarrassed earnest. It is a very special place, and I am so lucky and very proud to be a part of it. I thank especially: Patricia Juarez-Dappe, Jeffrey Auerbach, Richard S. Horowitz, Susan Fitzpatrick-Behrens, Thomas Devine, Clementine Oliver, Donal O'Sullivan, Erik Goldner, Josh Sides, and Merry Ovnick.

I owe many thanks to Gwen Walker, my extraordinary editor at the University of Wisconsin Press. She is the best. Working with her has been one of the most pleasant and valuable parts of this whole process, from start to finish. The manuscript has benefited tremendously from the care she took with it, as have I.

I am immeasurably, unspeakably, endlessly, tearfully thankful for my friends, who have provided encouragement, diversion, the best conversation, endless laughter, and so much happiness over the past many years. Many have read at least a part of the book with an eagerness that has touched me as deeply as their ideas have enriched the project. I thank especially Vince Cannon, Ian Chesley, Christine Evans, Sarah Horowitz, Michael Kunichika, Brad Reichek, Tom Roberts,

Victoria Smolkin-Rothrock, and Daniel Ussishkin. Anna Ruvinskaya, always in a category all her own, read and commented on substantial sections of the manuscript in addition to providing constant help with Russian translations. I am very lucky and so grateful to have found in Los Angeles a community of people who have given too much of our time together over to talk about this project, which would never have made it without them. There are two people who have really been with me through it all, and this book has been as much a part of their lives as mine, for my better and for their worse. They are Casey Santiago and Shawn Salmon, and if you look up friendship in a dictionary you'll find a picture of them there. I will spend the rest of my life thanking them for being my people.

Mostly, I am grateful to my parents, who made this, and everything I do, possible. I don't have the words to thank them. I can offer only those that follow, which are dedicated to them, with love.

Abbreviations

GARF	Gosudarstvennyi Arkhiv Rossiiskoi Federatsii (State Archive of the Russian Federation)
GOMETs	Gosudarstvennoe ob"edinenie muzykal'nykh, estradnykh i tsirkovykh predpriiatii (State Association of Musical, Variety Theater, and Circus Enterprises)
GUTs	Glavnoe upravlenie tsirkov (Main Administration of State Circuses)
Narkompros	Narodnyi komissariat po prosveshcheniiu (People's Commissariat of Enlightenment)
NEP	New Economic Policy
RGALI	Rossiiskii gosudarstvennyi arkhiv literatury i iskusstva (Russian State Archive of Literature and Art)
RGASPI	Rossiiskii gosudarstvennyi arkhiv sotsial'no-politicheskoi istorii (Russian State Archive of Social and Political History)
Soiuzgostsirk	Vsesoiuznoe ob"edinenie gosudarstvennykh tsirkov (All-Union Association of State Circuses)
TsUGTs	Tsentral'noe upravlenie gosudarstvennykh tsirkov (Central Administration of State Circuses)

Note on Transliteration and Translation

The transliterations in this book follow the Library of Congress system with a few exceptions for conventional English usage. Familiar last names have been rendered in a form without the apostrophe used as a soft sign (e.g., Gogol, Gorkii). Spellings in the endnotes and bibliography all cohere with the Library of Congress system. Translations are mine unless otherwise indicated.

When Pigs Could Fly and
Bears Could Dance

Introduction

Nikulin's World

On August 27, 1997, the *New York Times* reported the "most compelling event for Russians this year." It was the death of Iurii Nikulin, the seventy-five-year-old circus clown and comedic film star.[1] The day Nikulin died, Russian President Boris Yeltsin tearfully addressed the nation in mourning. "It is a day of deep grief for all of us," he said in a televised broadcast. "Nikulin, beloved by everyone, is no more."[2] Yeltsin, together with Prime Minister Viktor Chernomyrdin, First Vice-Premiers Anatolii Chubais and Boris Nemtsov, and the presidential Head of Staff, Valentin Iumashev, later paid his final respects to Nikulin, whose body lay in state for two days in the ring of the Moscow Circus on Tsvetnoi Boulevard. They were joined there by thousands of Nikulin's admirers, as "all Moscow seemed to be saying its farewell."[3] Mourners arrived at the circus on foot—the massive crowds had forced municipal authorities to close the streets and the metro station at Tsvetnoi Boulevard—and some waited as long as two hours to enter the building.[4] Those living outside of Moscow sent letters of sympathy just as earlier they had addressed their good wishes and offers of help to the clinic where Nikulin had lain in intensive care for more than two weeks. As his health declined, the nation held collective vigil, listening to reports on his status—"all the news began and ended with them,"[5] and they included "the kind of detail usually reserved for a head of state."[6] People of all ages and ranks had made their way to the clinic, hoping to donate blood or simply offering "any possible help," as Chernomyrdin had pledged upon his visit to Nikulin's sickbed. Iurii Luzhkov, the mayor of Moscow, and the Russian Health Minister, Tatiana Dmitrieva, also had stood by the ailing clown, as had the city's top medical specialists, who assembled each day to discuss any possible treatments.[7] Yet, sadly, there was no help to be given, and Nikulin died on August 21. In the words of the state press release, Russia had been "orphaned by the loss."[8]

Nikulin was buried at the Novodevichy Cemetery in Moscow, the final resting place of such renowned Russian and Soviet cultural figures as Anton Chekhov, Nikolai Gogol, Vladimir Maiakovskii, Konstantin Stanislavskii, and Dmitri Shostakovich. Two days after he was interred, the managers of Russia's leading diamond mining company named a large, recently unearthed diamond for the late clown, following a tradition of naming diamonds after such national gems as Aleksandr Pushkin, Andrei Sakharov, and Mikhail Bulgakov. Weighing 62.79 carats, the Iurii Nikulin diamond placed its namesake on the hierarchy of Russian luminaries well below Pushkin, whose nominal diamond weighs 320.6 carats, but very close to Sergei Prokofiev, whose diamond weighs 79.6 carats.[9]

At the time he died, Nikulin was, by all accounts, the "best-loved man in Russia," and he was, in fact, a clown.[10] His starring roles in such hit movies as *The Diamond Arm* (1968), *The Caucasian Captive* (1967), and *Twelve Chairs* (1971) certainly helped to secure his fame, but his film career was first launched by his success in Soviet circus rings, where he enraptured audiences for more than thirty years. Nikulin, himself, always insisted that, "by profession," he was a clown,[11] and his obituary in *Pravda* acknowledged that viewers of all generations considered Nikulin an excellent film actor, but emphasized that "many, many remember and love him as a brilliant circus master, a genial, but at times also caustic clown."[12] Valerii Kichin, reporting Nikulin's death in *Izvestiia*, remarked that "in a country divided by discord, where ill-will has become all but the specialty of the house, everybody was united in their love for a clown."[13] This love, he noted, was unique.

Kichin was not the only observer impressed by this uncommon love for a clown, which was shared by so many people with so little else in common. *Pravda*'s obituary began, simply, "Russia mourns. A person known and beloved in every home has died."[14] Ukraine also mourned, as did Kazakhstan. James Meek reported in the *Manchester Guardian Weekly* that Nikulin was beloved by "tens of millions" in homes across the former Soviet nations, while his obituary in the *Guardian* recognized the unique ability of Nikulin's humor to cross the class divide: "He drew affection from every sphere of today's divided Russian society, from the poorest pensioner to the richest New Russian businessman, from the most highbrow intellectual to the most brutal gangster."[15]

Even before his death, Nikulin's admirers marveled at the clown's power to unite people who were divided in nearly everything but their love for him. In 1996, the Moscow Circus held a jubilee celebration in honor of the clown's seventy-fifth birthday. "On the day of the jubilee," the accompanying almanac stated, "people gathered who could only gather together on this occasion." Scholars, businessmen, actors, writers, cosmonauts, artists, and statesmen came together to celebrate with the clown, and they were joined by many more who watched the event on television. The birthday of one man became a "mass [*vseobshchii*] holi-day," a reminder "that there are still things that touch everybody alike, as if time had not divided us."[16] Of course, it was not really time, or not only time, that had divided them. Gender, profession, age, education, nationality, religion, class position, and political loyalty divided them, just as it had before. But even then, in the Soviet Union, everybody loved Nikulin. As the circus magician Igor' Kio said in his 1999 memoir, "both Bolsheviks and democrats loved him."[17] No matter what, a clown could bring them together.

This may seem strange, but it is entirely consistent with the popularity and prominence of the circus in which Nikulin worked. Daniel Williams, writing for the *Washington Post*, attributed the outpouring of grief at Nikulin's death to the "Russian love of the circus, probably Russia's foremost communal experience." Like others, he emphasized the uni-versality of its appeal, noting that "rich, poor, Communist, dissident, Christian, Jew, Muslim or atheist, all Russians were taken to the circus as kids and take their own kids to the circus now."[18] Williams was right to associate Russians' love for Nikulin with their love for the circus be-cause, in more than one sense, Nikulin stood for it. Valeria Korchagina, writing for the *Moscow Times*, noted that Nikulin's performances in the Moscow ring won such wide renown that it became impossible to think of the one without the other.[19] After he retired from the circus ring in 1983, Nikulin served first as the artistic director of the Moscow Circus and then as its general director, a position he held until the year of his death. His name then became literally synonymous with the Moscow Circus when it was renamed for him. Still to this day, every afternoon before the circus begins, during every intermission, and every evening when it ends, throngs of children pile into a huge bronze car parked in front of the circus. Nikulin, also huge and bronze, stands with the door open for them, smiling with apparent approval at their refusal ever to hold still long enough for their parents to take a picture.

A Brief History of the Imperial Russian Circus

In short, everyone was so crazy about Nikulin at least in part because everyone was that crazy about the circus, and this was really nothing new. Neither Bolshevik nor democrat, dissident nor Jew, the first great Russian lover of the circus was, rather, an enlightened absolutist monarch, convert to Russian Orthodoxy, German by birth. Catherine the Great loved the circus. She first encountered the entertainment in the early 1790s, when Charles Hughes, the manager of London's Royal Circus, arrived in St. Petersburg. Hughes and his partner, Charles Dibdin, founded the Royal Circus in 1782 to compete with Hughes's former employer, Phillip Astley, who had established Astley's Amphitheatre in London in 1768. Astley is credited with having created the first modern circus, an entertainment that initially consisted only of his performance of tricks on horseback. Astley's equestrian displays made a hit with English men and women of high birth, but few others were so interested in the entertainment value of horses. The showman soon widened his production's appeal by introducing such popular fairground performers as jugglers, acrobats, tightrope walkers, sword-swallowers, strongmen, and clowns into the act. The Royal Circus did the same with similar success. In 1790, Hughes traveled to St. Petersburg with his stud of horses and a small troupe of performers, who, upon their arrival in St. Petersburg, staged Russia's first circus.[20] Catherine was so taken by the circus and its proprietor—Hughes was himself an accomplished trick rider and became, some speculate, Catherine's lover—that she ordered amphitheaters built for him in St. Petersburg and Moscow. Hughes spent three years in Russia, staging circus shows and teaching the equestrian arts. When he left, his horses, his students, and a market for the circus remained.[21]

In Russia, as in western Europe, the circus held a broad popular appeal, and, as a consequence, it attracted entrepreneurs who recognized it as a sensible business venture. In 1827, Nicholas I commissioned Jacques Tournaire, the founder of an itinerant troupe of riders in France, to build the first permanent circus building in St. Petersburg. In 1830, M. N. Zagoskin sponsored the construction of Moscow's first tent circus in the Neskuchnyi Garden, and in 1853, Guards Colonel Nikolai Novo-sil'tsev secured the support of Nicholas I for his construction of a winter circus in Moscow. In 1867, Karl Hinne erected a wooden circus in Moscow with the help of Gaetano Chinizelli, who gradually wrested control of the circus away from him. Chinizelli soon found his own rival in the person of Albert Salomonskii, who built Moscow's first stone circus in 1880 on Tsvetnoi Boulevard. Meanwhile, in 1873, three brothers, Dmitri, Petr, and Akim Nikitin, had become the first native Russians to launch a circus enterprise, which enjoyed great success throughout the provinces. Nicholas II confirmed the brothers' reputations as the foremost circus masters in Russia when he commissioned them to raise two circuses on the Khodynka Fields to take part in the public celebrations of his coronation in 1896.[22] In 1911, the brothers opened the last prerevolutionary circus in Moscow, one of eighteen rings they managed at the time.[23]

Well into the twentieth century, the Russian circus continued to appeal to all kinds of people for very different reasons. As a child in Pskov, the future revolutionary sympathizer and avant-garde film-maker Sergei Eisenstein attended the circus with his father, who was also a fan of the entertainment. Eisenstein recalled that his father preferred what he called "high class equestrianship" to the clowns that he him-self so dearly loved. "I have adored clowns since I was in my cradle," Eisenstein explained, admitting that he concealed from his father his "passion for clowns and pretended to be wildly interested in horses."[24] Eisenstein never outgrew his love for the circus, as his friend and corre-spondent Sergei Iutkevich recalled. The two were so "crazy about the circus" that in the early 1920s they made a habit of signing their letters to each other as "Pipifax." "It was a joke name in the fashion of clowns," Iutkevich explained. "Eisenstein was 'Pipi' and I was 'Fax.'"[25]

For different reasons, the circus also enthralled the young Aleksandr Benois, future director of the Ballets Russes, highbrow aesthete, political conservative, and snob. Benois fondly recalled the trained horses, balle-rinas, and acrobats of the Chinizelli Circus. He loved the musical clowns and the trained dogs and monkeys, but most enjoyed "the performance of a ventriloquist who manipulated a whole group of large comical dolls."[26]

Aleksandr Kuprin, a writer who left Russia after the revolution but returned to the Soviet Union in 1937, recalled that "the circus delighted, excited, and made all of us happy in our early youths." "Who of us," he asked, "escaped its miraculous, healthy, and fortifying magic? Who of us has forgotten that bright light, the pleasant smell of the stables, powder, and kid-skin gloves, the silk and satin of the brilliant circus costumes, the crack of the whip, the sleek, strapping, beautiful horses, the bulging muscles of the athlete?"[27] If anyone had forgotten, Kuprin's wildly popular tales of the circus and its performers might have reminded them. In "The White Poodle," the story of the adventures of an elderly organ grinder and a young acrobat named Sergei, Kuprin conjured the dream of joining the circus. After a long, hot, and thankless day, the two performers lay down to sleep, and "for a while the old man tossed and groaned and mumbled, but to Sergei the voice seemed to be coming from some soft and sleepy distance, and the words were as mysterious as in a fairy-tale." The old man was voicing "his favourite after-dinner thoughts about Sergei's brilliant future in the circus. . . . 'First of all I'll buy you an outfit: pink tights with gold, and satin shoes, also pink. In Kiev, Kharkov or, say, the city of Odessa—that's where they have real circuses! Lamps as thick as stars, all electric. Perhaps five thousand people sit there, or even more—I don't know exactly.'"[28]

In Anton Chekhov's rendering, this fantasy appeared to be more a nightmare than a dream, at least to the dog Kashtanka, who, upon returning to her cold-hearted owner after living briefly under the care of a kindly animal trainer, recalled the dingy room she had shared with her two colleagues, a gander and a cat, as well as the delicious meals they ate, the lessons they learned, and their performances in the circus, all of which "seemed to her now like a long, tangled, oppressive dream."[29] Iurii Olesha, a writer and Bolshevik fellow-traveler who became increasingly disenchanted with the revolutionary project, also represented the circus as a source of liberation in his novella *The Three Fat Men*, though without any of Chekhov's obvious ambivalence. The story's heroes are two circus performers who risk their lives to free an entire town from the oppressive reign of three opulent, corpulent men.[30]

Of all of the creative young minds entranced by the circus in Russia, Olesha seems to have been affected the most profoundly. He wrote that "as a boy and for many years afterward as an adult, the show I liked best of all was the circus."[31] On Saturday nights in Odessa, Olesha used money he had saved by skipping lunch all week to purchase a ticket into "that plush paradise, that paradise of marble and gold, of steps and little corridors, of arches, and frosted lamps, and echoes, and laughter, of shining eyes, and perfume, and the clicking of heels." The circus made such an impression on Olesha that he was tempted to say, looking back, that it lay at the "base" of his life. Scanning his past, he could most clearly see the "yellow ring with its scattered little figures of animals and people dressed in crimson velvet and in sequins." He could most distinctly hear "the crack of a whip like a pistol shot (and it pleases me to know that the whip was called a *chambriere*) and the shout of the clown." Though as a boy Olesha aspired only to be an acrobat, with no thought of becoming a writer, when he grew up he perceived that "perhaps the dream of being able to do somersaults was the first stirring in me of the artist, the first sign that my attention would be directed toward the world of imagination, toward the creation of things new and out of the ordinary, toward brightness and beauty."[32]

Of course, not everyone in Russia loved the circus because it awoke in them an impulse to create, and only very few became prominent writers, artists, cultural critics, and therefore memoirists. Most people left no record of their impressions of the circus, yet their love for it was not lost on those who made it their business to know the interests of the people.

A Brief History of the Soviet Circus

Vladimir Il'ich Lenin recognized the popular appeal of the circus and, for that reason, he liked it too. On August 26, 1919, Lenin signed a "Decree on the Unification of the Theatrical Concern" that, among other things, mandated the state appropriation of private circuses, "enterprises that are, on the one hand, profit-making and, on the other hand, democratic by virtue of the public that attends them."[33] The old Salomonskii Circus on Tsvetnoi Boulevard soon became the First State Circus, and the Nikitin Circus became the Second State Circus, both to be administered by the newly established Circus Section of the People's Commissariat of Enlightenment's theater department.[34] Within two months, the Second State Circus made its debut to a full house, and on September 1, 1920, the First State Circus staged its first performance.[35] In January 1921, the Circus Section supervised the incorporation of all private circuses within the Russian Republic into local departments of public education. Two years later, these circuses came under the centralized control of the Central Administration of State Circuses (Tsentral'noe upravlenie gosudarstvennykh tsirkov, TsUGTs), which had administered the two Moscow circuses since it was founded in 1922.[36]

The relative efficiency with which the Bolsheviks organized the circuses—they established the state cinemas, by contrast, only in December 1922—was the earliest indication of the prominent position the circus would long maintain in the Soviet Union.[37] In 1924, state circuses opened in Kiev, Nizhnii Novgorod, Leningrad, Orel, Tver', Rostov-on-Don, Kazan, Ivanovo-Voznesensk, and Tula. Together with the first Moscow State Circus—the second had since been closed—they attracted 1.5 million viewers in the 1924/25 season.[38] In 1927, Khar'kov also became home to a state circus, and total ticket sales reached two million.[39] Five years later, the number of circuses had grown to forty-six.

Since 1930, the State Association of Musical, Variety Theater, and Circus Enterprises (Gosudarstvennoe ob"edinenie muzykal'nykh, estradnykh i tsirkovykh predpriiatii, GOMETs), under the People's Commissariat of Enlightenment, had administered the circuses, but in 1936, the Ministry of Culture established the Main Administration of State Circuses (Glavnoe upravlenie tsirkov, GUTs) to manage them exclusively. In 1939, sixty-nine stationary circuses and fourteen traveling circuses operated in the Soviet Union, reportedly reaching nineteen million viewers annually.[40] During World War II, three "brigades" of Moscow circus artists performed more than 1,900 shows at the front, while still others made 10,679 appearances among military units and in hospitals.[41] By the war's end, only fifty-three, by some accounts fifty-two, circuses remained: at least thirty-four in Russia, one summer tent circus in Belorussia; two winter and four summer circuses in Ukraine; one each in Georgia, Azerbaijan, Uzbekistan, Kyrgyzstan, and Latvia; and one summer circus in Estonia.[42] Yet within ten years, sixty-five circuses were back at work, reportedly producing 71,910 shows for nearly twenty-eight million viewers annually.[43] In 1960, nearly thirty-four million people attended the circus, and, although no additional circuses were opened, more than thirty-nine million tickets were sold in 1965.[44]

In 1964, Laurens van der Post, a South African traveler, toured the Soviet Union and, wherever he went, he "never missed a circus."[45] He was thrilled that his own favorite Soviet pastime was so highly regarded by the Soviet people and so well funded by the state. He "found the circuses even more significant than ballet, theatre or opera, for the importance of the circus to the ordinary people themselves is evident."[46] As he explained in his travelogue, every major city featured a permanent circus, many housed in buildings of unparalleled opulence: "At Rostov-on-Don, for instance, the circus building with its front of soaring Corinthian columns and classical gable . . . has really to be seen to be believed. Inside it has more glittering tiers than a Hollywood wedding cake. Tier upon dazzling tier rise to a vast domed top and boxes, each lined with rich red velvet and finished off in curved cream and gold balconies festooned in plaster of Paris flowers, fruit and figurines *a la troisieme empire*, mount above them."[47]

The Soviet government invested in its circuses to the very end. In 1961, plans for the construction of a new circus in Moscow were announced, and ten years later the Great Moscow Circus at Vernadskii Prospect made its debut. It sold more than two million tickets in its first fourteen months.[48] In 1965, the Ministry of Culture authorized the All-Union Association of State Circuses (Soiuzgostsirk), which had managed the circuses since 1957, to borrow funds from the state building bank in order to finance the construction of twenty stationary circuses and twenty traveling circuses by 1970.[49] By 1976, more than twenty permanent circuses had been built from Alma-Ata to Zaporozh'e,[50] and within three years, box-office sales were estimated at eighty million annually.[51] In 1985, the Moscow circus on Tsvetnoi Boulevard was closed for renovations that lasted until 1989.

In 1986, Iurii Nikulin asked himself how many times a person in the Soviet Union attends the circus in his or her life, "not a person who particularly loves the circus, not a fan of the art of the ring, but a regular person." He concluded that in a city with a circus, of which there were quite a few, "a person goes at least three times: the first time his parents take him, the second time he takes his children, the third time he goes to the circus with his grandchildren."[52] Many people, of course, went much more often, though the weekly attendance by such fans as Olesha and I. I. Zheltov, the Assistant Chairman of the People's Commissariat of Turkmenistan, who admitted that in 1925 he had become so attracted to the circus that he could "not go for more than a week without it," probably was not typical.[53] Moreover, assuming grandchildren went once separately with their grandparents, Nikulin's reasoning actually placed the total number of lifetime visits to the circus at four. Yet Nikulin's arithmetical error is easily forgiven—by the time his career began elephants no longer solved math problems in the ring—and his point is well taken as anecdotal evidence for the fact, documented more objectively by the statistics, that most people in the Soviet Union went to the circus more than once.

Foreign audiences, some of whom hardly cared for their own circuses, liked the Soviet circus too. After World War II, many foreigners got the chance to attend it at least once in their lives. In 1945, audiences in Tehran received the Soviet circus "warmly," and circus performers were among the representatives of Soviet culture invited to tour India for six weeks in 1953.[54] During the three years between 1956 and 1958, around seven million people in twenty different countries attended more than 2,000 productions of the Soviet circus.[55] In 1956, circus per-formers embarked on a two-month tour of Belgium, a country whose twelve small native circuses were able to, at that time, "just get by."[56] To meet demand in Brussels, where the Soviets consistently sold out the Cirque Royal, ten performances were added to the itinerary. From Brussels, the performers traveled to Marseilles, Saint-Etienne, and, finally, to Paris, where an estimated 18,000 viewers attended circus per-formances.[57] That same year, the Soviet circus made its first appearance in England, where audiences attended a total of fifty performances in London and Manchester, despite the decline in popularity that the English circus had experienced since the turn of the century.[58]

In 1964, the Soviet circus launched its first tour of the United States. It debuted at Madison Square Garden before 8,000 viewers (half the seats were kept vacant to preserve the intimacy of the one-ring show). Admittedly, not everybody was pleased with the performance. "Many a United States circus man" was, according to the *Washington Post*'s Dorothy Kilgallen, "in a tizzy over the coming tour of the Moscow State Circus." They knew, she wrote, "that the Russian show . . . tops any-thing we've seen in Yankee-Doodleland for quite some time."[59] They were right to worry. The era of the great American traveling circus had long since come to an end, in 1917, to be exact. By 1956, the number of American circuses had fallen from ninety-eight in 1903 to only thir-teen.[60] Still, in 1964, American audiences came out for the Soviet show, which returned to the United States twice in 1967, a fourth time in 1972, and again in 1978. Ten years later, after traveling to twenty-seven coun-tries the previous year, Soviet performers again arrived in the United States, and they returned finally in 1989 for a tour of twenty-six cities, nearly double the number scheduled the previous year.[61] The circus might not have been "the biggest, most thrilling thing" in American life, as the artistic director of the 1967 traveling troupe claimed it was in the Soviet Union, but the Americans seemed, nevertheless, to like it.[62]

It is well known that the Soviet people did not always get what they wanted just because they wanted it, and certainly not because foreigners wanted it too. The popularity of the circus alone did not secure its favor among Soviet cultural administrators. They liked it for their own reasons, though these reasons differed in 1919, 1991, and at many points along the way. There were many reasons to like the Soviet circus, and not all of them were shared at all times by the state officials, schoolchildren, and grandparents, shock-workers and shirkers, atheists, Christians, Muslims, and Jews, collective farmers and cosmonauts, poets and gangsters, Russians, Tuvans, Azerbaijanis, and Poles, Bolsheviks, democrats, and everybody in between, or entirely indifferent, who patronized it. The circus became and so long remained the darling product of Soviet culture because it appealed to so many different people in so many different ways. To secure the favor of the Soviet state while maintaining the devotion of the Soviet people was no common feat for a product of Soviet culture, and this book explains how the circus achieved it. It asks what the circus meant to so many who loved it and why the circus came to mean so much in the Soviet Union.

Squaring the Ring

Part of the answer has to do with the circus and part of the answer has to do with the Soviet Union. Since European showmen first launched the modern circus in the late eighteenth century, the variety, "ambivalence," and "multiple meanings"[63] of the entertainment—"a theatre of contradictions"[64] that "has proved open to widely differing ideological inflections"[65]—have accounted for its appeal to socioeconomically, demographically, and politically diverse viewers, who recognized in the spectacle different and even contradictory meanings. Where horses failed to appeal, the clown still might succeed. If magic tricks disappointed, the trapeze artists still might stun. Different people liked different acts, and they might also have liked, or disliked, the same act for different reasons. The stumbling persistence of the clown could give heart to people down on their luck, or it could assure those of greater means that their superior position was well deserved. It could provoke in each of them, for different reasons, a feeling of shame, compassion, indignation, indifference, amusement, or confusion. The female aerialist might thrill or disturb some with her strength, some with her grace, and some with her simultaneous embodiment of both strength and grace. As a space of magic, dazzle, and play, the circus provided temporary relief from the routines of everyday life. Some might have seen in this the promise of permanent escape, while others simply were glad to go home with their hearts a little lighter. The topsy-turvy world of the circus could alert its observers to the frailty of the hierarchies that structured their world, or it could convince them that the social order suffered upheaval only in such strange and extraordinary spaces as the circus.

In other words, the circus meant so much because it meant almost nothing, or at least nothing to the exclusion of anything else. Does the acrobat's flip mean that gravity can be defied, or does the possibility of injury prove that the laws of nature remain a constant constraint? Do the aerialists' tricks convince viewers that with the proper persistence they too might fly, or do they provide a delightful spectacle of nearly inhuman achievement? Does a satirical barb inspire hatred or sympathy for its target? Is a trained lion a model of civility or a savage threat to its tamer? Do the performances of foreigners exaggerate or minimize the differences between people? Are the illusionist's tricks a lesson in the art of deception, or in the art of eluding it? Do the clown's irreverent antics convince the audience to break the rules or do they imply that only a fool would try? Does the circus transform its viewers or is it transformed by the dictates of their tastes?

The meaning of the circus and its various subgenres was indeterminate, often contradictory, and, consequently, open to more than one interpretation. While this helps account for the success of the circus as a capitalist enterprise, it only makes the Soviets' patronage of it more puzzling. Why did a government with an admitted interest in using cultural objects to propagate transparent, monosemic, and didactic messages adopt a medium whose meaning remained so unfixed? Paradoxical as it may seem, the circus appealed to its Soviet producers for the same reason it appealed to capitalist entrepreneurs. Precisely because the circus was an indeterminate and contradictory art form, it was capable of meeting multiple, changing, and even contradictory demands, including those that the Soviet state itself placed on the circus. The political, ideological, economic, social, and cultural imperatives of the Soviet state underwent periodic revision, and the official demands placed on the circus, along with all other cultural products, changed accordingly. At different times, the circus had to do different things. It had to convey different messages, construct different myths, please different constituencies, and promote different interests. Because the circus was a varied and flexible medium whose content remained ambiguous, it was able to perform these tasks with exceptional consistency throughout the succeeding periods of Soviet history.

Soon after the revolution, when all forms of culture were called to public service, the circus became an arena for the literal enactment of the revolutionary leap forward. Members of the former dominant classes fell from their horses, the autocracy was toppled by a clown, and viewers were exhorted to help secure the Bolshevik victory, which was repeatedly dramatized in pantomimes, *tableaux vivants*, and record-setting jumps. The circus could dismantle one regime as easily as it buttressed the next, which meant that even as the civil war raged on, it offered proof that a revolution in both Soviet politics and culture had already been achieved.

With the partial restoration of the market economy under the New Economic Policy (NEP) in 1921, new demands were placed on the circus, the most pressing of which was that it turn a profit. In order to increase ticket sales, a new staff of state producers purged much of the explicitly revolutionary content from the Soviet circus repertoire, which came to resemble its capitalist counterparts more closely than its socialist revolutionary antecedent. Yet, according to its producers and boosters, the circus lost none of its revolutionary significance. To their minds it remained a modern, international, authentically proletarian, enlightening, anti-religious, and, therefore, a properly socialist and naturally revolutionary form of art. During NEP, the most significant upside of the circus was that unlike other recognizably bourgeois entertainments that flourished at the time, such as foreign films, shopping arcades, jazz bands, beer gardens, and romance novels, it was a popular and arguably revolutionary entertainment. Official commentators who ascribed an ideological meaning to circus performances effectively articulated the myth that under NEP, the revolution had not been undone, and that neither state nor society wanted to undo it, no matter how much they all might have liked the new products on the market.

Official cultural demands changed again in 1928, when the circus was enlisted in Stalin's revolutionary campaign to modernize the Soviet Union by collectivizing agriculture and rapidly industrializing the economy. During the period of the so-called Great Transformation, the circus became a showcase for athletic performers whose flips, flights, and fantastic turns were said to demonstrate that where there was a will, along with proper methods of socialist labor and the most advanced technologies, there was a way for the newly perfected Soviet men and women to break the laws of nature. Producers, performers, and official commentators presented circus productions as proof that gravity could be defied, that darkness could be made light, that human nature could be perfected, and that any obstacle could be overcome, even one as overwhelming as Russia's economic backwardness.

Once Stalin's revolution had been declared a success in the mid-1930s, the circus was rhetorically remade yet again. Specifically, it was said to incarnate the better, more joyous future that all Soviets had been promised and that all of them could see embodied in the young, strong, and smiling performers who brought the Soviet circus to life every night. By the mid-1930s, a new generation of performers, forged during the period of the "Great Transformation," had replaced the last of the foreign and unreformed performers who had once populated Soviet rings. Most observers agreed that these performers—all perfect products of Soviet socialism—had succeeded in transforming crowds of circus viewers into new Soviet men and women, who were inspired by the superhuman feats they saw in the circus to perfect themselves too. According to the official rhetoric, the revolution in the circus had finally been achieved. Commentators claimed throughout the late 1930s that young Soviet performers, who literally embodied the future in the present, realistically reflected the optimism of the smiling circus viewers, for whom life had become, very visibly, "better, . . . more joyous."[66]

During World War II, the circus again answered the call to service by mobilizing the population against its enemies and helping to sustain its morale. Wartime circus programs alternately inspired hatred and disdain for an enemy that appeared by turns ferocious and feeble, frightening and frail, but always fell in the end. During the war, the circus and the rhetoric surrounding it articulated the myth that nobody, not even a person with his or her head in the mouth of a lion, had anything to fear. It told the Soviet people that no matter how unfamiliar life had become, everything would go back to normal in the end.

The war finally did come to an end, but not everything went back to normal. The Soviet Union's allies in victory soon threatened to overtake it, not only militarily but also economically. Food, clothing, housing, husbands, and parents remained in short supply, despite the government's repeated promise to provide for the material security of Soviet families. Postwar circus acts advertised Soviet consumer goods, dramatized scenes from family life, and championed the benefits of cultured living while simultaneously exaggerating the threat that the western powers posed to all three. Together they implied that material prosperity was essential to national security and that the state's legitimacy rested on its success in providing for them both. After the war, the circus offered proof that the Soviet government was the only able and legitimate provider for all the happy Soviet families residing in well-appointed homes throughout the prosperous Soviet homeland, no matter how difficult each of them had become to secure.

After Stalin's death, Nikita Khrushchev and Leonid Brezhnev each attempted to ensure the martial and material security of the Soviet Union, in both cases by preparing for another great war with the west, which they simultaneously sought to avoid. This was a confusing foreign policy, considered contradictory by most and specious by some, which is why the circus proved to be one of its more able proponents, both at home and abroad. In the mid-1950s, circus performers began to tour the world, offering tidings of peace, friendship, and goodwill to audiences they addressed in the universal language of movement, gesture, kind smiles, white doves, and big fake flowers. Marquee performances by grateful Central Asians and friendly Eastern Europeans portrayed the Soviet Union as a multinational state that was neither aggressive nor imperialistic, while magic tricks and "cosmic" aerial flights displayed its superior scientific, technological, and military might. During the Cold War, the circus offered proof of the Soviet Union's seemingly incompatible claims to be the world's best guarantor of peace, its most advanced military power, its sole sponsor of world revolution, and its most favored nation.

Stalin's successors sought to improve relations not only with foreigners, but also with their domestic constituents, many of whom had grown disenchanted with a system of government that had managed to produce Stalinism, smother free expression, and subjugate Eastern Europe, but could not adequately supply consumer goods, accommodate individual initiative, or discipline a corrupt bureaucracy. Between 1956 and 1991, the circus sought to maintain public confidence in the Soviet system. Even as political consensus collapsed, subcultural groups proliferated, and economic privations intensified, the late Soviet circus offered proof that the system was still capable of renewing itself. Individual performers were given center stage, where they demonstrated their novel, unique, and idiosyncratic achievements, which contributed to the collective strength of the circus troupe. At the same time, clowns mocked individual troublemakers—shirkers, idlers, and alcoholics, mostly—while causing all sorts of trouble themselves, without really doing any harm. The late Soviet circus thus maintained the myth that the Soviet government would rid itself of socially harmful deviant individuals, while tolerating socially harmless deviant individuals, and nurturing all other forms of individuality, the free expression of which was the greatest source of collective Soviet strength.

The circus was made to do many different things in the Soviet Union, just as it was made to do many different things everywhere. Yet in the Soviet Union, all these different things had one thing in common: the circus always offered proof of certain fictions. Because the circus could mean almost anything, it could be used to tell almost any story, and the Soviet state had more than one story to tell, few of which were altogether true. Regardless of what viewers had been told in the circus, the Bolshevik victory had not been achieved by 1920, bourgeois forms of culture and commerce did exist under NEP, many obstacles continued to impede Soviet economic development in the 1930s, the Terror offered little reason to smile, the Nazis were frightening, the promise of post-war prosperity remained unfulfilled, nuclear war was a persistent peril during the Cold War, minority nationalities remained subordinate to ethnic Russians, and dissatisfaction, dissent, and the free expression of individual opinion did threaten to destabilize the Soviet system in its final decades. All of this was very bad news for the Soviet government, which is why it cultivated forms of art that made none of it seem to be true.

Official commentators were able to spin politically productive fictions about the content of the circus because acrobatic flips, fakirs' feats, precocious elephants, conversational clowns, and talking dolls rarely communicated any monosemic message that precluded or necessarily refuted the meanings officially ascribed to them. Plus, when the messages either attributed to or clearly conveyed by any given act contradicted a message that might have been propagated in the past, little evidence of the difference existed. This was because circus performances left very little material trace. Unlike dramatic performances that rely on a script, music that follows a score, or opera and ballet productions that leave behind a libretto, circus performances are almost vanishing acts. Only those viewers who were willing to search the archives or read back issues of *Circus, The Theater Herald,* or *Soviet Circus and Variety Theater* had anything more than their memory—if they even had that—to confirm that the Soviet circus was, for example, first celebrated as a properly socialist form of art because it featured an international array of circus workers, only later celebrated as a properly socialist form of art because it showcased performers who had been born and brought up exclusively in the Soviet Union, and only after this celebrated as a properly socialist form of art because it championed the universal principles of peace and international friendship to audiences around the world. The impermanence of circus performances is part of what made the entertainment so flexible, and this helps explain why the circus so easily and very credibly accommodated the changing political messages and contradictory myths that Soviet officials relied on all cultural forms to communicate.

The circus was unique among Soviet cultural products for the variety and inconsistency of the myths and messages that it reliably propagated for more than seventy years. It also told all of these stories exceptionally well. Because the circus spoke in the language of live performance, it seemed more likely than any purely verbal or visual representations to be telling the truth. Any Bolshevik banner could claim victory for the revolution, but the social hierarchy really was inverted in the circus when once-marginal performers became privileged employees of a central state administration. A short story, or even a newspaper article, could describe a shock worker's glorious deed, but circus performers really did achieve feats of physical strength and mental discipline in the ring. They also really were healthy, smiling, and, unlike the new Soviet men and women depicted in paintings, described in prose, and portrayed in musical films during the 1930s, they really did exist, undeniably, in the present. The circus really was cheerful, animal trainers really did react fearlessly to frightening situations, female aerialists really were both graceful and strong, the Soviet circus really was a success with audiences at home and abroad, minority nationalities really did take center stage, discrete acts really were parts of a harmoniously integrated whole, and clowns really did cause all sorts of trouble without bringing down the show. Whatever the official fiction, the circus could both be said and be seen to confirm it consistently, which also helps explain why Soviet cultural administrators chose to produce a mass entertainment that was so different from the didactic media, narrative art forms, and monumental modes of representation whose prominence in the Soviet propaganda state has been so thoroughly documented.

Us versus the West

The polyvalence of the circus distinguished it from most other forms of official Soviet culture, and it is also what allowed Soviet producers to reshape the entertainment in ways that made the Soviet circus different from most other national circuses as well. Most significantly, the circus proved flexible enough to accommodate changing socialist ideals and to articulate official Soviet myths no less effectively than it advertised the virtues and values of capitalism to audiences in Europe and the United States. The circus was one of the earliest products to appear on the commercial entertainment market that emerged in the late eighteenth century, when more people in Europe and the United States began to have extra time and money to spend on leisure activities. To capitalize on this new demand, British entrepreneurs invented the modern circus by integrating the various entertainments of the fairground, the court, the hippodrome, and the cabinet of curiosities into a single profit-seeking program.[67] During the nineteenth century, the development of the circus remained closely tied to the rise of commercial capitalism, as showmen, especially in the United States, perfected the new technologies of advertising and market research, demonstrated the benefits of a disciplined division of labor, created and commodified star performers, and promoted the myth of the self-made man, whom they claimed to embody.[68]

By the turn of the twentieth century, Euro-American circuses had become so closely associated with capitalism that some among the makers of Soviet culture objected to including the circus among the new state-produced Soviet arts precisely because, to their minds, it exemplified the worst aspects of commercial entertainment culture. These critics argued that bourgeois entrepreneurs had used the circus to corrupt viewers by providing them with a spectacle of danger, degradation, and eroticism that catered to the basest tastes of the crowd. The circus was, to their minds, a counterrevolutionary entertainment that had no place in the necessarily revolutionary, proletarian culture of the Soviet Union.[69] This argument obviously proved unconvincing, and proponents of the circus, who insisted that the entertainment could be turned toward properly socialist purposes, had prevailed by 1919.

Once the circuses were nationalized by the Soviet government, their new producers did take pains, both rhetorically and in practice, to distinguish the Soviet circus from its capitalist counterparts. For example, during the 1920s, circus administrators waged a so-called Struggle Against Risk, in which they sought to remove the dangerous stunts that they claimed excited the nerves of bourgeois audiences at the expense of "circus workers'" safety. Although Soviet productions continued to feature gravity-defying feats of stunning skill, safety lines became a fixture of Soviet circus rings, to the dismay of some performers, and neither performers, producers, nor official reviewers sought to attract audience interest in these routines by exaggerating the dangers they posed to the performer.[70]

Animal trainers also deliberately downplayed the risks they took in Soviet arenas. With the exception of the period during World War II, when animal acts called attention to the bravery and patience that allowed trainers to cow savage beasts, animal trainers most often presented themselves as gentle teachers or loving friends to their animals. Trainers and their admirers in the press commonly offered the example of Soviet training methods, which were based on kindness, understanding, and Pavlovian conditioning rather than the more violent practices that were purportedly employed in the west, as further evidence that working conditions were more humane under socialism than capitalism.

This was the same story told by Soviet circus performers working in most every circus genre, many of whom testified to the improvement in working conditions, labor relations, and consequently in the quality of their performances once the circuses came under state control. In circus programs, press profiles, biographies, and autobiographies, Soviet circus people were not cast as self-made men, like American producers and performers, but rather as workers whom the revolution had liberated from danger, degradation, and exploitation by rapacious entrepreneurs.

Soviet circuses also rarely exploited the spectacle of physically abnormal people that attracted audiences to the sideshows and midways of the American circus in the nineteenth century. Instead, the Soviet circus became an arena for the demonstration of socialist bodies at their best. Circus performances and the rhetoric surrounding them consistently communicated changing official ideas about the human body, which served as a site for political inscription throughout the Soviet period. Whether athletes and acrobats appeared as models of discipline, whose physical training viewers were meant to emulate, or as proof of socialism's triumph over nature, or as so many silent, visually spectacular signs of the universality of socialist ideology, or as evidence of the feats that individuals could achieve when they participated in Soviet collectives, their bodies were always invested with new and ever-changing meanings that confirmed official political myths.

The bodies on display in western circuses also communicated ideological tropes—in this the Soviet case was not unique—only they promoted a rather different set of capitalist, nationalist, and imperialist projects. For example, in the English rings of the Victorian era, "this consummate age of industry and empire," the powerful, dynamic, and beautiful body of the performer "became a metonym for progress and power,"[71] just as it did during the Soviet industrialization drive during the early 1930s. Yet in the Soviet context, performers, producers, and official commentators all attributed the perfection of circus performers' bodies to the introduction of specifically socialist methods of organizing labor, including, for example, state circus management and the staging of collective competitions among performers. Similarly, whereas the aerialist's flight in nineteenth-century European arenas might have "confirmed a belief that European culture was headed towards an unstoppable domination of the natural world and non-European societies,"[72] demonstrations of nature's conquest in Soviet arenas were meant to presage the Soviet Union's development into a modern, internally self-sufficient, socialist economy.

Like circuses in the west, Soviet arenas also frequently featured foreign nationals, non-Russian national minorities, and the trained animals that represented them in routines that certainly did articulate myths about empire and ethnicity throughout the twentieth century. But unlike Euro-American performances that sought to establish a hierarchy of human relationships that either justified or anticipated the political, economic, or ideological domination of one national, ethnic, or racial group over another, Soviet routines instead told a tale, no less fictional, about the peaceful incorporation of minority groups into the multinational Soviet family. This was the same message conveyed by Grigorii Aleksandrov in his film *Circus* (1936), the final scene of which depicts the Soviet people, represented as a circus audience, warmly embracing non-Russian national minorities, international racial minorities, and even the foreign exile and main character, Marion Dixon, who found refuge in the Soviet circus from both American racism and exploitation by her European circus boss. Not surprisingly, the message of Aleksandrov's film about the circus was consistent with the official story being told about it, according to which all the members of the multinational Soviet family were eager to share the benefits of socialism with all the peoples of the world, and most especially with those who were struggling to free themselves from capitalist imperialist domination.

Like acrobats, aerialists, and animal trainers, clowns also appeared to be model Soviet people, even though in their clumsy, bumbling, and madcap antics, they typically had stood at the farthest pole from all other circus performers on the spectrum of human possibility that western and prerevolutionary Russian arenas commonly showcased.[73]

Although complaints about the enduring presence of buffoonish clowns in Soviet circuses continued to surface throughout the century, the most prominent and popular Soviet clowns did abandon their garish makeup, exaggerated clothing, and slapstick comedy in favor of more naturalistic personas that were meant to express the optimism, good cheer, and proper political points of view purportedly maintained by everyday Soviet people. Unlike clowns in American circuses, where the large scale of three-ring productions made speaking impossible, Soviet clowns continued to perform in the so-called conversational genre, most often by acting out small scenes from everyday life or addressing topics of common political concern. In this way, clowns performed an essential ideological function in Soviet arenas, both by articulating official political messages and by embodying the characteristics that were officially approved for emulation by all Soviet people. Yet this kind of clowning in the Soviet Union became a rather tricky business, especially when clowns who claimed to be typical Soviet everymen continued to behave like clowns—breaking the rules, subtly challenging authority, and performing ambiguous routines that contradicted the official messages that they seemed simultaneously to affirm.

The spotlight also closely followed women's bodies in circuses everywhere, but performances by female acrobats, aerialists, animal trainers, and occasionally clowns in Soviet arenas were meant to demonstrate a set of feminine ideals that differed considerably from those propagated in the west. Soviet critics of the bourgeois circus complained, from the start, about the eroticization of female performers, and Soviet circus producers, performers, and official commentators consistently claimed to depict women not as objects of male sexual desire but as exemplars of the new Soviet woman.[74] Throughout the Soviet period, and particularly after World War II, when women began to appear even more prominently in circus productions and in the press coverage around them, female circus performers were said and could be seen to embody the characteristics that, implicitly, every Soviet woman should share: strength, flexibility, beauty, grace, discipline, courage, and in the case of animal trainers, a maternal regard for their charges. Women in Soviet rings were frequently congratulated for achieving feats that rivaled those of men, yet, according to the official rhetoric, even when women successfully served in traditionally male performance roles, they did so in uniquely feminine ways. For example, female animal trainers claimed that their maternal instincts allowed them to tame wild beasts, while the beauty, ease, and agility of female acrobats and aerialists were celebrated as the source of their success. In contrast, their male counterparts purportedly relied on strength and courage alone to achieve their seemingly impossible feats. In this way, the story the circus told about the ideal Soviet woman served to enforce the social position of all Soviet women, who were doubly burdened as both wage earners and domestic laborers throughout the Soviet period.

This was an ideological lesson that differed significantly from those taught in western arenas, where American showmen eroticized semi-nude female performers while also depicting them as "dainty, domestic ladies" in order to undermine the "radical potential of these 'new women,'" whose greater visibility in the circus coincided with the growing prominence of women in the American public sphere during the late nineteenth century.[75] The feminine ideal established in Soviet circuses also stood in contrast to the entirely different case of the colonial Australian circus, where aerial performances by strong women in motion "defied social conventions" that restricted women's freedom of movement and prohibited them from displaying their physicality.[76] By doing so, these acts conjured the fantasy—one that might only have been realized in the marginal space of the circus—of freedom from "social categories of gender"[77] and from "ideologies surrounding the body"[78] more generally. In both Soviet and non-Soviet arenas, female performers obeyed conventional gender norms while simultaneously dramatizing their own liberation from them. Yet it was only in the Soviet circus that the point of showcasing this contradiction was not to enforce obedience, as in the American case, or to encourage liberation, as in the Australian, but to deny that any contradiction existed. The assertion that women living under socialism had been liberated from an exploitive ideology of gender that they nevertheless happily maintained was a myth that the circus propagated consistently in the Soviet Union.

Throughout its history, the Soviet circus served as a productive site for the propagation of legitimating myths and topical messages about, for example, the New Economic Policy, World War II, Khrushchev's peace offensive, and *perestroika*, while along the way producers, performers, and commentators also communicated official ideas about gender, the body, ethnicity, empire, economic modernization, the relationship between Soviet state and society, and socialist culture more generally. Throughout its history in England, Europe, and the United States, the modern circus also proved rich in thematic resources that, in the Soviet case, cultural officials deliberately turned to significant political advantage. This is another reason that the circus became a central institution within the Soviet Union, and it was this very privileging of the medium, which was produced by a central state administration, promoted in the official press, and put to explicit political use, that ultimately marked the clearest point of difference between the Soviet circus and its commercial counterparts in Europe and the United States.

The Audience

The consistency with which circus performances served as a site for the elaboration of ideological messages and legitimating myths certainly helps explain why the entertainment remained so popular among the producers of Soviet culture. This might also account for the entertainment's popularity among its many consumers. Some viewers might have liked the circus because it confirmed familiar stories that they wanted to believe or already did believe. Some Soviets might have wanted to be told, for example, that the revolution had not been betrayed by the introduction of NEP, that they were building a better and more joyous future, that they had nothing to fear from the Nazis, that they enjoyed unparalleled prosperity during the postwar period, that they lived in the best, most peace-loving place in the world, and that they were free to break the rules and express their individuality without disrupting life as they knew it.

Yet those same stories were also often contradicted by everyday experiences, and some viewers might have liked the circus because the tales it told were so easy to miss, so simple to ignore, and so often contradicted by the performances themselves. However thoroughly circus performances were made to accommodate the official demands placed on them, they maintained much of their indeterminacy. If the circus was revolutionary during NEP, why was it not revolutionary during the Terror, or during the thaw, or during the so-called era of stagnation? If it provided lighthearted entertainment at one time, why did it not at any other? Why did it celebrate individuality only during *perestroika* and not during the collectivization campaign? Even when it was meant to provide good cheer, the circus still involved grave dangers, just as it celebrated rule-breakers at the same time it indicted them, and alleviated fear even as it provoked anxiety.

The message of many circus routines remained confusing and contradictory, while other acts might have seemed not to mean anything at all. A stunning leap was no less stunning because a clown called it a symbol of the revolution. An aerialist's flight was as spectacular a sight as it had been before it was made to perform any political function. To see a lion leap through a ring of fire was to be amazed, whether or not a war was on. Magic tricks were no less enchanting if they failed to promote the superiority of Soviet science, Tuvan jugglers were entertaining whatever purpose their celebrity was meant to serve, and it was funny to see a clown chase a piglet around the ring, regardless of whose part the swine was playing. The circus could always just be novel, fun, and enchanting. Like no other form of official art in the Soviet Union, the circus offered its viewers a means of escape from the messages, exhortations, and tall tales that it, along with most other Soviet cultural products, was made to convey.

Circus performances alone could not compel all viewers to apprehend their significance correctly, which is why press reviews, pamphlets, and programs also told the viewers what the performances were supposed to mean. These publications undoubtedly helped some of them make sense of the show, and while they could not guarantee that all viewers considered, comprehended, cared, or concurred with what they had to say, the officially ascribed meaning of the circus might also have been reinforced by the simultaneous dissemination, through other media, of the messages the circus was meant to convey and the stories it was made to tell. For some viewers, this might have secured the meaning of the circus, though others might still have missed it.

The political meaning of the Soviet circus for its patrons was potentially as varied and ambiguous as the content of the spectacle itself. This conclusion refuses to assign any constant, universal, theoretically established political function to the circus,[79] and it might seem unsatisfying to scholars eager to understand whether the entertainment served or subverted the Soviet system. Yet the answer to this question must remain agnostic if it is to recognize the heterogeneity of Soviet audiences, who are often homogenized by observers of mass culture and, like Soviet subjects generally, essentialized by historians of the Soviet Union, as Choi Chatterjee and Karen Petrone have observed.[80] The modern circus was designed to appeal to diverse audiences who could discover in it many different meanings, and this helps account for its popularity among Soviet audiences as well. Some Soviet viewers might have been delighted to learn the lessons that others attended the circus specifically to avoid, and some might have become convinced of the myths that others thought circus performances belied. Despite the official rhetoric, some viewers continued to consider the circus a vulgar, bourgeois, inadequately revolutionized entertainment, and they might have seen it as a discredit to the government that produced it. Yet others might have appreciated the Soviet state for providing them with a purely enjoyable entertainment that lacked much overt ideological content.[81]

This was an uncommon situation in the Soviet Union, where the government consistently cultivated forms of culture whose meaning remained fixed, transparent, and resistant to subjective interpretation. Yet this was little cause for concern to its state producers, since, if nothing else, the circus always met the disparate demands of both state and society and, to all appearances at least, confirmed the congruity of those demands. Producers, performers, and official commentators consistently claimed that circus audiences patronized the circus for the same reasons that state officials purportedly produced it, no matter how far those reasons diverged or how often they changed. Circus audiences proved very easy to mythologize because so little indication of their real reactions ever existed. The absence of any reliable evidence regarding the reception of the circus is an obvious obstacle for historians, except insofar as it helps explain why Soviet officials privileged its production. For them, the virtue of the circus lay not only in its purported utility as a purveyor of political messages, ideological fictions, and legitimating myths, but also in the ease with which its audience could be idealized. Because audiences offered no indication of their responses to the show, other than those that were officially solicited and readily manipulated, Soviet commentators could effectively establish the myth that audiences clapped, laughed, and kept buying tickets to the circus for the same reason that state officials claimed to produce it. The essential fact for the producers and official observers of Soviet culture was that so many Soviet people had good reason to like the circus, which they also had good reason to like, regardless of whether, in truth, those reasons were the same. No matter how far the political demands, cultural desires, and basic perceptions of the Soviet people and the Soviet state diverged, they appeared to be consistent in the circus. In this way, the circus helped maintain what was perhaps the most essential legitimating myth for the Soviet government: the myth of popular consensus. The circus—both its performances and the rhetoric surrounding them—always offered proof that the Soviet people got everything they wanted and always wanted everything they got from the Soviet government. It told them that they all liked the same things and that they liked them for all the same reasons.

As far as the circus went, this even might have been true. It is possible that everyone liked the circus for the same reason, which, itself, might have been the reason why everyone liked it. State officials, school children, and grandparents, shock-workers and shirkers, atheists, Christians, Muslims, and Jews, collective farmers and cosmonauts, poets and gangsters, Russians, Tuvans, Azerbaijanis, and Poles, Bolsheviks and democrats all might have liked the circus because liking the circus was something they all had in common. The Soviet circus might have appealed to so many different people because it gave each of them the impression that neither gender, profession, age, education, nationality, religion, class position, political loyalty, nor anything else divided them. This was, after all, what it meant to be Soviet, which might be another reason why the circus became such a central part of life in the Soviet Union.

Perhaps it was for the loss of this experience, the experience of being Soviet, that so many people wept when Nikulin died. His was the death of the Soviet everyman, and perhaps when people mourned his passing, they also mourned the passing of the possibility that an everyman could ever exist again. Without him, they might have felt themselves bereft not only of their best-loved clown but of the best proof they had that the differences between people were not inalienable. The greatest sorrow they suffered might have been to know that they would never again be told that there was such a thing as a perfect community and that this community was theirs. This story—the story of the Soviet Union—died with Nikulin because his death was also the death of the Soviet circus, which might have been the one place in the world where this story really did come true. Maybe, in the end, that was the reason why everyone liked it.

Why not? When pigs could fly and bears could dance, anything was possible.

1

The Circus Turned Upside Up
Revolutionizing the Russian Circus

In 1918, Vitalii Lazarenko, the Soviet Union's "First Red Popular Jester," compared the Bolshevik revolution to a leap.[1] In the opening monologue of his circus performance, the clown announced:

Rossiiskikh groz bezumnye raskaty
Trevozhat mir prizyvom:
Schast'e kui.
"Bol'sheviki, o bud' oni prokliaty!"
Vezde tverdit vzvolnovannyi burzhui.
Skorei, skorei
im propisat' blokadu
Chtob slyshat' ikh rabochii nash ne mog
Prizhat', uniat',
no cherez ikh pregrady
V umy liudei my delaem pryzhok.
Pust' staryi mir pletetsia ponemnogu
I slavit trakt zaezzhennykh dorog.
K svobode, k schastiiu naidia svoiu dorogu
Chrez tsarskii tron
my delaem pryzhok.[2]

[The dreadful peals of the Russian storms
trouble the world with their call:
forge happiness.
"Bolsheviks, oh be they damned!"
repeats the nervous bourgeois everywhere.
Hurry, hurry
organize against them
so that our workers cannot hear,
clasp, or soothe them,
but we are leaping across their obstacles
into the people's minds.
Let the old world trudge along little by little
and glorify the path of hackneyed roads.
Finding our road to freedom, to happiness
we are taking a leap
across the tsarist throne.]

After reciting these verses, Lazarenko literally enacted the revolutionary leap by vaulting across a series of obstacles that had been placed before him in the ring.[3]

Lazarenko's leap goes a long way toward explaining why the circus—a western European import that was peddled by bourgeois entrepreneurs and patronized by the Imperial autocracy—was first incorporated into the Soviet cultural administration. Routines like Lazarenko's demonstrated that circus performances could accommodate the revolutionary messages that all forms of art were mandated to propagate at the time, which was an obvious upside of the circus from the Bolsheviks' point of view.[4] Just like songs, festivals, posters, and plays, postrevolutionary circus performances told the story of the revolution and celebrated its victory. For a time, the Soviet circus became an arena for the enactment of the revolutionary leap, and the Bolsheviks' successful transformation of a bourgeois entertainment into a form that championed the revolution was presented as proof that the leap really had been made.

It should come as no surprise that the circus was another of many popular prerevolutionary forms of culture that the Bolsheviks appropriated in order to propagate ideological messages. What does come as a surprise is that circus producers began to purge much of the new, explicitly revolutionary content from the circus repertoire in 1920, when some cultural administrators began to worry that the purity of the circus was being corrupted. Aesthetic concerns prompted this policy shift,

which was then institutionalized as a result of the economic imperatives that were introduced under the New Economic Policy (NEP) in
1921. In order to stabilize the Soviet economy after the civil war, NEP
provided for the partial legalization of private trade, the partial restoration of some property rights, and the partial elimination of subsidies for
cultural enterprises like the circus, which now had to compete in a
much more saturated cultural marketplace. In order to maintain ticket
sales, its producers restored the circus to its recognizably prerevolutionary form. All of this meant that evidence of the revolutionary leap
had become rarer and, therefore, as highly prized as the profits that
state circuses were now required to turn, which is why their producers
and boosters energetically insisted that the revolution in the circus had
not been reversed.

Between 1921 and 1929, the rhetoric surrounding the circus, rather
than the show itself, was revolutionized, as official commentators maintained that even entirely conventional circus programs provided edifying demonstrations of physical strength, the disciplined will, a conscious
attitude toward labor, and atheism. Because NEP-era productions once
again featured sequences of spectacular physical tricks that refused to
communicate any single message or tell any seamless story,[5] they readily
accommodated the novel meanings ascribed to them by Soviet commentators, who put ambiguous circus acts to political use by rhetorically
investing them with messages that were consistent with Bolshevik
political imperatives. During NEP, the most significant upside of the
circus was that unlike other arguably bourgeois entertainments that
flourished at the time, such as foreign films, shopping arcades, jazz
bands, beer gardens, and romance novels, it was a popular and arguably
revolutionary entertainment.[6] Official commentators who ascribed an
ideological meaning to circus performances effectively articulated
the myth that even during NEP the Soviet people and the Bolshevik
government together were taking a revolutionary leap, rather than a
step backwards.

This myth was essential to Bolshevik legitimacy, and it relied on
another official fiction that became central to circus rhetoric at the time,
namely, that viewers received the revolutionary messages that circus
producers claimed to be sending them. Though official commentators
offered little evidence to prove this claim, there was hardly any evidence
to dispute it, which made circus audiences very easy to idealize. The
absence of any reliable evidence regarding audience reception was
another significant, if unacknowledged, upside of the circus for its state

producers and official reviewers. Their assertion that Soviet viewers attended the circus to receive the political messages that it purportedly propagated was uncontested by any concrete evidence. The official endorsement of the circus as an ideologically instructive entertainment, beloved as such by crowds of Soviet people, helped maintain perhaps the most important legitimating myth after the revolution—namely, that an ideal Soviet public shared the principles and adored the products of a truly revolutionary Soviet state.

The circus was one of many popular entertainments, art forms, and mass media that the Bolsheviks pressed into political service after the revolution. Soviet officials relied on easily accessible mass media such as posters, newspapers, short films, and radio programs, to propagate political ideas to broad audiences while also entertaining them.[7] They also sponsored the production of novels, fables, plays, festivals, and monumental sculptures that narrated the history of the revolution, depicted its heroes, and mythologized both.[8] James Von Geldern explains that the Bolsheviks also subjected more playful forms of popular culture, whose political significance was less certain, to "structural changes" so that they might more clearly communicate unambiguous messages and articulate political myths. Marline Otte locates a similar case in the context of interwar Germany, where the "eagle cowboy" Erich Rudolf Otto Rosenthal, alias Billy Jenkins, made deliberate "aesthetic choices" that transformed his once polyvalent Wild West circus act into "a useful tool for Nazi propaganda." When Jenkins first staged his act after World War I, he ensured its appeal to diverse audiences by relying on the "multiple meanings" of the eagle—"an 'empty sign' that could be filled with a wide range of potentially contradictory meanings" by symbolizing, for example, both internationalism and nationalism. Yet when the political situation in Germany began to change during the 1920s, Jenkins altered his acts—he "even trained his eagles to impersonate the living emblem on military standards, posing over an oversized German flag"—so that their "ambivalence . . . receded." Otte concludes that "what had once found special appeal on the basis of its multiple meanings came to represent one single meaning, and turned into a powerful endorsement of Nazi ideology."[9]

What makes the history of the Soviet circus in its first decade so surprising is that its producers so briefly and only ever incompletely made similar aesthetic choices to alter the structure of circus performances in order to secure their ideological valence. Instead, they preserved the circus in its conventional form and left its content ambiguous. Yet by doing so, they did not forfeit the political utility of the entertainment. Unlike other products of Bolshevik culture, the circus was not made to educate audiences, mobilize people politically, revolutionize Russian culture, transform the Soviet Union into a propaganda state, or unify the Soviet populace in its adherence to the ideology of socialism. It did, however, perform an entirely different, but no less essential political function: the circus helped maintain the myth that these incredible leaps had already been achieved.

The Revolutionary Circus

In 1919, the Circus Section undertook the task of "cleansing" the newly nationalized circuses of "unhealthy elements" and overseeing the further development of their artistic productions, as the decree of August 26 mandated.[10] Prominent members of the Soviet artistic avant-garde, such as Boris Erdman, Il'ia Ehrenburg, the poet Ivan Rukavishnikov, the ballet choreographer Kas'ian Goleizovskii, the painter Pavel Kuznetsov, the sculptor Sergei Konenkov, the theater director N. M. Foregger, and the sole circus "specialist" M. A. Stanevskii (also known as the clown "Bom") joined the staff.[11] Since few of them had any training in the circus arts, they were uniquely qualified to carry out their more specific mandate: to reform the circus by replacing its individual, discreet routines with long narrative pantomimes that dramatized revolutionary themes.[12] In this they largely succeeded. The state circuses' first three seasons did feature didactic theatrical spectacles that incorporated various circus attractions, as well as more classic circus acts that were invested with new ideological lessons.

The first revolutionary pantomime to make its debut was Ivan Rukavishnikov's "Political Carousel," which was staged at the Second State Circus in 1919 under the direction of Foregger on a set designed by Kuznetsov. The performance dramatized the struggle between labor and capital and culminated with the "joyous celebration of the liberation of labor."[13] That same season, the First State Circus also staged a pantomime on a less obviously revolutionary theme. Konenkov's "Samson and Delilah" featured circus wrestlers who created "living pictures" by assuming various poses to illustrate the events of the story. Konenkov later explained the ideological message that his spectacle was meant to send. He claimed to have been inspired by Maksim Gorkii's comparison of the prerevolutionary fate of the Russian people with the biblical image of Samson: "thrust to the ground by the heavy and rude mechanism of the poorly constructed state machine, the Russian people were constrained and blinded like Samson, who was truly a great sufferer." Konenkov claimed that viewers responded warmly to the parable of their own recent liberation from oppression.[14] Though Konenkov did not offer any evidence for this claim, his ideological message appealed to at least one person. Lunacharskii was an enthusiastic fan of Konenkov's project, and he explained its significance in an article advertising its debut. Lunacharskii identified the story of Samson and Delilah not as a biblical tale, but as one of the "most miraculous myths in the treasure trove of popular poetry." "A Titan," he continued, "who defends the freedom of his people, falls victim to female cunning, is degraded and blinded, finds in himself the strength to break his chains and emerge victorious."[15] Lunacharskii considered this to be one of the "most ancient stories of the struggle for freedom. . . . of the eternal struggle of light and darkness."[16] Konenkov's production was, in Lunacharskii's view, a true circus routine—a "routine of that circus of which we can dream, a circus of exceptionally noble beauty, capable of directly relating the physical perfection of the human being to a deep internal content."[17] Whether viewers recognized the ideological significance of the routine is not a question Lunacharskii addressed directly. His statement simply assumed that they did, and yet his explication of the pantomime's message could indicate some concern that the audience might otherwise have missed it.

By the following year, Lunacharskii's dream circus appeared incarnate in the arena of the First State Circus, at least according to Vitalii Lazarenko, who introduced the program:

Grazhdane!
Nash tsirk vstupil na novyi put'!
Otbrosim poshlost'.
Podnimem my svoe iskusstvo,
Chtob v tsirke
vy smogli dushoiu otdokhnut'
I radost' prinesti i zriteliu i chuvstvu.
I my, sluzhiteli areny tsirkovoi,
Na etot novyi put vstupaem smelo:
Vas shutkoi rassmeshim
razumnoiu, zhivoi,
Pokazhem krasotu i moshch',
i gibkost' tela!

Ekstsentriki, shuty, s trapetsii polet,
Uchenyi umnyi kon' i muskuly iz stali
Vse zdes' slivaetsia v odin vodovorot.
Otvaga i talant, pryzhok sal'to-mortale,
Ogni Areny vnov' segodnia zablestiat.
Artisty tsirka, my na
novyi put' vstupaem.
Seichas fanfary vam otkryt'e vozvestiat.
Itak—
My nachinaem![18]

[Citizens!
Our circus has set out on a new path!
We will cast vulgarity aside.
We will improve our art
so that in the circus
you can thoroughly
rest, and to bring happiness to the viewer.
And we, servants of the circus arena,
bravely set out on this new path:
we will amuse you with
smart and lively jokes,
we will show you the beauty, power,
and flexibility of the body!
Eccentrics, jesters, the trapeze flight,
the educated, intelligent horse and muscles,
everything here merges into one maelstrom.
Bravery and talent, the aerial flip, and
the Lights of the Arena will shine anew today.
Artists of the circus, we are setting out on
a new path.
Now the fanfares will announce the opening
And so—
We begin!]

After the cast of the show paraded around the arena, one group of performers entered again, dressed like workers and peasants, carrying saws, axes, blocks and poles, which they used to assemble several buildings. The performers concluded the pantomime by freezing in their positions to create a tableau vivant of "Workers Creating a City," as the act was titled.[19] The program also featured other miniature pantomimes that caricatured vulgar, infantile bourgeois women and mocked cowardly members of the Entente. The show then culminated in the second act, with the staging of Rukavishnikov's mass pantomime, "Chess." The spectacle featured a ring-sized chessboard, which served as the field of battle between "oppressors," in white, and the "oppressed," in black. The two sides were represented by well-known literary, theatrical, and folkloric figures, including, on the side of the oppressed, Freedom, Don Quixote, Carmen, a Traveling Minstrel, and a Balalaika Player, pitted against a Sultan, a Yankee, a Toreador, an Iron Knight, and a Friar. The combatants engaged in a lively struggle, using animals, illusion tricks, music, and most other conventional means of waging war in the circus. The side of the oppressed won the day. When the Workers' Leader captured the Sultan, he proclaimed, "Check," and the other black figures cried "Mate," prompting the vanquished oppressors to flee from the battlefield in a panic. The victors celebrated with a dance that ended in a still pose featuring Freedom, raised high above the rest, beckoning all the liberated peoples toward him.[20]

Like Konenkov, Rukavishnikov, and their collaborators, Vladimir Maiakovskii and his collaborator, Vitalii Lazarenko, also attempted to convey ideological messages through a conventional and very popular circus genre: the wrestling bout. Maiakovskii's "Championship of the Universal Class Struggle,"[21] which was staged by the Second State Circus in 1920, dramatized the struggle between the Bolshevik Revolution and an entire team of its enemies, who also competed among themselves for the spoils of the "Imperial War." Contenders included Lloyd George, Woodrow Wilson, Alexander Mitterrand, the White Army General Baron Petr Wrangel, the Polish nationalist Joseph Pilsudskii, and the "Almost Champion," a Menshevik. Lazarenko played the roles of Uncle Vania and the Revolution itself. Appearing as the former, he officiated the wrestling match. After introducing each competitor with a satirical monologue, he announced that a gold crown inscribed with the phrase, "Profit of the Imperial War," would be thrown into the ring. The wrestlers battled each other for the prize until finally Lazarenko announced the entrance of the "Champion of Revolution," a role in which he appeared after rushing backstage to change costumes. In a skirmish between "Revolution" and "Entente," the clown dexterously flipped his opponent, but failed to pin him. Suddenly transforming himself back into the character of the referee, Lazarenko proclaimed:

Ne mozhet poborot'
Ni eta storona, ni ta.
Peremirie.

T'fu!
Pereryv na desiat' minut.
Vse kto khochet
Chtob
Krasnye pobedili cherez desiat' minut,
pust' idut po domam—
—A zavtra na front dobrovol'tsami—
I Vrangeliu sheiu namnut.
A Ia
Uzhe
segodnia tuda zhe
a dlia skorosti
V ekipazhe dazhe.[22]

[Neither side
can defeat the other.
Truce.
Bah!
Break for ten minutes.
All who wish
that
the Reds will win, in ten minutes
should return home
and set off tomorrow to the front
as volunteers
to wring Wrangel's neck.
And I
already
am heading there today
and, for the sake of haste,
in a carriage, no less.]

By refusing to enact the Red victory, Maiakovskii exhorted viewers to carry the revolution to victory themselves. This device also introduced some suspense into the event, since a wrestling bout was hardly worth watching if everybody knew which side was going to lose.

Some circus performers did go so far as to dramatize the revolution's victory. For example, a troupe of equestrian clowns staged the defeat of the revolution's class enemies at the premier of the Second State Circus. In a classic circus sketch, known as "The Riding Lesson,"[23] or, in this case, "Madame Deni's Riding Lesson," the "Countess Deni" revealed herself to be a miserable student of the equestrian arts—a particularly damning failure given her class position. In the course of her riding lesson, Madame Deni lost her wig, became entangled in her crinoline gown, and drooped from her horse, from which she hung "suspended in the most surprising and amusing poses."[24] Monsieur Deni groaned in horror as the Denis' servant futilely attempted to right his mistress. In the climactic sequence, Madame Deni caught her foot in a loop fastened to the saddle and rode through the ring upside down. Circus artists similarly unseated the bourgeois family Brown, in "Mr. Brown's Riding Lesson." Mr. and Mrs. Brown entered the ring, arguing loudly with their grown son until the ringmaster managed to get their attention by announcing the management's intention to pay a large sum to whomever succeeded in standing upright on a moving horse. After attempting unsuccessfully to climb onto the horse all at once, the Browns decided that Charlie, the son, should try his luck. After a safety harness was attached to the performer, he cautiously mounted the horse, only to fall off as soon as it set out at a trot. Supported by the safety line, Charlie flew through the air, clinging desperately to the horse's tail. Mr. and Mrs. Brown chased after them, straining to grasp Charlie by the legs. They finally succeeded, and Charlie landed happily on the ground. Mr. and Mrs. Brown, no longer interested in taking their own turns, fled from the arena and abandoned their son, who was, literally, the future of their class. They soon lost their way and began to run toward the stables rather than the exit, provoking a last burst of laughter from the delighted crowd.[25]

Lazarenko was the performer best known for his dramatic enactments of the revolution, which he continued to figure as a stunning leap throughout the civil war—a period when the revolution's victory was hardly secure. If Iurii Nikulin was the last best-loved clown of the Soviet circus, Vitalii Lazarenko was the first. For nearly twenty years Lazarenko remained a fixture of the Soviet state circuses, where he served as the model Soviet clown, praised in his life, remembered for decades after his death, and given much of the credit for turning the circus upside up.[26] When Lazarenko launched his career as a clown in 1906, he adopted the *ryzhii*, or red-headed clown persona—a common, buffoon-like figure typically paired with a white-faced clown, known in Russia as the *belyi*, or white clown. The *belyi* clown, often called a *clown debonnaire* in France, was an elegant figure whose subtle makeup and fashionable costumes contrasted sharply with the stiff red hair and outlandish makeup of his madcap comrade, the *ryzhii* clown. In the traditional clowning team, order was maintained by the *belyi* clown, who attempted to discipline the disorderly *ryzhii*. For his part, the *ryzhii* flouted the *belyi*'s authority, regularly violating his partner's cherished rules and, more often than not, getting away with it.[27] For example, in "The American Duel," a classic prerevolutionary routine, the clowning duo, Lepom and Eizhen, challenged each other to a duel, which they executed by placing two scraps of paper, one marked "life" and the other "death," into a hat. The clown who drew "death" lost the duel and would be shot. Predictably, Eizhen, the *ryzhii* clown, drew "death" and, recognizing the horror of his predicament, he bid a dramatic farewell to Lepom and the distraught onlookers. Eizhen stumbled out of the ring and, soon after, a shot resounded in the wings. Melodramatically clasping his hands, Lepom moaned, "Oh, what have I done?" Within seconds, however, Eizhen reappeared, joyously announcing, "Thank God, a misfire!"[28] Although the disobedient clown obviously would have missed intentionally, he claimed to have obeyed the rules of the duel, attributing his survival to happenstance. In addition to demonstrating the *ryzhii*'s characteristic reliance on chance as a pretext for his own willful rule-breaking, this routine also exemplified the *ryzhii*'s immunity from the dictates of language—a synecdoche for systems of order and authority more broadly—since the written words "life" and "death" failed to dictate the enactment of the experiences they signify.

Although Lazarenko performed without a white-faced partner, he directed his typically red-headed irreverence toward the higher authorities of the Imperial Russian state.[29] In one exemplary prerevolutionary sketch, Lazarenko announced that the parliamentary Duma was so named because its only task was to think (*dumat'*)—it was not given anything to do. Lazarenko then read an explicitly anti-tsarist monologue condemning autocratic violence:

Za granitsei silu pushek
Izuchaiut Kruglyi god
I v svoikh tam ne streliaiut,
A u nas—naoborot.[30]

[Abroad, they study the strength of guns
the whole year round
and they don't shoot their own.
And with us, it's the opposite.]

In 1922, Lazarenko wrote that in his performances, he tried to respond critically to the social evils of the day, and his early routines often did address viewers' everyday problems. For example, after the February Revolution, the clown lured the ringmaster—the figure of highest authority within the circus ring—into a satirical dialogue. He asked the ringmaster, "Tell me, can a dog grow back a tail that's been cut off?" When the ringmaster replied with a resolute "No," Lazarenko responded that a dog could indeed grow back a tail and guaranteed to prove it. He explained that one must simply hang a sign from the dog announcing that flour is given out here, and the dog will grow five *khvostov*—*khvost* meaning both "tail" and "line."[31]

Whether or not it was actually funny, this joke exemplified the satiric humor that, according to Lunacharskii, Soviet performers should wield as an effective weapon in the revolutionary struggle. In a 1920 essay titled "We will laugh," Lunacharskii celebrated the kind of satire that provoked the indignant laughter in which could be heard "the snap of the whip and at times the peal of the approaching thunder of battle." For Lunacharskii, laughter was the "aspen stake that is driven into the recently slaughtered dark wizard, who is prepared to return from his coffin." It was "the hammering of sturdy nails into the black coffin of the past." Lunacharskii explained to his readers that they must not consider any victory over a vile enemy to be decisive, especially if the enemy is an entire class or an entire culture. Such an enemy, he wrote, "entangles you from every side with thousands of poisoned threads, and he has thrust some of these tentacles into your very mind, into your very heart, and, like any hydra, he can be born again from any shoot." Lunacharskii insisted that laughter could prevent this regeneration: "There is such a substance, such a disinfectant, that makes everything foul evaporate—that is laughter, a great cleanser!" Lunacharskii concluded that "in our time, when we have thrown down a gigantic enemy only in Russia, when we are entangled by the miasmas of the old culture that poison all our air, when that enemy still triumphs all around us, waiting for the moment to inflict a new blow, in this time, without dropping our swords from one hand, we take in our other hand a weapon that is already sharp—laughter."[32]

Lazarenko needed both his hands and two strong legs to wield the revolutionary whip-thunderclap-stake-hammer-cleanser-antidote-sword of laughter, and he put them to good use. After the October Revolution, he continued to perform politically tendentious routines, which now, however, were directed not against, but in support of the established authorities. The irreverent *ryzhii* persona hardly suited Lazarenko's new role as the champion of the Bolshevik regime, and he modified his appearance accordingly. Lazarenko abandoned the *ryzhii's* red wig and exaggerated face paint in favor of a sanitized costume more typical of the *belyi* clown and, therefore, more appropriate to the serious work of cleansing the enemy from the hearts and minds of the Soviet people. Fulfilling Lunacharskii's mandate that the Soviet clown dare "to be a publicist," Lazarenko trumpeted the achievements of the new Soviet state, often casting himself in the role of Revolution in his individual monologues, as in his work with Maiakovskii.[33] For example, Lazarenko began one routine he performed in the Second State Circus by reading several couplets about freedom. He then pointed to an inflated bladder, shouted, "Attention—the old regime," and jumped onto it, causing the bladder to "burst with a deafening bang."[34]

The introduction of explicitly ideological routines like Lazarenko's into the Soviet circus repertoire has led several historians of Soviet culture to conclude that the Bolsheviks turned the circus upside down. Richard Stites numbers the circus among the many forms of popular culture that the Bolsheviks "infused" with "revolutionary content," with the result that "this was no longer folk nor popular culture; it was elitist revolutionary enlightenment and pseudo-religious missionary work for moral uplift and political persuasion."[35] James Von Geldern also concludes that a contemporary Soviet critic was correct to accuse the Circus Section of "destroying the circus" with acts like Rukavishnikov's "Political Carousel."[36]

Yet the comic equestrian genre, for one, was hardly destroyed when it was made to ridicule members of the upper classes. Some viewers might not have even noticed that the hapless rider was named "Countess Deni" or "Mr. Brown," just as they might not have known that the story of Samson and Delilah was told as an allegory for the revolution. Similarly, while some viewers might have appreciated Lazarenko's performances because they celebrated the Bolshevik victory, others might have been thrilled by his leaps alone, which were no less stunning because he called them a symbol of the revolution. Others might have simply been excited by the bang of the exploding bladder, no matter what it was supposed to signify, and many might have remained unconvinced, in the midst of the civil war, that the Bolsheviks' revolutionary leap had, in fact, been achieved. A life-sized game of chess was a novel enchantment, as were the illusion tricks and trained animals that Rukavishnikov's pantomime also featured, and viewers might have enjoyed them regardless of whether they thought the Friar belonged on the side of the "oppressors" or "oppressed." Conventional circus acts that were infused with new revolutionary content or integrated into didactic theatrical spectacles still retained much of their appeal as extraordinary and amusing entertainments. The Bolsheviks did not manage to destroy the circus—or, from their point of view, to revolutionize it—by transforming it into an exclusive medium for ideological propaganda immediately after the revolution. While Stites's and Von Geldern's conclusion can be more convincingly applied to the few most didactic pantomimes, monologues, and *tableaux vivants* featured in the first several seasons of the state circuses, it still does not account for the fact that in 1920, Soviet cultural administrators began to remove these routines, for fear that they were destroying the circus.

Revolutionary Circus Rhetoric

In December 1920, the theater department repudiated the Circus Section's attempt to replace varied circus attractions with long narrative pantomimes and appointed a new staff of more experienced circus professionals to reverse the reform that had been implemented the previous year.[37] The administration denounced the "persistent striving to fundamentally 'theatricalize' the circus," which had "radically destroyed the pure forms of circus art and made it impossible to preserve tried and true circus traditions."[38] This reversal was initiated by Vsevolod Meierhold, who had been appointed to head the theater department in September 1920 and had long deplored efforts to "theatricalize" the circus, though Maksimilian Nemchinskii convincingly argues that economic imperatives, in addition to purely aesthetic concerns secured the policy shift. He notes that the Soviet circuses continued to feature large-scale, narrative pantomimes through the 1921 season, well after Meierhold's tenure had ended in February. He also explains that the Circus Section, which was renamed the Central Administration of State Circuses (TsUGTs) in 1922, was reconstituted as a self-financing trust at that time. According to Nemchinskii, this meant that "the administration had to solve the problem of devising programs according to old methods whose success would be guaranteed."[39] As a result, between 1920 and 1922, the pure forms of circus art were revived, the tried-and-true circus traditions were preserved, and the popularity of the circus was restored. Yet what Nemchinksii fails to note is that its producers continued to insist—vigorously, if not convincingly—that the revolution in the circus had not been reversed.

From 1922 until 1929, Soviet state circuses more closely resembled their western European counterparts and Imperial Russian antecedents than their immediate postrevolutionary predecessor. Programs featured conventional circus attractions that lacked much of the overtly ideological content with which they had been invested during the State Circuses' first three seasons. For example, one typical NEP-era routine was performed in Moscow in 1924 by the German acrobats Peters and Billy. The arena was set with tables, chairs, and barrels to resemble a bar, in which the acrobats staged a series of tricks seemingly for their own amusement. Billy climbed onto the shoulders of Peters, who jumped into and out of the barrels, and onto the tables. Peters assembled the furniture into an elaborate pyramid and topped it with a chair. Billy sat on the chair, placed an apple on top of his head, and held a sword above it. Peters then leapt over Billy's head and pressed down on the sword with his leg so that it sliced through the apple. For their act's final trick, Peters jumped over four chairs that were standing in a row.[40]

This was hardly Lazarenko's revolutionary leap, which was a fact not lost on some NEP-era observers who noted that very little had changed in Soviet circuses since 1917. A delegation from the Voronezh circus reported to have "found no particular difference between the prerevolutionary and contemporary circuses" that they attended in Moscow even as early as 1921.[41] According to one review, the debut production of the First State Circus in 1922 was comprised entirely of "old acts."[42] That same season another critic complained that the "perfidious administration fed" those attending the Second State Circus "the worst numbers of past years."[43] As late as 1929, Sergei Sokolov stated that there was "still no Soviet circus."[44] He decried the absence of the "revolutionary agitator, the proletarian organizer of the masses" from Soviet circus productions, which continued to rely on "convention, the old traditions left to us from the bourgeois circus."[45] A. K. Finikov, a "working viewer" who was employed at a textile factory, agreed. In his statement, "The Circus Is Conservative," which was also published in 1929, Finikov complained that circus programs had not changed at all over the past ten to fifteen years: "It is possible that in the course of a season one or two contemporary, tendentious numbers will appear, but as a rule, the circus is still just marking time." In Finikov's view, acrobats, animal trainers, and clowns had yet to be mobilized effectively for the creation of "our authentic revolutionary circus."[46] Although this view had become canonical by 1929, it was not universally held or officially endorsed during NEP.

Precisely because the Soviet circus was so vulnerable to this criticism throughout the 1920s, its producers and many official observers insisted that the revival of what some considered a typically bourgeois circus actually marked the emergence of an authentically revolutionary entertainment—one that did serve as a political agitator and organizer of the masses. In 1925, Lunacharskii described the circus as being "close to the masses,"[47] which implied not only that the entertainment was popular but also that it could be used effectively to enlighten, instruct, and influence the Soviet people.[48] He explained that the Soviet state appropriated the circuses with the intention of using them as "one element of the new artistic-educational policies."[49] As Moris Gorei reported in 1928, it was precisely the edifying function of the Soviet circus that made it authentically revolutionary from its producers' point of view. Gorei quoted two circus officials who explained to him that "in the Soviet Union, the circus has been made into a 'school for the education of the worker and peasant masses,'" whereas the circuses of the capitalist west were useful only to the extent that they made a profit.[50] In the Soviet circus, he concluded, "the artist is not a phenomenon, but an instructor, who can be successfully imitated."[51] Yet neither Lunacharskii, nor Gorei, nor any other Soviet commentator was able to identify what distinguished Soviet performers, who could be imitated, from their capitalist counterparts, who could only be admired. This was because nothing at all, not even the profit motive itself during NEP, distinguished their performances, which was a point that seems only to have fueled the proliferation of official claims that the Soviet circus was an educational and, therefore, a revolutionary institution.

In May 1919, the animal trainer Vladimir Leonidovich Durov also assigned a pedagogical role to the "new healthy art of the circus," which he claimed would contribute to "the urgent enlightenment of the popular masses."[52] Durov considered this "key to the successful building of socialism,"[53] and he attempted to contribute to this project himself by literally transforming the circus ring into a "model school." In his memoir, Durov described the "school" he organized in the arena for his "four-legged and plumed friends" who "sat on benches like real school children."[54] The public, he recalled, was astonished to see his "pupils" turn the pages of specially made wooden books with their snouts, beaks, and fins. Even the ass, who sat on the last bench, turned the book's pages with his nose and roared loudly when asked to recite a lesson. All of the animals were diligent students, but Durov's elephant, appropriately named Baby, was the "head pupil" in the school and often received a 5+, the highest mark, for his demonstrations of knowledge and skill. When asked to add three plus four, for example, the elephant picked up an enormous piece of chalk with his trunk and drew seven lines on the blackboard. Seeing that the elephant had solved the problem, the pelican hissed in approval, but was immediately chastised by Durov, who shouted, significantly, "No prompting please! Mine is not an ordinary school, but a model school." Durov admitted that Baby occasionally drew too few lines, a mistake that would be corrected quickly by his dog Lord, who barked once for each line still needed. Sometimes Baby also drew too many lines, in which case Leo, the sea lion, would erase the extra lines with his fin. "The public applauded me and my pupils and laughed uproariously," Durov recalled. "It seemed to them an incredible thing."[55] Durov's act was meant to serve as an analogy for the custodial relationship that circus viewers and performers and, by extension, Soviet state and society, were meant to maintain during this period.

Even when they did not perform in actual model schools, trained animals were officially presented as the exemplary pupils of beneficent educators, as Karl Krane explained in 1926. In an article titled "The Secrets of the Tamer," Krane informed his readers that "first of all, there are no tamers, and secondly, there are no secrets."[56] Krane hoped to correct viewers' mistaken impression of the animal tamer as an embodiment of strength and courage. He insisted that a wild beast could not be trained by means of physical strength alone. "The psyche of an animal can be influenced only through calmness, kindness, and an innate love for animals," he wrote.[57] Krane concluded that "there are no tamers, only teachers [*vospitateli*]."[58]

According to the official rhetoric, other Soviet circus performers, whose work was less literally pedagogical than animal trainers', also taught viewers important lessons. In a 1925 essay on "The Child and the Circus," Lunacharskii claimed that athletic circus performances instructed children in the value of hard work. He described the performer as a "worker who achieves miracles by means of a persistent desire to attain perfection," and, consequently, provided children with a model of the "conscious relationship to labor."[59] According to Lunacharskii, children saw in the circus an example, which they might imitate, of physical strength and agility that had been achieved through patient lessons, systematic labor, and courage.[60] Later that year, another reviewer explicitly attributed an edifying function to athletic circus performances that, in his view, demonstrated the same rhythm and precision of movement demanded of industrial laborers. These performances acquired an "educational meaning," he claimed, when they were parodied by clowns, who repeated the actions of jugglers and acrobats more slowly and schematically in order to demonstrate the potential of the human body to move quickly, intensely, and dynamically.[61] "In general," he concluded, "many circus numbers can serve as a good method for the propagandizing of the principles of scientifically organized labor and for convincing the masses of its utility and necessity."[62] "Scientifically organized labor" was the Soviet term for Frederick Taylor's methods of scientific management.

In 1925, V. V. Shvetsov provided a somewhat different explanation of how athletic circus performances achieved edifying effects. He claimed that the strength and agility of acrobats first caused viewers to be stunned and then amazed. This sensation, in turn, provoked a feeling of jealousy, which prompted viewers to recognize their own incapacity, since, he claimed, they would not envy people who were weaker and worse than they were. "Envy," Shvetsov wrote, "is the first cruel reproach of oneself," but, he continued, "if I begin to feel envy, then that means that I not only have become conscious of my ugliness, but also that I want to rid myself of it. I want to possess those strong arms and legs, those strong muscles and teeth. From here, the step toward imitation, toward the re-education of myself is not so far."[63] Shvetsov left it for viewers to determine how their re-education would proceed, though push-ups, sit-ups, and the local physical culture circle, undoubtedly, would have been involved. As for the imitation of good teeth, it remained unclear what was to be done.

One of the more dramatic examples of Soviet rhetorical acrobatics during NEP was provided by fakirs and their promoters, who claimed that their performances convinced the Soviet people of the utility and necessity of possessing a strong will. In 1926, the circus director A. M. Dankman heralded the arrival in the Soviet Union of the internationally renowned fakir, To-Ramo (which meant "The Conqueror" in Sanskrit). To-Ramo was famed for the strength of his will, by means of which alone he purportedly was able to conquer the will of other creatures and overcome his own physical pain. In one routine that Dankman described, To-Ramo removed a wild eagle from its cage in the arena, and though the eagle beat its wings malevolently and threatened To-Ramo with its claws, the fakir instantly compelled it to lie lifeless before him. To-Ramo similarly subdued a boa constrictor with a single glance, forcing it to look indifferently upon a rabbit he had set before it, just as he had placed an unresisting chicken safely into the mouth of a pacified crocodile.[64] When asked to explain why he chose to perform in the circus, To-Ramo insisted that the promise of fame and fortune hardly enticed him into the ring, and that "only the conviction that I might show my viewers the strength of will a person can possess and inspire them to follow my example carried me into the arena."[65] "Strength of will," he continued, "is the most valuable thing that we can acquire in our heroic century. We have conquered and tamed nature, but we remain slaves of our will. A weak will is the scourge of contemporary society."[66]

Although To-Ramo and his admirers encouraged circus viewers to imitate his disciplined will rather than his actual "experiments," one Soviet promoter of the fakir arts did encourage viewers to try these tricks at home so that they might learn another lesson, namely in the deceits of religion. In a small pamphlet published in 1928, Izmail Urazov heralded such fakir tricks as fire-eating, walking on nails, and live burials as "miracles of will" that "debunked divine occurrences" and thereby served as "anti-religious propaganda."[67] He explained that circus fakirs modeled their performances on the feats of physical strength and discipline achieved by true Indian fakirs, and described how readers could train their bodies to perform some common tricks. For example, to prepare for performances of the "Human Aquarium," in which the artist vomited up thirty to forty glasses of water along with live fish and frogs that he had swallowed, one should swallow increasingly large amounts of water and, with the last sip, a vomit-inducing emetic. Over time, the dose of emetic should be reduced until none was needed to activate the gag reflex after the last gulp of water was consumed. Urazov warned readers that to prevent injury, fish must be swallowed head first, and added that while swallowing frogs posed no physical risk, it could be unpleasant when a frightened amphibian urinated into one's mouth.[68] Urazov hoped that this and other examples would convince readers of the "tremendous training, will, and self-control" required of these artists, whose performances revealed all purported "miracles" to be merely the result of "training, knowledge, and will."[69] For Urazov, the circus provided lessons in both self-discipline and atheism.

Another author similarly mouthed the official line on the circus in an article on ventriloquism, a conventional circus genre that he or she claimed propagated anti-religious principles. The author explained that viewers had once considered ventriloquism to be a "mysterious, inexplicable, almost supernatural" phenomenon, before, that is, the cheerful, satirical genre of speaking dolls rescued ventriloquism from the "lot of 'miracles.'"[70] Since religious miracles were never presented as amusing or cheerful—"with the exception of the evangelical legend of Christ's turning water into wine in the Sea of Galilee"—the author doubted whether even the most devout person could discern a "mystical foundation" in the following trenchant dialogue between a ventriloquist and his doll: "Karlusha, why is your nose red? Because I'm treating my anemia with vodka."[71] This conclusion was consistent with the official claim that the circus itself provided an alternative to religion, which had been offered two years earlier. A commentator observed that the circus arena, which was usually topped with a cupola, "somewhat resembles a church, and all of its 'acts' and 'numbers' are adorned in the brightly colored clothing and brilliant lighting that is, more than anything, customary for rituals." In this writer's view, the circus promoted a belief not only in the physical power of human beings, but in their power over the world of animals and objects. In the circus, such modest and humble objects as dinner plates, bottles, and children's balls "fly into a frenzy with the wave of human hands and fingers, and they move and dance in completely uncharacteristic ways."[72] He or she argued that when confronted with the enchantments of the circus, viewers learned to forsake their belief in a supernatural divinity and began to worship, in its place, the all-mighty human being.

Another ideological lesson that the Soviet circus demonstrated, according to the official rhetoric, was that the Bolshevik revolution had liberated circus workers from bourgeois owners who had exploited and abused them. Circus performers frequently testified to the improvement in their labor conditions that resulted from the revolutionary dispossession of bourgeois circus owners. In 1922, for example, Vitalii Lazarenko briefly recounted the story of his life, which began in 1890 when he was born into a working-class family living in the Donbass. His father had worked as a miner, but he died when Lazarenko was only four, leaving him to the care of his negligent, often drunken mother. When he was seven years old, she sent him to live with an uncle who managed a troupe of fairground performers and who had agreed to employ Lazarenko in exchange for such a meager quantity of food that the youngster was forced to steal in order to survive. Eventually, Lazarenko left his uncle to join a private circus where he learned to perform on the trapeze, the horizontal bar, the rings, and on horseback. He confessed that, looking back, he could hardly believe how he managed to learn all of these numbers, which demanded "constant, protracted, agonizing, exercise," while also completing all of his other chores. After morning rehearsal, Lazarenko was required to care for the horses and to distribute advertisements for the show and post them around town. He was required to rake the arena, roll up the curtain, fill thirty-six lamps with kerosene before the performance, and extinguish them when it ended. He was required to undress all of the performers and clean their boots. He was required, every evening, to perform four different numbers. For all of this he received beatings and food—"the beatings were healthy (with a *tambur'er*—with a whip) and drew blood, but the food was not healthy." For eight years he worked without a salary, sleeping under the table or the bed, all because, since childhood, he had loved to jump and flip. Even so, he finally left for another circus, where he was paid 20 rubles a month. At this point his career took off, and he was soon earning 550 rubles a month to perform as a carpet clown in the Nikitin circus.[73]

Other performers told similar tales of abuse, neglect, and exploitation by rapacious capitalists, and Aleksandr Kuprin dramatized their plight in his 1902 short story, *In the Circus*. He told the story of a wrestler named Arbusov, who had a heart ailment from which he was suffering particularly badly on the day before a performance. Although the doctor forbade him to appear in the ring, Arbusov could not sacrifice the 200 rubles that he would lose if he forfeited the match. The night of the event, as he prepared to enter the arena, "it came to Arbusov's mind with extraordinary clearness how wild, useless, foolish, and cruel the thing he was getting ready to engage in was. But he also knew and felt that he was being forced to do it by some anonymous and merciless power. And he stood motionless, looking at the heavy curtain folds with a dull and dismal obedience."[74] He succumbed to the mysterious merciless power, entered the ring, and, minutes later, fell before his opponent. As he lay on the mat, surveying the audience, he recognized that the dream of the circus was a senseless fantasy: "The spectators, jumping from their seats, were yelling like maniacs, moving around and waving handkerchiefs, but all this seemed like a long known dream to Arbusov—a dream senseless, fantastic, and at the same time petty and boring in comparison with the anguish that was eating his heart."[75] He gathered up enough strength to stagger to his dressing room, where he collapsed and died.

In their memoirs, many circus performers testified that they were spared Arbusov's fate by the Bolshevik revolution, which finally liberated them from the murderous yoke of bourgeois entrepreneurs.[76] In

1929, an editorial in *Tsirk* (*Circus*) celebrated the revolutionary improvement in the conditions of circus labor: "From being essentially the slave of the director, who forced the artist to be a nanny for his children, fetch groceries from the market for his family, and clean the stables, the circus performer has become one among the number of workers."[77] The revolution made circus performers workers and, as a consequence, brought them especially "close to the masses." Because they were themselves members of the Soviet public, who had purportedly benefitted from the revolution they now served, circus performers were recognized as being among those best equipped to instruct the Soviet public in the lessons they had already learned: lessons in the benefits of the perfected body; the disciplined will; a conscious attitude toward labor; atheism; and, most important, the Bolshevik revolution, which, of course, was equal to them all because it led to them all.

Between 1919 and 1929, producers and boosters of the Soviet circus consistently claimed that its performances propagated ideological messages to viewers who, they assumed, readily received them. Yet it is hard to imagine that the spectacle of a fakir vomiting frogs and a ventriloquist talking to his doll convinced everyone in the crowd to give up religion, just as it is difficult to imagine that every child who saw a trapeze act developed a conscious attitude toward labor, and that every worker who enjoyed a juggling act came to recognize the utility and necessity of Taylorism. It is likely that at least some viewers who found clowns' jokes funny did not experience their own laughter as "the hammering of sturdy nails into the black coffin of the past," as Lunacharskii insisted. It is possible that only very few viewers realized that the lives of the circus performers they loved had been spared when they entered the employ of the Soviet government. Not everyone who witnessed one of Lazarenko's leaps during the civil war allied with the Bolsheviks, just as trained animals did not always present themselves to their viewers as products of a successful educational system. One animal trainer reported in 1928 that a group of peasants who had seen his act refused to believe that his performing dogs were trained at all. "Although they were amazed," he stated, the peasants insisted that his dogs were "'not dogs, but some peculiar type of things' that are born trained."[78] His viewers had clearly missed the message, though they were still amazed and obviously entertained by the novel spectacle.

Acrobatic displays, riding lesson skits, animal acts, To-Ramo's feats of will, various ventriloquists, and sundry human aquaria were no less entertaining than fake wrestling matches and slapstick equestrian acts.

They were as entertaining as they had been in the past and still were in the west, which is why they were harnessed to the project of mass enlightenment in the first place. This meant that circus viewers might not have comprehended, concurred with, or been at all concerned with the messages these performances intended to send, and they could still have enjoyed the show. Lazarenko continued to combine politically enlightening rhetoric and amazing displays of physical prowess throughout the 1920s and into the 1930s. Because his monologues remained only one element in a dazzling circus act, viewers might have appreciated Lazarenko's topical satire—as they were meant to—or they might have tolerated it for the chance to see the clown's record-setting leaps. Aside from those of Lazarenko, very few circus performances during NEP could be considered deliberately propagandist, despite official claims to the contrary, and even when more explicitly ideological content was included in circus programs before 1921, they did still provide exceptional entertainment. Even viewers who had read Durov's description of his training methods, Lunacharskii's essays on the virtues of the circus, Urazov's pamphlet on the ideological relevance of fire breathing, and Sokolov's article on the circus worker as a Taylorized laborer might have liked the circus for reasons other than the contribution it made to their own ideological education.

Reception

The possibility that audiences might have missed the messages rhetorically ascribed to postrevolutionary performances threatened to dismantle the myth that the Soviet public eagerly attended an authentically revolutionary circus, which is why this possibility was effectively denied by the makers and most official reviewers of the Soviet circus between 1919 and 1929. Assertions regarding audience reception were an essential component of the Bolsheviks' earliest arguments advocating the incorporation of the circus into the Soviet cultural establishment. In his 1919 article, "Tasks for the Renewal of the Circus," Lunacharskii invoked and effectively mythologized the Soviet audience in his defense of the circus against critics who considered it a lower form of entertainment that had no place in Soviet culture. Lunacharskii scolded communists who promoted the "vulgar point of view," characteristic of the "petty-bourgeois [*meshchanskaia*] intelligentsia," that melodrama, variety theater, and the circus were "art of the third sort, like inferior tobacco or margarine that even corrupts the people." He explained that any communist sincerely interested in the question of culture should sooner feel sympathy than disdain for "everything that bourgeois *kulturtragers* have stained with the word 'boorish.'" Lunacharskii acknowledged that "the rapacious entrepreneur, the most repellent type of bourgeois," did indulge popular tastes in an attempt to poison "the people as much as possible when preparing an artistic fare for them," but he insisted that popular tastes were not at all boorish. The tastes of the crowd "cannot be entirely ugly . . . they are, of course, for the most part higher, better, and stronger than the tastes of cultured people." Lunacharskii argued that by pursuing their own class interests, bourgeois entrepreneurs had unwittingly propagated an art form of considerable virtue, otherwise it could not have appealed to the necessarily lofty tastes of the popular masses. "When we look closer at a spectacle that is successful with the crowd," he continued, "we will see that the popular masses are attracted to it not by the whitewash and rouge, not by the squalid luxury of the costumes in which the entrepreneur-ponce has dressed them, but by the healthy beauty and vital temperament that is hidden beneath all of this." For the circus viewing public—"our public . . . nine-tenths Red Army soldiers, workers, and their families"—the circus was not at all the poisonous spectacle that bourgeois owners meant it to be. Lunacharskii's argument pointed to the conclusion he explicitly drew at the end of his article: namely, that the circus still did have an upside, which would be turned back up again once ownership of the means of circus production was seized from the bourgeoisie by the socialist state on behalf of the working masses, whose necessarily lofty cultural demands would then be met.[79]

Lunacharskii's argument clearly proved convincing—the decree nationalizing the circuses identified them as capitalist enterprises that were, in spite of being profitable, "democratic by virtue of the public that attends them"[80]—and his rhetoric became canonical during the 1920s, as official commentators insisted that the Soviet state had revolutionized the circus by satisfying Soviet viewers' demands for an enlightening and ideologically instructive spectacle. For example, in 1924, Andrei Shibaev observed that, in the nineteenth century, the circus was a favorite entertainment of the workers, who particularly appreciated the "well-aimed though veiled gibes at the tsarist government and its agents." He added that manual laborers knew the importance of physical strength and agility and naturally appreciated displays of physical prowess. Yet workers, he lamented, were not the only admirers of the prerevolutionary circus, and it was not their tastes but the tastes of petty-bourgeois viewers that entrepreneurs hoped to satisfy with magic tricks and enchantments, equestriennes in short skirts with winking eyes, risky tricks, and clowns who ridiculed cooks, firemen, and house-maids while boxing each other's ears.[81] Like Lunacharskii, Shibaev acknowledged that some elements of the circus might not be appropriate for Soviet culture, but he insisted that these elements were alien to "our public"—a line of reasoning that had become commonplace by the mid-1920s. In 1925, I. I. Zheltov, the assistant chairman of the People's Commissariat of Turkmenistan who confessed to attending the circus once a week, shared his opinion of the entertainment with the readers of *Tsirk*. He admitted that in the past he had considered the circus some kind of vulgar fairground entertainment that simply amused people. Now, however, he was convinced that the circus was a serious and useful spectacle, since it was attended by the "true proletariat," which comprised 90 percent of the circus audience. "The worker," he wrote, "goes where it is understandable, intelligent, and free."[82]

These commentators defined the circus by what it meant to the working class and, in so doing, they, themselves, defined both the circus and the working class. When they argued that the circus must be healthy, intelligent, and free because the proletariat liked it, they were defining the proletariat as healthy, intelligent, and free—an assertion they then proved by interpreting the circus as healthy, intelligent, and free. This circularity in their reasoning might not have given anybody pause, because this interpretation of the circus performed the primary function that was assigned to the circus itself during this period: it told the Soviet people who they were supposed to be.

In the 1920s, both producers and official observers of the circus admitted that, for them, part of the appeal of the circus lay in the contribution it might make to the transformation of the Soviet people, a function that, to their minds, did not contradict their vow to transform the circus in accordance with the demands of the Soviet people. They simply maintained that the Soviet people demanded a circus that would transform them. The official rhetoric surrounding the circus invested an ideal-typical proletarian audience with authority over the entertainment and, thereby, legitimized a project of cultural enlightenment over which the state maintained almost exclusive authority. More than that, this interpretation of the circus not only legitimized but also contributed to the fulfillment of the mass enlightenment project, since it told the Soviet people that, before all else, they were supposed to be people who wanted to be told who they were supposed to be. In 1925, for example, E. Magilevich, the head of Glavkurupr, opened his review of the year's circus premiere with the familiar statement that the "main viewers of the circus are the working masses, and, therefore, the circus program should correspond to their demands." He wrote that the task of the circus was, therefore, "to give healthy, cultured entertainment and also to be a stimulus for the political and cultural education of the viewer." This was a task the circus could achieve with a program built on "political satire, healthy laughter, the beauty of the healthy, agile, and strong body, and calculated, certain, rhythmical movement."[83]

Studies of viewer reception conducted in the 1920s claimed to offer empirical evidence for Magilevich's assertion that Soviet audiences demanded ideologically instructive circus programs. The question of the audience's response to the circus, and to the theater, film, and newspapers, was first systematically addressed during the NEP period, when the partial reintroduction of the market allowed for a degree of social differentiation that undermined any assumption of a socioeconomically homogenous audience.[84] Yet while studies of circus viewers recognized the heterogeneity of the audience, acknowledged that the circus appealed to different groups of people in different ways, and might have represented a sincere attempt to identify viewers' responses, those responses were interpreted in ways that confirmed assertions about circus reception that had been articulated in advance of any study. In the 1920s, audience studies were publicized less to offer any insight into reception than to promote a normative model of proper circus viewing and to provide evidence that Soviet audiences already conformed to it. Official discussions of reception were an essential element of the revolution in circus rhetoric that was achieved during NEP, when much of the revolutionary content had been removed from the rings in order to ensure that the show would be well received.

In 1925, for example, Lunacharskii reported the results of surveys distributed by the editors of the journal *Tsirk*, who received one hundred responses from children aged twelve to fifteen years and fifty responses from workers. The survey, which asked respondents to compare the circus, theater, and film, solicited "completely unexpected" results from the schoolchildren, according to Lunacharskii.[85] Nearly 90 percent of young viewers claimed to prefer either theater or film to the circus, with preferences evenly split between the former two. According to Lunacharskii's summary of the results, the children found nothing interesting, noble, or instructive in the spectacle of people "spinning around, risking their lives for a piece of bread, cracking dim-witted jokes, and laughing stupidly." They concluded that the circus is only for NEPmen, who love rude spectacles.[86] The children's interpretation of the circus closely resembled Lunacharskii's own earlier critique of the bourgeois circus as a vulgar spectacle of human degradation, valued as such by bourgeois entrepreneurs.[87] From the point of view of a Soviet audience, however, this interpretation was hardly acceptable and, to Lunacharskii's mind, entirely inaccurate. He attributed the children's failure to identify the virtues of the circus to their own unhealthy and incorrect sensibilities. Lunacharskii admitted that he was slightly horrified that these "already intellectualized young men and women have lost their taste for the delights of physical achievement and concentrate their attention, instead, on the simple and irresponsible delights of the theater."[88] He doubted that a single athletic young person would consider the circus a spectacle fit only for NEPmen. These children, he insisted, would appreciate the achievements of physical culture in the circus, which would be for them a continuation of their own sporting lives, rather than a hostile, alien spectacle. Lunacharskii took as proof of this claim the warm reception the circus found among working viewers, who "love" the circus because they "have a much more conscious attitude toward the significance of the circus as an educational spectacle."[89]

Lunacharskii refused to acknowledge that the circus clearly had failed to teach children the benefits of physical development. His own argument implied that health, strength, and agility lay in the eyes of the beholder and that those eyes could not be opened by the spectacle of health, strength, and agility alone. This interpretation seemed to contradict his contention that the circus was an effective educator, yet Lunacharskii offered it in order to idealize those viewers who preferred the circus precisely because, he claimed, it was an educational spectacle. Lunacharskii insisted that the children surveyed disliked the circus because they failed to recognize its ideological significance, which, according to his reasoning, only proved that viewers who liked the circus did so because they apprehended its educational messages. He presented viewership data less as an index of viewers' real responses than as proof that those who liked the show were already ideal.

In 1927, researchers at the Theatre Research Workshop surveyed viewers at the Moscow state circus and also discovered that, like Lunacharskii's schoolchildren, some viewers "uniformly disapproved of the circus as a form of art."[90] They noted, though, that these negative opinions were expressed in "clumsy, uncouth" phrases by viewers who

had arrived in Moscow from elsewhere and who were, the authors
noted, mainly peasants.[91] Just as Lunacharskii had discounted the
children's criticisms, the authors of this study simply dismissed those
viewers' distaste for the circus, implicitly attributing it to their igno-
rance and abnormality. Like Lunacharskii's, their evaluation of viewers'
response was meant to idealize those viewers who did like the circus
precisely because, the researchers implied, it was an instructive, politically agitational medium. The study did offer evidence that some of
these ideal audience members already existed. Its authors reported that
respondents generally approved of demonstrations of "the agility of
the healthy body" and that they disapproved of clown acts that were too
often "'boring . . . monotonous . . . not funny enough . . . not satirical . . .
repellent . . . outdated . . . pitiful.'" The researchers considered this last
criticism valid because even though it indicated an absence of agitational content from the circus repertoire, these responses confirmed the
official claim that agitational content is what Soviet circus audiences
sought.[92]

In 1928, the Theatre Research Workshop provided additional evidence that ideal circus viewers really did exist in the Soviet Union, or at
least in Tula, where the study was conducted. Their report included the
example of a twenty-two-year-old Red Army soldier who recognized
the edifying function of gymnastic routines, as was evident in his suggestion that sportsmen should be showcased in the circus so that "each
worker might achieve as much."[93] The report also cited a twenty-seven-
year-old worker, who noted that the "grand art" of physical performance "attracts young people to physical culture."[94] The authors also
endorsed viewers' demands for improved clown acts that included
"more satire, more humor," as a twenty-five-year-old student demanded.[95] A thirty-two-year-old white-collar worker similarly suggested that "more topical [*zlobodnevnoi*] satire be introduced" into
performances.[96] According to the researchers, viewers responded posi-
tively to the routines of Vitalii Lazarenko, who told satiric jokes on the
themes of hooliganism, drunkenness, and alimony payments, while
also performing more commonplace clown acts. They noted that 62
percent of blue-collar workers favored Lazarenko's performance,
whereas 62 percent of white-collar workers found it dissatisfying.[97]
Although the authors neglected to comment on this discrepancy, their
reference to it implied that white-collar workers failed to appreciate the
agitational content of Lazarenko's act, unlike the implicitly ideal Soviet
viewers, who did.

In the 1920s, studies of Soviet audiences concluded that official commentators were correct to claim that viewers liked the circus because it featured edifying displays of physical feats and political messages. The evidence they offered was highly selective, interpreted subjectively, and therefore unreliable, but nothing more credible existed to contradict it. Any claim that Soviet viewers patronized the circus because it was novel, spectacular, and largely lacking in ideological content must remain merely speculative. As a result, what remains the greatest source of frustration for the historian of the Soviet circus—the almost total absence of any reliable evidence regarding audience reception— was one of the most significant virtues of the circus for its producers and official reviewers, who could credibly claim that circus audiences received the messages that performances purportedly communicated.

Conclusion

Between 1919 and 1929, the ideological message that the official circus rhetoric conveyed most consistently was the legitimating myth that a homogenous Soviet public unanimously embraced the enlightening product of an authentically revolutionary Soviet state. Because the meaning of NEP-era circus acts, just like conventional circus acts performed in most other times and places, remained ambiguous, they readily accommodated the political messages rhetorically ascribed to them by producers, performers, and official commentators. They also continued to attract a wide audience whose members might have included some Soviets who hardly embodied the characteristics with which they too were effectively rhetorically inscribed. As a result, the Soviet circus proved to be a productive site for the elaboration of political myths that were said and could be seen to be true in the circus arena, which helps explain why Soviet cultural administrators chose to produce a mass entertainment that was so different from the didactic media, narrative art forms, and monumental modes of representation that thrived in the propaganda state.

Yet by the late 1920s, the myth of the revolution's victory had become much more difficult to maintain. After more than a decade of Communist rule, the Soviet population, including much of the governing elite, had grown impatient with the regime's inability to fulfill the promises of a revolution that appeared, increasingly, to have failed. Soviet society under NEP remained divided by class, as market conditions had allowed some to grow fat while others were lean in both town and country. Managers and technocrats, rather than workers and peasants, continued to administer the workers' and peasants' state. Circus producers and official observers were beginning to acknowledge that the Soviet circus was closer to the bourgeois entertainment it had been than the socialist form of art it was said to have become. At the end of the decade, many people agreed that the Bolshevik revolution in the circus, as in Soviet state, society, and culture more generally, had fallen short. Yet most were eager to take the leap again.

2

The Great Transformation of the Stalin-Era Circus

Circus performers do impossible things. They turn three flips in the air and land on their partners' shoulders. They juggle six plates while spinning a hoop on one foot. They stand perfectly still on a slack wire. They fold their bodies in half, and in half again, and in half again. They change their clothes in the blink of an eye. They disappear and reappear. They dance with bears. They make everybody laugh. They fly, and so do their pigs. Circus performers do impossible things, and sometimes they do stumble, slip, or drop the juggling pin. But when they fail, they try and try again, until they get it right. Then the crowd goes really wild.[1]

In 1928, Stalin introduced a series of policies intended to transform the Soviet Union so profoundly that some historians refer to this period as a second revolution. He brought NEP to an end by outlawing private ownership and bringing the economy under the complete command of the state. He introduced the "Five-Year Plan for Industrialization and Socialist Construction" and forcibly collectivized agriculture in an attempt to propel the Soviet Union out of economic backwardness once and for all. He led the Soviet Union in a campaign literally to build socialism by constructing factories, plants, industrial towns, and collective farms whose inhabitants would become the newly perfected men and women of the Soviet Union—as much the products as the producers of Soviet socialism. If everything went according to plan, within five years the nature of the Soviet Union would be transformed, and not least affected would be Soviet nature itself, in all of its vegetable, mineral, and human varieties.[2]

This was a difficult if not impossible task, which is why some people thought the circus might help to achieve it. While the period's ubiquitous slogans exhorted people to engage in heroic feats of labor, and short stories and novels illustrated the human transformations that would result from the changes made to nature,[3] only the circus offered real, live displays of human beings who, it was claimed, had broken through the bounds of nature by adhering to proper methods of socialist labor and by making good use of new technologies. At the time of the so-called Great Transformation, the circus demonstrated that gravity could be defied, that darkness could be made light, and that human nature could be perfected. Circus performances and the rhetoric surrounding them told Soviet people that the impossible was possible, even if only on the second try.

Circus performances between 1929 and 1939 still remained almost entirely conventional, with two significant exceptions: they featured more elaborate demonstrations of technology and they were less likely to feature the foreign performers who had populated circus rings through the NEP period and were steadily being replaced by young, Soviet-trained performers. By the time the new Soviet Constitution declared that socialism had been achieved in 1936, most observers agreed that these performers—all perfect products of Soviet socialism—had succeeded in transforming crowds of circus viewers into new Soviet men and women, who were inspired by the superhuman feats they saw in the circus to perfect themselves too. According to the official rhetoric, the revolution in the circus had finally been achieved, and commentators claimed throughout the late 1930s that young Soviet performers, who physically embodied the future in the present, realistically reflected the optimism of the smiling circus viewers, for whom life had become, very visibly, "better, . . . more joyous." By the end of the 1930s, the second revolution in the Soviet circus had been declared a success, even though, as some observers still complained, the content of real circus performances had hardly been transformed.

Production Gymnastics

Things would, of course, be done differently this time. In the 1920s, official commentators claimed that the circus had been revolutionized when it was made to satisfy Soviet viewers' demands for an enlightening and ideologically instructive spectacle. By 1929, however, most observers agreed that this first attempt to revolutionize the circus had failed and that if the second attempt were to succeed, an agent of revolutionary change more reliable than the Soviet people—namely, the Soviet state—would be needed. Circus producers no longer claimed to have reconstructed the circus according to viewers' demands, but rather insisted that they would transform circus viewers by presenting them with spectacles of performers who had recently perfected themselves. In this way, Soviet commentators resolved the contradiction implicit in earlier official conceptions of the circus as a form of art that would produce a perfect proletariat once its performances satisfied the demands of a proletariat that was presumed to be perfect already. After 1928, Soviet officials understood the proletariat to be less perfect than perfectible, and it followed that circus audiences and performers were newly recognized as being the objects rather than the agents of the circus's revolutionary transformation. During this period, Soviet state officials claimed for themselves complete command over the means of producing the circus, which was understood to be one means of producing a new and better proletariat. To some, this reversal might have marked a retreat from purely socialist principles, but to many more, it facilitated the introduction of properly socialist methods for producing the circus, which, if produced by any other means, could be neither a proper product nor an effective producer of socialism.

By the early 1930s, mass taste had lost even its nominal authority over circus production, and, consequently, the audience's demands became largely irrelevant to the circus administration. The last recorded study of audience reception was conducted in 1931; thereafter, commentators began to encourage the circus administration and the press to provide viewers with an authoritative interpretation of the show. In a report on the "Tasks of the Soviet Circus" submitted in 1931 to the Kievan Circus's Office for the Study of the Circus Process, A. V. Vladimirskii conceded that whatever circus producers intended their shows to mean, ultimately, the circus meant only what it meant to its audience. Yet, unlike earlier adherents to this view, he refused to cede absolute authority over circus production to the dictates of mass taste. Instead, he insisted that the circus administration and the popular press "provide the working masses with a proper approach to the interpretation of the true meaning of the circus and its role in proletarian reality."[4] Another report, titled, "Toward the Reconstruction of the Circus," also submitted to the Kievan Office that same year, insisted that the administration wage a "struggle for the *reconstruction of the viewer's perception* . . . a struggle against the remnants of capitalist consciousness" by providing viewers with an ideologically correct interpretation of the spectacle.[5] The author suggested that short lectures explaining the tasks of the circus and analyzing individual circus genres be read to circus spectators and that longer lectures and public debates about the tasks of the circus be organized regularly. Printed matter on the circus and other arts, along with showcases of circus literature, reports on other circuses, and photographs of the best circus numbers were also to be displayed in the circuses' "viewers' corners."[6]

In accordance with this program, on February 28, 1930, a group of workers was invited to preview Vladimir Maiakovskii's circus pantomime "Moscow Is Burning" and to join the author in a discussion of the production. Maiakovskii's dramatization of the 1905 Revolution was staged two months later, one week after the author's suicide on April 14, 1930. It featured a montage of scenes that parodied Nicholas II, whose part was played by a dwarf; it condemned the prerevolutionary class system, which was represented by a pyramid with Nicholas on top and "shackled workers" on the bottom; and it celebrated the valiant revolutionaries, one of whom distributed incendiary pamphlets while swinging from the trapeze. In "Moscow Is Burning," Maiakovskii endowed classic circus forms with explicitly revolutionary content, just as he had in the immediate postrevolutionary period. Yet while this production, together with the previous year's dramatization of the Red Army's defeat of Nestor Makhno in "Makhnovshchina," revived an earlier form of revolutionary spectacle, the discussion surrounding it marked a departure from the previous conception of the relationship between the audience and the performance.[7] In his discussion with the workers who previewed the show, Maiakovskii stated that he sought to solicit their instructions and opinions, but only after he had fulfilled a prior objective: "to explain" the meaning of the production and the significance of its various elements. He explained to viewers, for example, that "for us, water is not simply water, but it fulfills another duty—it washes away lies and barriers." He also explained that "Moscow Is

Burning" was meant to demonstrate "how the working class proceeded through a general rehearsal to arrive at the present day."[8] The viewers seemed to have been unimpressed—the show was a flop.[9] Yet a review published in the May issue of *Tsirk i estrada* (*Circus and Variety Theater*) praised the show anyway, not because it met viewers' demands, but because it was "one more step toward our circus, which alongside the other arts, should contribute to socialist reconstruction and should not only provide healthy rest and exercise, but should also organize consciousness."[10]

The new rhetoric surrounding circus reception was consistent with the official celebration of art's ability to reconstruct Soviet men and women during the period of the first Five-Year Plan. In an article titled "The Socialist Education of the New Man," published on the front page of *Zhizn' iskusstva* in June 1929, M. Rafail explained that during the epoch of the socialist reconstruction of the economy, the work of state cultural departments should be directed toward "the alteration of human material." Rafail admitted that it was more difficult "to remake people" than to construct an economy, but he insisted that it was not impossible. In order to secure the participation of millions of Soviets in the construction of socialism, to "extend the tentacles of cultural revolution into the private lives of each worker," and "to educate the psyche of the proletariat in the direction of the continuous raising of its socialist consciousness," it was necessary, in Rafail's opinion, for cultural workers to adopt socialist competition as both a political slogan and as their own method of labor. Practically, this involved creating cultural programs that promoted the principle of socialist competition, that explained the challenges of socialist construction, and that propagated the general line on industrialization and collectivization. It also entailed programming events throughout the workday, rather than just at the lunch hour, and holding them not only at factories and plants, but in the streets and squares of workers' neighborhoods.[11]

Other commentators also endorsed socialist competition as an appropriate method for producing the circus, and many thought that the best way to implement this method was by staging actual socialist competitions between circus performers. On December 29, 1929, the Moscow and Khar'kov circuses agreed to participate in a socialist competition to be held in 1930.[12] That same year, an editorial in *Tsirk i estrada* identified the circus and variety theater as "shock-work forms [*udarnye formy*] of spectacular art." Its author noted that the shock-labor movement pervaded all spheres of life in the Soviet Union, including the theaters, whose most active workers had organized shock-labor brigades in order more efficiently to fulfill the plan, reduce overheads, and elevate the artistic and ideological level of the shows. The author congratulated those circus and variety theater performers who had also established shock-labor brigades and encouraged others to join their movement. He insisted that as mobile forms of art capable of responding quickly to current affairs, the circus and variety theater must respond to the most important events of the time. They were obliged, in his view, not only to keep pace with the general tempos of socialist construction, but also to serve as the pioneers of the shock-labor movement, in which, as in the circus itself, the best results were achieved with the least expenditure of energy and resources.[13] To this end, A.V. Vladimirskii called for the circus administration to implement methods of socialist work, such as shock-labor, socialist competition, and *shturmovye* weeks in his report on the "tasks of the Soviet Circus," issued the following year.[14]

During the period of the "Great Transformation," when all of nature, including human nature, was to be transformed, Soviet workers themselves were understood to be products of socialist labor methods no less significant than the coal they mined, the steel they forged, and the performances they staged. According to the official rhetoric, socialist labor was the best method for altering human material, which meant that the first new Soviet men and women to be produced by the newly revolutionized circus were the circus workers themselves. Circus performers were presented literally as being the products of their own labor; once perfected, they would be capable of producing properly Soviet performances and properly Soviet audiences.

In April 1928, one month after Stalin introduced the Five-Year Plan, a memorandum appended to the annual production plan for the Central Administration of State Circuses (TsUGTs) explained the relevance of the circus for the project of socialist construction. The authors maintained that the "first and most significant" element of the circus remained the demonstration of the physical education, development, beauty, and hygiene of the human body. They claimed that by means of the "strictest self-discipline and self-education," circus artists mastered the techniques of their profession, which is what brought the circus so "close to our epoch." Inherent in the skill of the circus artist were "tremendous initiative and a vast reserve of energy, directed toward overcoming all imperfections conditional upon the structure of the human body." This spectacle of the physically self-perfected human being was then thought to inspire viewers to exercise their own energy, initiative, and discipline in order to overcome the imperfections of their own bodies.[15]

Circus performers were officially celebrated as model products of socialist labor, and as such they were also thought to be effective producers of socialist laborers. The official endorsement of the circus as an educational and therefore potentially revolutionary arena—a place where both performers and spectators were ultimately perfected—resembled the official claim that circus was an enlightening spectacle, which had been asserted consistently since 1919. Discipline, will, and education remained essential means of achieving this transformation, whose benefits were understood to be professional. Yet energy, initiative, and technique were now considered essential to a process whose result was precisely defined as the transgression of natural human limitations that were recognized as being primarily physical. This was a subtle shift of emphasis, but one that marked a significant revision of the official rhetoric surrounding the Soviet circus.

For example, one month after the TsUGTs memo was issued, Moris Gorei asked whether the circus was a "revolutionary spectacle." His answer was "yes, if it convinces us that by means of the exertion of energy, a strong will, and a methodical approach [*metodichnost'*], that which had seemed impossible becomes feasible."[16] This was a big "if," and by 1929, most commentators agreed that the circus had failed consistently to infect the audience with the necessary energy, will, and confidence to overcome their physical imperfections so that they might perform impossible feats. Yet by 1930, few doubted the potential of the circus to produce a perfect Soviet populace, capable of performing impossible feats.

In 1930, the director of the circus administration, A. M. Dankman, and Alekseev, a representative of the Union of Art Workers, issued reports on the "Conditions and Prospects of the Work of TsUGTs," whose conclusions identified the basic task of the circus arts as "the agitation and propaganda of the ideas of socialist construction." The authors encouraged circus administrators to organize the constituent elements of the program—physical culture, technical prowess, the word, music, dance, and more—into a "single complex of influence," directed toward the promotion of socialist forms of labor, the advancement of Soviet technology, the obliteration of old traditions, and, finally, "the activation of the mass viewer in accordance with . . . the creation of a new type of person to be a member of the new society being built on socialist beginnings."[17] In a discussion of the tasks for the development of circus arts held that same year, one TsUGTs administrator explained that the circus could influence viewers to transform themselves into proper socialists by presenting models of human perfection. In his view, "our athletes" were already endowed with all of the qualities necessary for their future perfection, and it remained "the task of our Soviet circus . . . to show how the person of the future socialist society will be constituted."[18]

A year later, Ia. K. Tsveifel' accorded a more literally didactic function to physical circus routines. In his own report for the Office for the Study of the Circus Process, Tsveifel' demanded that every acrobatic number include a moment of educational significance. He considered the circus a "school of healthy life," in which viewers encountered models of physical omnipotence, beauty, and dynamism—models on which weak and ineffectual people might then mold themselves. He called for more "'marble' people" to illustrate the hardiness, beauty, and training of the body, for more gymnasts and acrobats to demonstrate the miracles that could be achieved by ordinary people who systematically and methodically pursued their physical development, and for more riders and jugglers to teach workers the value of agility, decisiveness, and precision.[19] Tsveifel's identification of physically perfected circus performers as the harbingers of a perfected social order was consistent with the Soviet imagination of the new man as an athlete, "a natural analogue to . . . the hero-worker," during this period. As Toby Clark explains, the image of the athlete promoted the "'production gymnastics'" that characterized industrial labor in the 1930s while simultaneously projecting the Marxist utopian vision of the transformation of labor into a recreational pursuit. As Clark writes, the "sporting worker is fit for the everyday tasks of building socialism, and also foreshadows his non-alienated descendants."[20]

According to the official rhetoric, circus performers not only foreshadowed their descendants, but literally brought them into being. In 1931, for example, Vladimirskii extolled the circus as a powerful producer of future Soviet men and women. He began his report on the "Tasks of the Soviet Circus" by acknowledging that the road to communism was "not strewn with roses," and proposed that only by waging a victorious struggle against "an aggressive and resistant environment [*sreda*]" could the proletariat safely traverse it. Vladimirskii identified both the natural "elements" and "social maladies" that threatened to hinder the proletariat. The former included "such difficulties of disorganized nature" as impassable rocks, precipices, and deserts that impeded the progress of the proletariat along the path to "new forms of life." These hindrances could be overcome, Vladimirskii claimed, by the strength of human muscles and the machines that they built. The second threat consisted of the "hostile social front, that either by virtue of inertia or aggressive intransigence still stands in the path of the working class in the struggle for communist forms of life." Though Vladimirskii identified class enemies as a "social" threat, he attributed their persistent presence to a defect in human nature. He counted the "inertia of human nature" among the *"elements* that inhibit progress" and that, implicitly, could be overcome by the strength of human muscles and the machines that they built. Communism's victory would be nature's defeat, and, according to Vladimirskii, nature suffered a stunning defeat in the circus.[21]

According to Vladimirskii, the performances of acrobats, trapeze artists, and jugglers displayed the "limitless potential of the human body." He claimed that their performances convinced viewers of the "elasticity and functional riches that lie within any human body and that are fruitlessly lost on millions of people who are not even aware of their potential, which they could realize if they deliberately organized and systematically developed these hidden rudiments [*zachatkov*]." Vladimirskii argued that the "models of perfected form" on display in the circus inspired viewers to realize their own potential for physical perfection, which was no small feat for the circus. Given that Vladimirskii understood the class struggle to be largely a struggle against the rule of nature, it is not surprising that he considered physical training to be a "citizen's duty and a political act directed toward the creation of a generation of fighters" capable of waging a successful battle for Communism. The circus, in Vladimirskii's opinion, encouraged viewers to take up arms—their own arms—and join the fight against nature's imperfections.[22]

Even Vladimirskii admitted there were some natural limitations that even the most physically developed individuals could not overcome. Yet fortunately, he noted, these fighters were armed with more than their own musclebound appendages. He explained that unlike animals, whose physical endowments restricted their behavior, human beings "breached this biological armor" by making machines that propelled them into a "limitless expanse of functional potential." Humans, for example, were born without wings, but they could fly higher than any bird. Their eyes were weaker than an eagle's, but they could look through a microscope to see the smallest bacterium. Their hearing was not as sharp as a dog's, but they could distinguish words whispered across great expanses with the use of a telephone or radio.[23]

Iurii Olesha made the same point in "We Are in the Center of Town," a short homage to the zoo that he wrote in 1937. Olesha recorded a remark that one youth made to another while they watched an Australian parakeet, which was adorned with a brightly patterned throat, move across a swath of netting using its forehead for balance. Referring to the bird's labored gait, the young man exclaimed, "'How hard it is to do that!'" prompting Olesha to respond in the text, "Actually: how difficult it is to make that pattern! And to devise the entire coloring? To create that gamut, these striking tints." Olesha identified "nature" as "this brilliant master." "It is in her laboratory," he continued, "that the amazing azure is prepared which decorates the breast of the peacock," just as nature "devised the construction of the jumping kangaroo" and created the gull, which "is a torpedo . . . a monoplane of the most perfect appearance with low-placed wings."[24] Olesha marveled at the inventions of nature that were on display at "nature's exhibition, her booths" in the zoo. Yet his enthusiasm only quickened when he took leave of the zoo and entered the city anew: "And again we are in the city. We are among machines. How difficult it is to make a machine! A bridge. An airplane. Or little gadgets. The magical eye of a microscope. We are in the fantastical world of technology." In this world, humans' creative powers not only matched but exceeded those of nature, which was tamed and made submissive in their hands. In the world of technology, he concluded, "a man can show himself to be a master with just as much power as nature. He is more powerful than she. He takes away her secrets and forces her to serve him. He tames her, and she snarls less and less and purrs more and more in his hands, like the little tamed snow leopard in the baby animals' area in the zoo."[25] As Olesha explained, technology allowed humans to escape the strictures of nature.

Showcasing Soviet Technology

The circus was a place where the laws of nature appeared to be easily defied, and, as such, it provided an appropriate showcase for Soviet technological achievements. Since its inception in late eighteenth-century England, the modern circus had celebrated humans' triumph over nature's laws. In his history of the early English circus, Marius Kwint identifies the circus as an aesthetic counterpart to modern industrialization. He argues that in the context of industrialization, traditional fairground acts were newly recognized as demonstrations of the limitless capacity of human beings to defy the constraints of nature. Kwint reads William Wordsworth's descriptions of "'The Horse of Knowledge, and the learned Pig . . . All jumbled up together to compose, / A Parliament of Monsters'" as "the products of a single 'Promethean' impetus; a panoply of infinite technological and political possibilities for the self-recreation of humankind and its environment." Kwint concludes that in the circus, spectators found "optimistic signs that modern human beings could transcend, by secular and enlightened discipline, the fallen state that had always appeared natural."[26]

The horse of knowledge and the learned pig performed human feats alongside humans who performed inhuman feats in a setting that stood, itself, in violation of the laws of nature. As Helen Stoddart explains, the circus was the first American entertainment to feature electric lighting and other electrical experiments. It came to be associated with modern technological innovations, which helped fulfill "the circus's drive to demonstrate visually the human capacity to dominate the natural world."[27] The American example, in turn, inspired European showmen to incorporate new technologies into their own circus productions. Marline Otte discusses one German circus director's incorporation of such novel technologies as automobiles, airplanes, and film into his shows, which also featured an unusually large number of animal acts, including beasts riding bicycles, wearing boxing gloves, and dancing to exotic songs.[28]

Entertainers in prerevolutionary Russia also promoted the circus as a showcase for modern technologies. In 1911, the Nikitin brothers cele-brated the opening of their new circus building by staging Russia's first "aquatic pantomime," which, according to the program's libretto, was produced in compliance with the standards for such productions in the largest cities of Europe and America. The libretto praised Aksim Nikitin for the enormous material investment he made in the capital improve-ments of his circus, which now featured an arena floor that was made out of coconut fibers, weighed 120 poods (1 pood = 36.11 pounds), and was specially commissioned from the famous Berlin firm Fisher and Wolf. This modern import protected spectators in the front row from the dust and mud that normally splattered them during equestrian routines. Most significantly, the stadium was now lit by thousands of electrical bulbs that created a "sea of fire and light." Though the meta-phor was mixed, its implication was clear: by means of modern tech-nology human beings had not only reproduced but also surpassed nature's own products. No amount of water could extinguish the artifi-cial seas of fire created by electric bulbs, which was especially impor-tant for Nikitin, whose greatest innovation was the construction of a circus ring that, by means of a "complicated mechanism," automatically lowered itself to transform the arena into a "deep lake" containing, as the libretto detailed, 480,000 liters of water at a temperature of 25 degrees Celsius. As a result of these modernizations, "that which could not have been achieved in today's circuses and theaters due to their imperfect construction, has been achieved brilliantly in the enormous arena of the Nikitin circus."[29]

In 1929, the Soviets also attempted, with less success, to celebrate the supernatural powers of modern technology by staging "The Black Pirate," an aquatic pantomime adapted from an 1881 Chinizelli circus production. In his review for *Zhizn' iskusstva*, Simeon Dreiden celebrated the show as a "brilliant" demonstration of the "superb" capacity of the circus to stage mass pantomimes. Dreiden praised the State Circus Administration, whose representatives "displayed excellent team-work, discipline, and an ability to clearly, quickly, and accurately realize the plan of the producer." Yet while he claimed that proper methods were used in the production of "The Black Pirate," Dreiden thought that it still failed to realize the full potential of pantomime as a properly Soviet art form. Dreiden admitted that "we will not search for that which is called ideology in this 'gala-presentation,'" and quoted a "bilious" viewer who remarked that "here there is not as much ideology, as there is water!"[30] The viewer did have a point. The pantomime dramatized the misadventures of a petulant aristocrat, the titular Black Pirate, who assembled a gang of rowdy bandits to torment the gentle peasants who inhabited the northern French countryside. Without the help of the local police, who sold their allegiance to the bandits after vowing to bring them to justice, the peasant mob defeated the aristocratic rabble, rescued an abducted maiden, and presumably liberated any other booty with which the pirate might have absconded.[31]

Dreiden considered this "sentimental, old-fashioned . . . assortment of pompous trivialities" to have been nothing more than an excuse to play in the water. As a consequence of its ideological vacuity, Dreiden concluded, "The Black Pirate" could not be considered a Soviet pantomime, but only its rehearsal. A truly Soviet pantomime would benefit, necessarily, from the technology of the twentieth century and an enthusiasm for contemporary industry, both of which were, in Dreiden's opinion, entirely incommensurate with the scale and technological means of the circus productions of the eighteenth and nineteenth century, of which "The Black Pirate" was one. Dreiden insisted that "film, the car, the city, 'the rhythms of contemporary life'" should be introduced into the circus arena. "Without these new means of expression," he concluded, "a contemporary Soviet pantomime cannot be built."[32]

Other commentators argued, more generally, that modern technology was a necessary component of genuinely Soviet circus programs, not only circus pantomimes. Dankman himself encouraged circus workers to modernize their productions by introducing new technologies into their acts. In 1930 he read a speech on the development of variety theater and circus arts before the Vserabis plenary session in which he identified "workers' inventiveness" as the most significant engine driving the evolution of the circus arts. He explained that "each artistic number is, in essence, an original combination of the definite laws of mechanics or physics, in the case of athletic and mechanical numbers, or psychology, in the case of trained animal acts, etc." The number of ways these different laws could be combined to produce artistic routines was, in Dankman's opinion, "limitless," and it was the task of circus workers "to discover new combinations of the laws of dynamics, psychology, and physics" that might then serve as the basis for new artistic routines.[33]

Whether or not they deliberately set out to recombine scientific laws, many circus performers did incorporate new technologies into their acts during this period. In a 1979 biography of the acrobat Raisa Nemchinskaia, her son, Maksimilian Nemchinskii, explained that in the early 1930s, aerial performers often constructed sets for their routines that evoked mechanized flight. He reminded his readers that this was the time of the first flights across the ocean, of attempts to conquer the stratosphere, and of fantastical plans to study other planets. "Behind each of these projects," Nemchinskii asserted, "stood human daring and perfect technology," and since "the circus always strived to display the latest technological innovations," such as bicycles, motorcycles, and automobiles, it was little surprise that circus performers also introduced airplanes, dirigibles, and rockets into their acts.[34]

In 1929, for example, the gymnasts Eder and Beretto enacted the "Flight of an Airplane around the Eiffel Tower." They constructed a large bamboo apparatus that was equipped with a trapeze. In Nemchinskii's opinion, their apparatus was as traditional as the tricks they performed. He explained that the true novelty of their act was that the artists had devised a way to maintain a motorless airplane in orbit around the tower using cords and cantilevers. Similarly, in 1934, the gymnasts Valentina and Mikhail Volgin, who performed under the name Duglas, built a smaller scale flying machine in the shape of a rocket. The rocket hung from the dome of the circus and rotated horizontally, while the two gymnasts balanced on bamboo poles that extended from the rocket's tail and performed synchronized tricks.[35] It was around this time, too, that Durov's pig Chuska took the first of her thirteen flights around the ring in a hot air balloon,[36] and she was soon outdone by Snowdrop, Durov's rat, who piloted a tiny airplane, motored by a propeller and a rubber band. Durov explained that "of his own accord, from a sense of self-preservation, the little animal balanced himself in flight, unconsciously maintaining the equilibrium and thereby helping the even flight of his airplane."[37] Achievements in aviation provided some of the best evidence that the new Soviet men and women could, if equipped with the most advanced technology, conquer nature. It made sense, therefore, that circus performers, especially acrobats and animal trainers, whose feats most dramatically flouted the laws of nature, would associate themselves with aviators. These innovative accoutrements not only advertised the successes of Soviet technology but also helped to secure the identity of circus performers as model Soviet men and women.

The Failed Transformation and Minor Transgressions of Clowning

Clowns were also among the new Soviet men and women who broke the rules of nature in circus rings, though not always to appropriate ideological effect. For example, in 1933, the clowning duo Vitalii and Eddi cheated, deceived, and, according to all appearances, did break the rules of nature by employing, among other devices, the trappings of sport, which was one of the more significant means by which the Soviet people were encouraged to perfect themselves physically. In this sketch Vitalii invited the ringmaster, Kadono, to play a game with him, but Kadono declined after he saw Vitalii stretching out a rubber switch that he was wearing around his neck. Just then, Eddi entered the ring carrying various vials and tiny boxes, "shouting: who needs toadstools and bed-bug traps?" He approached Vitalii, who offered to show him a "good sport," which he claimed was better than any of those remedies. Eddi agreed, and Vitalii placed the rubber switch on the other clown's neck. He stretched it out as far as it could go before he released it, so that Eddi received a strong blow to the face. Eddi fell to the ground, but soon stood up and, grabbing a stick, began to chase Vitalii around the ring. Vitalii shouted to a nearby stagehand that he was being pursued by a hooligan and needed help. The stagehand caught Eddi and handed him over to Vitalii and Kadono, who agreed to put Eddi in Vitalii's large sack and then drown him in the river. Yet as soon as they lifted the sack onto their shoulders, it tore in half, releasing Eddi, who was now dressed like a woman, wearing a long white blouse and a long-haired wig. Kadono and Vitalii shrank back in fear, and Eddi began to beat them with a stick until they stood up and fled the arena. In this routine, Vitalii used the cover of sport to injure Eddi, whose reprisal Vitalii then evaded by taking advantage of a virtuous citizen's willingness to help maintain public order. Eddi, in turn, took advantage of his concealment in the sack to transform himself into a woman (the Russian term for a quick-change routine is the cognate *transformatsiia*). Eddi defied a law of nature, in this case the law of gender identity, in order to defy an unjust civil authority, which did not communicate an appropriate ideological message at all.[38]

Another routine featured a "sport" in which the *belyi* clown attempted to use a mace-like weapon to extinguish a candle he had placed on his partner's head. Not surprisingly, he ended up smacking the *ryzhii* in the face. The *ryzhii* then challenged his rival to a duel, which, at the ringmaster's suggestion, the two clowns agreed to fight by strapping boxes of dynamite to their backs, arming themselves with burning torches, and chasing each other around the ring. When the *ryzhii* stumbled and fell, the *belyi*, who proved to be both unathletic and a cheat, exploited his advantage and ignited the dynamite, which sparked and smoked as the defeated clown ran from the ring in tears.[39] In a different skit, the *ryzhii* did eventually avenge himself by magically evading the laws of physics in order to best his opponent in a shooting match: the *ryzhii* clown fired his gun in every direction other than that of the target, which he nevertheless hit every time.[40] Like most clowns before them, Vitalii and Eddi entertained an ambivalent relationship to order, authority, and the rules of the game in routines that were also simply silly. This might be why, to some, it became increasingly obvious that this type of clowning broke the rule requiring cultural forms to support the Soviet state and promote its plans. At worst, though none admitted it, the unruly antics of such clowns as Vitalii and Eddi exposed the potentially dangerous consequences of the official exhortation of the Soviet people to flout the authority of nature.

Between 1930 and 1936 commentators periodically decried the failure of Soviet clowning, the one circus genre whose potential to propagate an ideological position was understood to be limitless. For many, clown acts provided the best evidence that the nature of the Soviet circus remained far from transformed. In 1930, *Sovetskaia estrada i tsirk* (*Soviet Variety Theater and Circus*) published a provincial worker's critique of the Vladikavkaz circus's "unsuccessful program," in which the clown acts were "amazing in their absurdity" and distinguished themselves "by their enthusiasm for outmoded styles."[41] That same year, representatives of the circus administration joined *komsomol* members in a discussion of the circus and, specifically, its shortcomings. The active participation of the *komsomol* members betrayed, according to the account in *Sovetskaia estrada i tsirk*, a "keen interest in the circus" on the part of the working youth, who, one after the other, noted the circus's shortcomings and offered suggestions to improve the entertainment. In addition to complaints about high ticket prices—it cost workers five to six rubles to attend the circus with their families—*komsomol* workers voiced concern about the poor state of clowning, "which rather than addressing current events articulately and keenly, overlooks them." The article explained that over the past thirteen years the working viewer had matured, while clowning had "marked time, without changing its already obsolete clown types." Vitalii Lazarenko was the one exception. In the present day, the author concluded, the Soviets needed "intelligent laughter and not laughter for laughter's sake."[42]

Clowning was not the only circus genre that remained inadequately reconstructed, according to much of the official commentary published in the mid-1930s. By 1932, for example, some commentators had begun to admit that viewers did not necessarily recognize gymnastic routines, aerial numbers, and trained animal acts as being the demonstrations of humans' capacity to transcend the limitations of nature that they were officially understood to be. In May 1932, the directors of the First State Circus invited viewers to participate in a discussion of the tasks and achievements of the circus. The Assistant Director of the Ministry of Enlightenment's arts department, L. I. Novitskii, opened the conference with a strong critique of the circus, which he claimed was still viewed "not as an art imbued with ideological content, but as a place where naked technique is demonstrated." In his opinion, the Soviet circus remained subject to the influence of the bourgeois, western European circus, which was characterized by a "pure demonstration of technique, physical agility, and no ideological content at all." One viewer, Comrade Gribkov, a worker at the AMO plant who had attended the circus two to three times a year for the past twenty-five years, agreed that nothing had changed in the circus. "The numbers are the same, only of a lower quality," he stated. In Novitskii's opinion, this was a great shame, because the circus, like any form of art, was capable of exerting a powerful ideological influence over millions of people. For that reason, he concluded, every circus number should be saturated with ideological content.[43]

The Transformation of Circus Personnel

Novitskii and Gribkov's complaints were hardly unique at the time. In fact, they were leveled in the midst of a purge of the State Association of Musical, Variety Theater, and Circus Enterprises (GOMETs), a division of the Ministry of Enlightenment that had administered the Central Administration of State Circuses (TsUGTs) since 1931. In February 1932, the People's Commissariat of Workers' and Peasants' Inspection assembled a commission to purge the GOMETs apparatus.[44] As N. Oruzheinikov explained in *Sovetskoe iskusstvo* (*Soviet Art*), the commission's task was to identify the "concrete culprits of the disgraceful situation in which the viewer, to this day, is presented with gypsy acts and vulgar, narrow-minded anecdotes and couplets, and in which the ideological line of the repertoire of the variety theater and circus is not at all in keeping with the level of the tasks of the fourth, conclusive year of the five-year plan."[45] From his point of view, it seemed that neither performances of "The Black Pirate," demonstrations of modern technologies, nor athletic demonstrations, which comprised 75 percent of the circus repertoire in 1929,[46] had "radically directed the circus and variety theater toward the problems of socialist construction, toward the problems that concern millions of proletarian viewers."[47]

The commission concluded that the problem with GOMETs was personnel. Specifically, the circus administration had failed to impose proper methods of socialist labor upon circus workers, who, as a consequence, could hardly be considered new Soviet men and women, capable of producing ideologically proper circus performances. Two articles published in *Sovetskoe iskusstvo* by the *chistka*, or purge, brigade attacked the management of GOMETs for administering the circus according to an "assembly line [*konveier*] system," in which managers in Moscow commissioned acts, assigned them to artists, and then assigned and reassigned artists to perform in circuses across the Soviet Union. The commission concluded that this system did less to impose centralized control over the circuses than to reduce the entire administration to chaos. In Sverdlovsk, as one article noted, six identical acts were performed in the same program while one artist was assigned to appear in both Stalino and Dnepropetrovsk at the same time.[48] More important, the circus management, happily ensconced in Moscow, could not "attend to the perfection of numbers, the improvement of the quality of production and . . . the strengthening of labor discipline among artists."[49] GOMETs was further accused of neglecting the education and material welfare of its cadres of circus performers. Members of the brigade chastised GOMETs for mismanaging the world's only technical college devoted to training circus performers. They considered it the fault of GOMETs that the college continued to lead a "beggarly" existence in a "neglected" circus ring with students who were deprived of dormitories.[50] The consequences of this negligence were apparent to at least one participant in the May viewers' conference, which featured performances by graduates of the technical college that were so weak as to convince comrade Nemirskii, a worker at the New Dawn factory, that the college produced circus performers who were no different from those appearing abroad. "In regard to ideology," he concluded, graduates of the technical college "give nothing, and in regard to technique they are much worse" than their foreign counterparts.[51]

By the end of 1932, months after the GOMETs apparatus had been purged, the situation had still not improved, according to Soviet cultural officials, who continued to criticize the circus administration in similar terms for the next several years. For example, on the eve of an all-union conference of GOMETs, Mikhail Imas, the manager of GOMETs, published a catalogue of the administration's shortcomings in *Sovetskoe iskusstvo*. He admitted that, to date, "the basic working method of the circus and variety theater enterprises remains the demonstration of western European genres and the imitations of those models by Soviet artists; the commission of ready-made numbers that were prepared by an artist without any direction; and an aspiration to maintain traditional, conservative forms." Imas called for the reconstruction of all circus genres and, in the first place, clowning, which, he admitted, had made no progress since its emergence as a genre in the modern circus.[52] Apparently, none of this had been achieved by the following year, or by the following. In 1934, the chief director of GOMETs, I.S. Ganetskii, rebuked circus administrators at an all-union conference, where he attributed the "poor quality of artistic production in the circus" to the failures of leadership and administrative oversight.[53] A review of the program that debuted that year at the First Moscow Circus complained that it demonstrated old familiar routines that failed to transcend the limits of what had already been achieved in a given genre.[54] Yet in little more than a year, by the time the First Moscow State Circus made its premiere in September 1936, the story had begun to change. A. Nazarov noted in

Pravda that the circus continued to suffer from serious inadequacies, including some "vulgarity" that remained in the repertoire, but his review emphasized the improvements that were also evident in the program, including, most especially, its reliance on young artists who were raised under Soviet conditions, rather than foreign performers, and that "in the circus it is cheerful and interesting."[55] This story of the circus's steady improvement would become canonical through the rest of the decade.

Even when the official rhetoric surrounding the Soviet circus did less to celebrate its revolutionary achievements (as it had during NEP) or highlight its ideological potential (as was more commonly the case during the first years of the Five-Year Plan) and more to enumerate its shortcomings, the circus still served as a productive site for the rhetorical elaboration of an important legitimating myth—in this case that the proper method for reconstructing Soviet institutions involved the re-forging of personnel through political reeducation and improved administrative oversight. Not surprisingly, once all of this was said to have been put in place, with the result that the victory of socialism in the Soviet Union was finally declared, the circus helped to maintain that myth too. Beginning in 1936, the circus was once again officially celebrated as a form of culture that had been successfully revolutionized.

Getting Real

The Soviet Union was a happy place to be, at least officially, after 1935, according to Stalin, who announced that year that "life has become better, comrades, life has become more joyous." Life in the Soviet Union was so happy because the Soviet Union was the country of "victorious socialism," according to the 1934 Party Congress, which was known as the "Congress of Victors." Things became happier still in 1936, when the Stalin Constitution officially declared that socialism had been built in the Soviet Union.[56] Socialism also appeared victorious in the circus, where a new generation of young performers, forged during the first Five-Year Plan, replaced most of the foreign and unreformed performers who had once populated the Soviet rings. These happy products of victorious socialism could now meet the new demands of Soviet viewers, who were themselves celebrated products of victorious socialism. According to the official rhetoric, viewers demanded spectacles that would delight them by reflecting their own happiness. Clowns proved well-suited to the task of expressing the good cheer of an ordinary Soviet person, and many of them abandoned their face paint and exaggerated costumes in favor of personas they claimed to have modeled on the happy, smiling viewers they were hoping to amuse. The Stalinist circus, with its young, healthy, Soviet-born performers, whose happiness reflected the audience's own good cheer, was presented as proof that life in the Soviet Union really had become better and more joyous. Circus productions and the rhetoric surrounding them told the Soviet people that socialism really had been achieved and that there was good reason to believe that an even better Communist future was imminent, since Soviet youth were, literally, the embodiment of that future in the present. This certainly was something to cheer about, and, in the circus, happy cheers could always be heard.

According to the official rhetoric, by 1936 the means of circus production lay securely in the hands of newly improved Soviet viewers, who were once again imagined to be the producers rather than the products of the Soviet circus. A 1936 review by A. Nazarov in *Pravda* criticized Soviet circus art, "the favorite art of the popular masses," for continuing to "lag behind the demands that the culturally matured viewer" had set before it.[57] Two years later, at a meeting of leading state circus workers, Kholmskii, the director of the circus administration's artistic section, discussed the shortcomings of the circuses in similar terms. While he acknowledged that significant progress had been made, particularly in the replacement of foreign performers with Soviet youth, he insisted that the development of the circus continued to "lag behind the cultural growth of the viewer. . . . And further, more and more the circus lags behind the demands and political tasks that stand before us, those just desires and hopes, that the wide mass of viewers has placed before us."[58]

The Soviet state no longer demanded that the circus transform its viewers—officially, this task had already been accomplished—but rather that it transform itself in accordance with viewers' demands. And what the audience demanded was to be happy: "The people love the circus for its mirth, cheer, humor, festiveness, and elegance," an *Izvestiia* editorial stated in 1939.[59] The best way for the circus to make viewers happy, most commentators agreed, was to present them with young Soviet performers, the real products of socialism, whose happiness reflected their own.

As Kholmskii remarked in 1938, the most significant step the circuses had taken toward meeting the demands of Soviet viewers was to replace foreign, bourgeois performers—according to Evgenii Kuznetsov's

1939 account, more than 75 percent of Soviet circus routines were performed by foreigners in 1925[60]—with young Soviets, who were born after the revolution, reared under socialism, and trained in the state circus school. Similarly, even as A. Nazarov criticized the circus for failing to have met viewers' demands, he offered the Moscow Circus's opening program of the 1936 season as an exemplary show, though he noted that it was the exception. He identified "two particularities" that distinguished the production from earlier Soviet programs. First, the "bright spectacle" relied "exclusively on the strength of Soviet artists," who were accompanied by only one foreign artist. His second and related point was that the program was "composed of the forces of young performers, who have grown up under Soviet conditions." Nazarov went on to add a third feature, that "in the circus it is cheerful and entertaining," and singled out the clown Karan d'Ash (Karandash), a member of the first class to graduate from the State Circus School in 1930, whom he praised for "provoking a cheerful reaction from the viewers' hall."[61] In his review of the season's third program, Viktor Ermans similarly noted that only one foreign number was scheduled to be performed, and even that artist had not yet arrived in the country. He went on to note that even in provincial circuses, where foreign artists continued to appear, "with each month there are fewer and fewer of them." Ermans did, however, lament the failure of young performers to have fully mastered their technique and encouraged the circus administration to "continuously attend to the growth and development of young circus performers and help them to improve."[62]

By the following year, they did seem, to many, to have improved. In his review of the Moscow Circus's 1937 winter program, S. Dikovskii noted that of the fourteen numbers included in the show, only two were performed by foreigners. Young Soviet circus artists presented the others: "It is joyous [*radostno*] to see on the stage capable young people, to read in the playbills such ordinary last names as Anisimov, Likhachevich, Drozdov, in place of fanciful pseudonyms."[63] That year's program at the Leningrad Circus also featured "'Contemporaries of October [*Sverstniki Oktiabria*]' . . . the pupils of the Soviet circus, the students of the Soviet circus school, our wonderful artistic youth." According to the playbill, "the amalgamation of the best representatives of the October generation into one program emphasizes the essence, in terms both of principle and artistry, of Soviet circus art."[64]

Programs produced in the Moscow Circus's 1938 season were also greeted with unanimous praise by reviewers who congratulated young

Soviet performers for infecting the audience with their own happiness, which itself reflected the happiness of the current Soviet epoch. Al. Al'evich raved in *Izvestiia*: "Today is the day of youthful actors." He wrote that "all of the participants in the program cheerfully sing at the beginning of the production," and reported that "after the very first sounds of the song the viewer is immediately infected with the feeling of cheerfulness, merriment, and happiness."[65] Al'evich claimed that this feeling did not abandon viewers until the very end of the show, during which they all observed "how happily, easily, and fearlessly these young people work."[66] Iurii Dmitriev lauded the young acrobats Ingo and Darvest in similar terms. "When they enter the arena," he claimed, "you feel their youth. . . . They work so cheerfully, they make the most difficult leaps and formations so easily and happily that they unintentionally transfer their happiness to the people." Dmitriev concluded, without registering any contradiction, that "the cheerfulness of our epoch could not but be reflected in one of the most cheerful of the arts—the circus."[67]

In other words, circus programs made audiences happy by showing them how happy they already were. A review of the opening program of the 1938 winter season also celebrated the "successes of the young Soviet circus," which, though still insufficient, were indisputable. The reviewer insisted that the Soviet circus was proceeding along the proper path, toward "the creation of a bright, cheerful, and healthy spectacle," a development he attributed implicitly to the participation of "Soviet youth."[68] Viktor Ermans's review in *Sovetskoe iskusstvo* hailed the program as a "holiday of youth." Ermans described the "army of Soviet circus performers, who have grown up in the years after the revolution," as a "great cultural force, which has provided for the flowering of the beloved popular spectacle, the circus." Ermans attributed the recent success of the Soviet circus to the youthfulness of its performers who were "easy to work with" since they were not "burdened by the weight of the traditions and experience of the old circus."[69] Yet Al. Morov, writing the same year, added another explanation: these young people were not simply young, they were also Soviet, "raised and educated in Soviet reality," as, in 1938, only young people were.[70]

These cheerful, young, Soviet performers were the circus's so-called *vydvizhentsy*. As Sheila Fitzpatrick explains, in the mid-1930s, former workers and peasants, who were educated during the first Five-Year Plan, were promoted into prominent positions within various Soviet governmental, technical, and cultural institutions.[71] With their ascendance, the Soviet state would finally become a workers' and peasants' state, and the Soviet circus would finally become a workers' and peasants' circus. As Viktor Ermans explained in his 1938 review, the majority of young circus artists "are Soviet *fizkul'turniki*. From factories and plants, through the circus technical college, they have arrived in the arena."[72] In his brief account of the history of the Soviet circus, published by *Pravda* in honor of the twenty-year anniversary of the circus's nationalization, L. Nikulin similarly explained that the foreign performers, who had once populated Russian circus rings, had recently been replaced by "tens and hundreds of new young Soviet artists." According to Nikulin, these young cadres were athletes and physical culture enthusiasts, who were recruited to enter the Circus School from "factories, plants, railroad workshops, collective farms, and mines." Nikulin concluded by extending a warm greeting to the jubilee, "which has given birth to and cultivated strong, beautiful, agile, and courageous artists, who have significantly elevated the art of the circus."[73]

At this time, most Soviet institutions were giving birth to, cultivating, and, most importantly, employing properly Soviet young people, who were, in turn, elevating those institutions. Yet this was a particularly happy development in the circus, where young "replacements," as the Leningrad Circus's 1937 program billed them, did not, according to the official rhetoric, literally replace older, improperly Soviet cadres, many of whom, in other fields, had been purged from their positions.[74] In the circus, foreigners were being replaced, which implied not only that a socialist circus could be built in one country but also that the circus was free of any unhappy involvement in the Terror. Circus performances in the late 1930s even sought to demonstrate the close relationship maintained between the two generations of Soviet performers, the older of which facilitated the younger's advancement, without, apparently, suffering as a consequence of it. For example, the circus exhibition featured at the 1938 All-Union Agricultural Exhibition staged a competition between young and older performers, according to Viktor Ermans's account. While the young performers, many of whom had recently graduated from the Circus School, displayed their "precision" and "balance," the older performers "invariably perfect their own outstanding skill" and demonstrate "how excellent their strength and knowledge is." Ermans did not fail to note that the program was composed entirely of Soviet performers, with one exception: "The sea lion Fritz, a native of far off California, is the sole foreigner."[75] Another account of the development of the Soviet circus over the previous twenty years

also emphasized the continuity between the older and younger generations. According to M. Khrapchenko, writing in *Pravda*, the prerevolutionary Russian circus strove to "play on the basest feelings, indulge
backward tastes" and "to stun 'the public.'" In contrast, he continued,
the work of Soviet circus artists is "imbued with an awareness of the
dignity of the citizen of the Soviet country. . . . Soviet artists display
wonderful models of strength, agility, and inventiveness; they demonstrate bright and cheerful art, which excites and captivates viewers with
beauty and perfection." Not surprisingly, Khrapchenko attributed the
evolution of Soviet circus art to the work of young Soviet performers,
but he also gave some credit to the older generation: "Together with the
most advanced masters of the older generation, young masters created
their own particular style of circus art."[76]

In 1938 the Moscow Circus offered a program that showcased two
generations of circus artists, both "fathers and sons," as B. Ermans described them in *Sovetskoe iskusstvo*. Ermans explained that "they say
that in the Soviet Union there are no old people," which, he continued,
was particularly apparent in the circus, where "all are young." Ermans
meant, of course, that in the circus everybody was youthful, regardless
of their age. What it meant to be youthful, he went on to imply, was to
be properly Soviet. Ermans offered the example of Vitalii Efimovich
Lazarenko, long recognized as the first and most properly Soviet circus
performer of them all: "Look at how much ardor Vitalii Lazarenko puts
into his monologues that are directed against 'feeble people' [*shliap*],
truants, and slovenly individuals. Can you really believe that before us
stands an artist who has given forty years of uninterrupted work to the
circus? His genre is political clowning. He is able to hold the attention
of the audience, arouse in it patriotic feelings and provoke good laughter." Ermans proceeded to offer his opinion that one of the best numbers
in the program was performed by Vitalii Efimovich Lazarenko and his
son, Vitalii Vitalevich Lazarenko, who had mastered a variety of genres,
including dancing, juggling, and jumping. To conclude their routine,
the two exchanged "pleasantries": Vitalii Efimovich cried, "Long live
children!" to which his own son replied, "Long live fathers!" and then
concluded with the shout: "Comrades, value elders."[77] Vitalii Vitalevich
heeded his own command. In an interview printed in a 1939 issue of
Sovetskoe iskusstvo, he stated that "working jointly with my father helped
me greatly. . . . Under the direction of my father I perfected my art" and
succeeded in jumping across eight horses. The interview concluded

with Lazarenko's recitation of a pair of couplets that he composed in honor of the twentieth anniversary of the Soviet circus, "a great holiday" for circus artists and viewers:

S molodezh'iu nashei boevoiu
Khorosho zhivetsia vam i mne.
Ia svoe iskusstvo molodoe
Posviashchaiu molodoi strane.

[With our fighting youth
you and I will live well!
I dedicate my young art
to a young country.][78]

Lazarenko identified himself as one of the fighting young people who would help all the inhabitants of the young country to live well. His sentiment was consistent with the celebration of youth at the time, a category from which, to his mind, the older generation need not be excluded. As Ermans similarly implied, to be young was to be Soviet and to be Soviet was to be young—a strange claim to which the "young art" of the circus seemed, to many, to lend credibility.

The appearance of the "Soviet generation" of happy, youthful, upwardly mobile performers in circus rings across the country was presented as tangible proof that socialism really had been achieved in the Soviet Union. Unlike the bountiful harvests depicted in paintings, the colossal construction projects celebrated in the press, or the positive heroes portrayed in novels, these performers really did exist, flawlessly, in the present. Yet they were real in another sense too, at least according to the official rhetoric. In the 1930s, circus performers were thought to reflect and, in the case of clowns, to give expression to Soviet reality. Ermans and Vitalii Vitalevich Lazarenko maintained that the circus was young, just like the Soviet Union. Iurii Dmitriev argued that the circus was cheerful, just like life in the Soviet Union, and that circus performers were optimistic, just like all Soviet people were. In a 1939 pamphlet on P. Maiatskii's motorcycle attraction, A. A. Dorokhov stated that "the young artists of the circus, who have been cultivated by the Great October Socialist Revolution, strive in their grand and valuable work to reflect the hero of our construction, to show the valor, courage, and strength of our people, to glorify the great Soviet motherland."[79]

Real Soviet Clowning

It was at this time, too, that clowns began to present themselves, or their personas, as real Soviets, whose thoughts, feelings, and appearance were identical to those of the Soviet people who surrounded them in the audience. In 1938, for example, Vitalii Efimovich Lazarenko explained that after the October Revolution he adopted a less exaggerated costume and a more topical repertoire as a consequence of his internalization of the viewers' attitudes and ideas. At the time, he explained, "I did not set for myself the goal of studying political propaganda. But insofar as I was strongly connected to my viewers and not only was not ashamed of being a gallery *ryzhii*, but even took pride in this, then naturally, I began to live by the ideas and interests of my viewers, and these were the ideas and interests of the masses, the interests and ideas of the working people."[80] According to Iurii Dmitriev's profile of the clown, published in *Sovetskoe iskusstvo*, Lazarenko was well aware of the interests and ideas of the working people, with whom he had come into frequent contact while working as an itinerant performer in the pre-revolutionary Russian circuses. According to Dmitriev, for fifteen years Lazarenko "traveled from one provincial city to another, always in third class, among the simple folks, he listened to much, inquired about much, and knew very well the ideas and mood of his audience. He was one of the first circus clowns who turned to the themes that concerned the viewers in the galleries, who reflected their mood." Dmitriev maintained that Lazarenko's strength as a performer lay "in his topicality, in that he found himself in constant contact with the audience and reflected their ideas and mood." He concluded that Lazarenko became a Soviet actor when he began to present exclusively topical material. The ideal Soviet clown was, in other words, a real Soviet clown, who looked like a real Soviet person, thought like a real Soviet person, and was concerned with real life in the Soviet Union.[81]

Like Lazarenko, Mikhail Rumiantsev began performing as a carpet *ryzhii* but quickly rejected this mask in favor of a persona that he claimed realistically represented the ordinary Soviet individual. Rumiantsev graduated from the Circus School in 1930 and made his debut as the *ryzhii* Vasia later that year. In a revealing passage of his postwar memoir, Rumiantsev attributed his decision to perform as a *ryzhii* clown to the limited availability of costumes in the Second State Circus, where he had no choice but to appear in the dated costumes of the old Nikitin circus. Yet he claimed in spite of this impediment to have done everything he could to transform his character into an everyday person. He chose the common name "Vasia" because he wanted to create a character who represented the "soul of society," and he "strove toward an everyday image and not toward the trite figure of the circus *ryzhii*."[82] It was not until 1936, however, that Rumiantsev finally developed a more naturalistic clown character. Performing in his first season with the Leningrad circus, he appeared in the ring without makeup, wearing a baggy jacket with a striped shirt and slightly oversized pants. He named this character Karan d'Ash (Karandash), after the Russian-born, French cartoonist Caran d'Ache, who derived his own playful penname from the Russian word *karandash*, meaning pencil. Rumiantsev explained that the name suited the everyday nature of his new persona, "above all because a pencil is a widespread, popular, pedestrian object."[83] The clown then claimed literally to have drawn his new character from the masses of healthy, happy, ordinary Soviet citizens who surrounded him in the streets and in the ring: "My hero is a normal, healthy, smiling person, very active, who rushes everywhere and reacts to every funny situation with a child's directness. . . . His smile is healthy and calm, and the optimistic feeling of the contemporary Soviet person is already reflected in it."[84]

It was Karandash's happy smile, his youthfulness, and his optimism that made him a recognizably Soviet person, according to his creator. Tat'iana Tess agreed. In her 1939 review of Rumiantsev's repertoire, she described the clown's typical entrance into the ring and emphasized his youthfulness and good cheer: "As always, he enters the ring cheerfully and unburdened, as if he is concerned only with entertaining himself. From a running start, he slides across the carpet just like children do on icy pavement. . . . With him it is simply very cheerful, around him there is a pure and good atmosphere of cheer." As a result, she explained, "the sympathy of the hall is always on his side. In all his escapades, the hall is his accomplice."[85] This was not surprising, given that the clown was created to be just like one of the viewers. As Rumiantsev wrote,

Today I feel myself at times not so much in the ring, as among the public. Sometimes it even seems to me that I am one of the viewers, perhaps, the most immediate, who did not sit in the amphitheater, but came down into the ring in order to watch everything more closely, and himself try to imitate the artists' tricks. My Karandash is a liaison between the arena and the amphitheater. The public immediately recognizes something of itself in him and eagerly awaits his first appearance, as if they are meeting an old friend. Between Karandash and the public, close relations are immediately established. He expresses aloud the public's opinion of the previous number, at times astonished, at times skeptical. It is as if he invites the viewer to be an accomplice in his tricks. He does not especially try to make the public laugh, to the contrary, together with it he laughs at his own pranks and eccentricities.[86]

Rumiantsev's repertoire included a series of skits in which he really did appear to be an ordinary member of the audience, who suddenly found himself in the ring and attempted to replicate the trick he had just witnessed. In one routine, Karandash paraded a small dog around the ring, mimicking the ceremonious entrances of the animal trainers. The clown then produced a plate and a string of sausages, which he dramatically displayed before the audience. With a flourish, he tore off one of the sausages and placed it on the plate. He then set the plate before the dog and the sausage instantly disappeared. The clown raised the empty plate and, beaming with pride, bowed to the delighted audience, and the two ran out of the ring like a pair of pranksters.[87] In another routine, Karandash expressed the audience's presumed skepticism toward the conjurer by making a bottle vanish and then stepping to the side so that it fell out of his pants. The clown also revealed the trick to Igor' Kio's "magical" ability to levitate people. Karandash agreed to allow the famous magician to levitate him, but insisted on wearing his hat during the trick. When the magician adamantly refused, the audience learned that Kio's powers actually depended on an apparatus attached to the volunteer's head.[88]

In one of the clown's most celebrated routines, he played the role of an eager but inept student of the art of tightrope walking. According to Nikulin's description of the historic skit, one of the tightrope walkers who had just performed invited Karandash to join him on the high wire. The naïve, overly optimistic clown decided to try his luck and began to walk gingerly across the rope, clinging to the performer's shoulders. After crossing half the rope, the clown was distracted by an itch and he lowered his arms to scratch his leg. Oblivious to the clown's hesitation, the artist continued to walk forward with the balancing pole. When he realized that he had been abandoned, Karandash sat down astride the rope: "The small man, left to the mercy of fate, cowering and clinging tightly to the rope, timidly looked back, then down, and let out a heart-wrenching scream."[89] The clown gradually pulled himself together and began to devise a solution. He looked down at the netting, ten meters below. As if trying to estimate the distance, Karandash dropped his hat, then took out an actual tape measure and calculated the distance. Glancing slyly at the audience, the clown produced a skein of cord, long enough to be tied at one end to the rope and then lowered down to the netting. Yet he simply threw the cord across the rope, so that the two ends dangled above the net. Karandash confidently grasped both halves of the cord and began his descent. When he reached the end of the shorter half of the cord, the entire cord slipped down and Karandash flew into the netting from a great height. As he fell, the terrified clown surreptitiously flung off his wig to reveal a bushy head of hair standing on end. He jumped down from the net and fled behind the curtain. Although this skit actually required the skill of a well-trained professional, Karandash appeared to be walking the wire for the first time, just like any ordinary man given the chance to try his luck at something new.

Karandash's young, cheerful, heroic persona, when taken to be a realistic reflection of everyday Soviet people, implied that everyday Soviet people really were young, cheerful and heroic. Viewers' obvious affection for the clown was also taken to be a realistic reflection of their demand for young, cheerful, heroic Soviet clowns. Rumianstev's routines, like Maiatskii's and all those performed by smiling young Soviets, told the Soviet people who they had become. Yet they also told the Soviet people who they were supposed to become, since these performances were less descriptive of real Soviet people than they were prescriptive of an ideal Soviet person, who would, as a consequence of these performances, be incarnated in the future. Recall that Iurii Dmitriev considered the circus to be a reflection of happy Soviet life, and yet he also thought that circus performers transferred their own happiness to the audience. A. A. Dorokhov insisted that heroic young performers, like Maiatskii, strove to reflect the heroic products of socialist construction, and yet he also thought that they strove "to aid in the cultivation of steadfast, resolute, and strong defenders of our native borders." Dorokhov quoted Maiatskii's own stated intention that his performances transform the audience: "I hope . . . that the viewer left the circus infected with good cheer, bravery and courage."

The idea that properly Soviet audiences demanded a properly Soviet circus that would make them proper Soviets resembled the formula proposed by students of audience reception during NEP, which is not surprising, given that, in both cases, the circus was introduced as evidence of the revolution's success. The difference was that in this period, Soviet viewers laughed and clapped, stomped and cheered for the young performers who really were the products of socialist construction. Moreover, the possibility that everyday Soviets had not yet become the brave and cheerful heroes they would be in the future did not render their representatives in the ring any less realistic. Soviet circus performers were youthful and, as such, they were still in a process of development. They were, literally, the future in the present. Their performances and the rhetoric surrounding them, which identified being young with being Soviet, implied that all real Soviets were still in a process of becoming. This story helped account for the less cheerful aspects of the socialist present, and it also implied that people whose development had halted—the implicitly unreformable victims of the purges—were not real Soviets and never would become real Soviets, since, as the story went, their development had been halted.

In the mid-1930s, young smiling Soviet circus performers and the young smiling Soviet people whose happiness they purportedly reflected were said to signify socialism's recent victory and communism's future achievement. Their performances and the rhetoric surrounding them relied on a system of signs that they simultaneously refused, since, unlike other "representations of reality in its revolutionary development," circus performers and their audiences really did exist, literally, in the present. In the circus, things really did appear to be exactly what they were said to be, which was something Mikhail Rumiantsev understood very well. In one well-known skit, Karandash entered the ring after a troupe of bronze-painted acrobats had completed its routine. The clown began to chase them around the ring, and when he finally caught up with one and kicked him soundly on the leg, a bronze gong resounded through the arena. In the circus, the painted bronze man really was made of bronze. Karandash's donkey, when equipped with a bicycle seat, handlebars, and tiny license plate, also really was a bicycle: when, halfway across the ring, the donkey refused to budge, Karandash hopped off to fetch a bicycle pump, which he tied around the donkey's leg and pumped. With the "flat tire" repaired, the two continued on their way. For the clown, everything really was exactly what it was said to be, which was another aspect of his youthful, childlike sensibility. His viewers might have taken these routines to be a lesson in the very method of representation on which socialist realism relied. They might have been convinced that, like the bronze men and the bicycle, they, themselves, and the circus performers who represented them in the ring, really were so many smiling young Soviets, who really were, or were at least becoming, incarnations of the socialist present and the Communist future.

Yet the bronze man was not really made of bronze, and the donkey was not really a bicycle, which is what made Karandash's skits so funny. He mistook these things to be exactly what they were said to be, as only a fool would do. His routines thus might have prompted viewers to wonder whether anything was what it was said to be and sometimes even did appear to be. In one routine, titled "The Incident in the Park," Karandash actually dramatized his own failure to have become the very thing he was trying to be, which was, in this case, a model of perfection. The scene took place in a summer garden where a statue of the Venus de Milo stood guarded by a young man who was responsible for maintaining the park. Karandash entered the garden carrying a washbasin and a birch bough, evidently returning from the *bania*. Hoping to rest for a bit, the clown approached one of the benches, but the guard shooed him away, explaining that the benches had been painted recently and were not yet dry. The insistent clown sat down anyway, and his suit, cap, and hands were covered with stripes of green paint. In order to scrub his hands, the clown reached into his wash basin for his soap sponge, but he dropped the slippery soap, which slid from his grasp a number of times. As he bent down to get it, he accidentally bumped into the statue, which tipped over and broke into pieces—an indication, already, of the fragility of seemingly substantial artistic representations. The clown tried to put the statue together again, but he confused all of its parts. Suddenly, he heard the guard approaching and hurried to find a hiding place. Finally, he stumbled upon a solution. The clown pulled his long white shirt out from his pants so that it covered his legs, stuffed his arms into the shirt, and climbed onto the pedestal. The guard approached and noticed the debris, which he began to sweep up. Karandash thought his disguise had saved him, but a sudden wind blew his cap away, which caught the guard's attention. The guard finally noticed the interloper and chased him out of the ring to the laughter and applause of the audience.

In this skit, the clown had failed to become the statue, and his routine might have been taken as a lesson in the impossibility of transforming oneself into any model of human perfection. It might have encouraged some viewers to wonder whether all circus performers were, like Karandash, merely imposters. It might have encouraged other viewers, who did not doubt that circus performers were who they were said to be, to wonder whether they, like Karandash, might find it impossible to assume the identity of any artistic representation. Yet others, most likely including the state officials who approved the act, might have taken the routine to be a lesson in the impossibility of falsely assuming any identity. For them, what might have mattered most was that the guard discovered the imposter, who would not get away with wrecking the statue. Yet other viewers might have found their sympathies to lie less with the guard than with the clown, who was, after all, one of them. They might have discovered in his routine a potentially effective, if poorly executed, tactic for avoiding reprisal and evading figures of authority. Yet what mattered most was that Soviet viewers always laughed and happily clapped, regardless of whose side they took in "The Incident in the Park," whatever significance they attributed to the performances by the two Lazarenkos, and no matter what they took the new generation of circus performers to represent. Circus performers really were young, smiling Soviets, just as their viewers also really were joyful and maybe even more optimistic in the circus, which really was a product of Soviet socialism.

Conclusion

Between 1934 and 1939, producers, performers, and official reviewers presented the circus as proof that the revolution in the Soviet Union had succeeded, just as they had between 1919 and 1929. Only now, evidence of this myth was located not in the purportedly revolutionary content of circus performances that offered audiences an education in socialist values, which they supposedly demanded. Instead, proof of socialism's victory could be seen in the young performers who had been raised in the Soviet Union and trained according to the properly socialist methods that they continued to employ in their performances. According to the official rhetoric, these performers, who were themselves the products of the Great Transformation, helped to secure this second Soviet revolution by forging new Soviet men and women from among the viewers who saw them on display. Circus performers accomplished this task with such success that by the end of the decade, they were instructed to work even harder to meet the new demands of the new Soviet viewers, who were recognized, once again, as being not only perfectible but the already perfected subjects into whose hands the means of Soviet cultural production could again be placed. According to all accounts, by 1939, the revolutionary transformation of Soviet circus performers and viewers—and by extension all of Soviet culture and society—had succeeded. The only aspect of the Soviet circus that seemed to escape the revolution was the content of the repertoire itself, which continued to feature purely athletic routines and slapstick clowning skits—Karandash's reprises were an exception, but they did as much to dismantle as to establish the official myth that new, smiling, optimistic, Soviet men really existed. In this respect, the second revolution in the circus had failed as thoroughly as the first, and though there would be no third revolution declared in the circus, the ideological content of Soviet circus performances was finally fully transformed during World War II. This was, oddly, a period in which the official myth surrounding the circus was that it had not changed at all.

3

Roaring, Laughter
The Circus at War

In early September 1941, less than three months after the Soviet Union entered World War II, the Moscow circus launched its winter season. G. Aleksandrov described the scene on opening night: "In a blacked-out, bleak, and war-torn Moscow, thousands of people gathered at the circus. Bright lamps burned and spot lights shone under the circus top as if there were no black-out, as if the war had changed nothing at all in the circus." Yet, he continued, this impression was a false one. Rather, like most things, the circus changed when the war came. Aleksandrov observed that viewers' eyes gleamed and that they exchanged glances and applauded thunderously at the conclusion of the program's opening monologue, which celebrated the feeling of fellowship enjoyed by all Muscovites at war. He noted that viewers took the program's politically inflected routines to heart and also enjoyed its more comedic moments, gratefully bursting into "sincere, cheerful" laughter whenever something funny happened in the ring. Aleksandrov concluded that "only people certain of their future, certain of their victory can laugh like that."[1] The laughter that Aleksandrov heard that night was no different from the laughter that had always resounded in the circus ring, which was precisely why it came to mean something new in the

92

context of war. The audience's laughter was now understood to be an expression of its confidence in the certainty of victory, of its fearlessness in the face of danger, and of its unflagging morale. Paradoxically, the very constancy of the circus enabled it to propagate the new myths that producers, performers, and official commentators relied on it to elaborate during the war.

As soon as the Germans invaded, the circus was enlisted to serve in the war effort alongside most other forms of art and entertainment. Wartime posters, poems, press pamphlets, and films depicted the Germans as inhuman beasts and sought to mobilize the population to defend itself against a hateful, terrifying enemy. At the same time, cartoons and caricatures of feeble, foolish, and ridiculous Germans inspired confidence in the inevitability of their defeat. Popular songs and poems extolled the Soviet motherland and aroused patriotic sentiments, while novels, films, paintings, and plays celebrated courageous frontline heroes and tragically fallen martyrs. Classical music concerts lifted morale by bringing listeners together to experience something of normal life in times of peace.[2]

The circus did all these things too, and, by doing them all at once, it also did something more: it sought to conquer fear. In the wartime circus, Soviet enemies appeared by turns ferocious and feeble, mighty and meek, frightening and frail. Animal trainers and their promoters in the press exaggerated the dangers posed by the powerful, bloodthirsty, and vicious beasts, who were, nevertheless, almost always cowed by their skillful, courageous, and patient human adversaries. These routines aroused and then allayed viewers' fears of the grave and mortal threats that they themselves faced outside of the circus. For their part, clowns deployed laughter as a potent antidote to fear, most often by depicting the Nazis as absurd creatures of a lower order. The wartime circus was presented as proof that nobody, not even a person with his or her head in the mouth of a lion, had anything to fear. It helped maintain the myth that no matter how unfamiliar everything had become, it would all go back to normal in the end.

Laughter

One week after Germany invaded the Soviet Union, the artistic director of the Main Administration of State Circuses (GUTs), Evgenii Kuznetsov, outlined the new demands that the state had placed on the circus. He identified the "most immediate task of the Soviet circus" as the "fast, efficient" introduction of "an up-to-date and highly agitational military and anti-fascist repertoire." He explained that "now more than ever the circus should 'resound,' 'resound' with the pointed, well-aimed political word of the publicist, the satirist, and the poet." Kuznetsov went on to identify various forms of the "spoken genre" that might best purvey politically agitational content, including the emotional monologue, the politically pointed feuilleton, the tendentious couplet, the clever ditty, the buffooning pamphlet, and the pithy political reprise. He concluded his report by reminding any readers who doubted the circus's readiness for war of the great military tradition of the Soviet circus, whose performers served the Red Army during the civil war by propagandizing military and revolutionary themes. Predictably, Kuznetsov cited the example of Vitalii Lazarenko, "that strong and colorful revolutionary satirical jester," who "spoke in a loud voice on the themes of the intervention, the civil war, and the defense of the motherland."[3]

Eight months later, Kuznetsov signed an order recognizing the particular significance that "the sharp political word, which inspires the Soviet people to new military and industrial feats and which stigmatizes the enemy with vicious and accurate satire," had acquired under the conditions of war. The order explained that, "with great rapidity, events on the fronts of the Fatherland war are unfolding, the heroic Red Army is routing the fascist aggressors, more and more frequently, the radio announces that Soviet lands have been liberated from the enemy and provides new evidence of the heroism of the Soviet people and the vandalism of the fascist aggressors. The home front is growing stronger, with its powerful burst of labor productivity, which is helping the Red Army to defeat the enemy." The order directed the circus to respond quickly and broadly to these events with topical anti-fascist routines. Circus directors were given one month to incorporate into their programs introductory monologues that detailed the most recent military events and mobilized the audience on behalf of the struggle against German fascism. Artists and writers were notified that they would be paid only for submissions to the repertoire that addressed military and anti-fascistic themes.[4]

In response to Kuznetsov's directives, as well as the financial incentives offered by GUTs, many Soviet clowns did return to the genre of politically tendentious clowning that was first made famous by Lazarenko. As a result, the wartime circus became, once again, a safe place for language. In order to forecast the Soviet victory, praise Soviet soldiers, and ridicule the enemy, clowns relied on both direct speech and the kinds of metaphorical devices that had often been employed to ridicule Soviet enemies in the past.[5] In the 1920s, Lazarenko had made frequent use of metaphor to malign the enemy—recall his identification of an inflated bladder that he went on to pop as "the Old Regime"—and to dramatize the revolution, which he represented most often as a leap. This was precisely the kind of metaphorical device that Karandash undermined to such comedic effect in the 1930s, and to which clowns returned during the war.

Even Karandash, the clown most suspicious of language in the 1930s, adopted a new repertoire, rich in verbiage and metaphor, to address the themes of war.[6] The clown later explained that during the war, "our art needed to be raised to the battle. Satire needed to be directed against the enemy, needed to affect those people who didn't help us enough in the struggle against fascism. . . . It was necessary to search out and find a way to combine serious political themes with the particularities of my genre."[7] One of the ways he did this was by introducing satirical elements into conventional comedic routines. For example, Karandash devised a skit in which he failed to discipline an unruly animal, which represented the target of his satirical barb. In this routine, Karandash entered the arena carrying a briefcase, which he set down beside an orator's podium. The clown then produced a small dog from his briefcase and sat it down in front of the microphone. He placed the dog's paws on the lectern in an orator's pose, and the dog began to bark loudly into the microphone. Finally, Karandash decided to coax the animal down from his perch, but his efforts were for naught; the dog continued to bark. The exasperated clown finally erupted, "Stop blathering!" and the dog obediently climbed down from the podium. But as soon as Karandash let him out of his sight, the dog jumped back onto the lectern and started to bark again. After finally completing his speech, the dog climbed back into the briefcase, and Karandash announced, "The speech by Minister of Propaganda Goebbels is finished."[8] This routine relied on metaphor to identify Goebbels as a dog, while it further secured the status of language by associating its absence, or, more precisely, its distortion, with the enemy's perfidy.

In another frequently performed skit, Karandash entered the ring dressed in a tin pot helmet, wielding an axe and a club. He confidently climbed onto a fascist "tank," which was represented by a barrel on wheels with a swastika and skull and crossbones painted on its sides.

As he mounted the tank, the "German commando" shouted, *"Nach Moskau!"* Yet contrary to the soldier's bold pronouncement—again, the enemy's words failed to signify their intended meaning—the tank merely rolled a couple of inches before it let out a bang and fell to pieces. The unfortunate soldier crawled out from under the wreckage and, with his clothes in tatters, hobbled out of the ring on crutches.

Other clowns also relied upon speech, metaphor, and narrative to execute routines that heralded the Soviet victory and ridiculed anybody who might stand in its way. Some clowns made fools of Soviet enemies simply by playing their parts in the ring. One clown, for example, appeared as Ion Antonescu, who was dressed in women's clothes and repeatedly subjected to the abuses of a Nazi soldier, who was also played by a clown, until both were blown up by a bomb that Soviet partisans had disguised as a music box.[9] Most often, however, clowns used animals to represent the objects of their derision. For example, in December 1941, Vladimir Durov introduced a wartime routine that he had developed in collaboration with Demian Bednyi. As each of his charges entered the ring, the trainer recited a series of satirical verses identifying the animals as various enemies of the Soviet Union. To accompany the goose, which marched around the ring with a dignified air, Durov read:

Vot gus'. Solidneishaia ptitsa.
On slavoi pradedov gorditsia.
Byl predkami ego
kogda-to Rim spasen.
Rim nynche varvarstvom fashistskim
potriasen.
Ves' mir shmeshat
ego besslavnye pokhody.
Uzh on nad propast'iu
stoit odnoi nogoi,
No v etom vsem povinen
gus' drugoi
Chernorubashechnoi, bezdarneishei porody.[10]

[Here is a goose. A most respectable bird.
He takes pride in his forefathers' glory.
Once upon a time,
his ancestors had saved Rome.
Today Rome has been shaken
by fascist barbarians.

The whole world is amused
by his inglorious marches.
He already stands on one leg
above the abyss,
But for all of this, another goose,
of a black-shirted, third-rate breed
is to blame.]

Later in the act, a group of dogs dressed as "diplomats" fought each other furiously as they were conveyed around the ring. Durov addressed the crowd:

S podruchnymi svoimi psami
Pes Gitler, znaete vy sami,
Igraet v druzhbu—napokaz.
Na nikh kul'tury vneshnei znaki,
Diplomaticheskie fraki.
A soberutsia glaz na glaz
Peregryzutsia kazhdyi raz.
Zver'e! Oskalennye pasti!
Pred nami vrazheskaia "os'"
Ona treshchit i vdol' i vkos'.
My razdrobim ee na chasti.[11]

[With his lapdogs
the dog Hitler, as you yourselves know,
plays at friendship—just for show.
They wear outward signs of culture,
all sorts of diplomatic gowns.
But when they get together
they go for each other's throats.
Beasts! Teeth bared!
Before us is the enemy "axis"
It is cracking along its length and width.
We'll break it to pieces.]

In another case, Durov cast his dog Nera as the victorious Soviet soldier rather than the vanquished enemy. Durov recited a series of verses explaining how Nera would behave if she were personally to meet Hitler, who was represented as a cannibal (Germans were often labeled man-eaters and cannibals in the Soviet press and posters[12]):

Nera metnulas' by
liudoedu na grud'
I vpilas' zubami v ego glotku.
Eto byl by otvet
V pokaze nagliadnom i tochnom
Vot chto tebia, liudoed,
Zhdet na fronte Vostochnom.[13]

[Nera would leap up
onto the cannibal's chest
And take him by the throat with her teeth.
This would be an answer
Given clearly and precisely
As to what awaits you, cannibal,
On the Eastern front!]

Finally, Hitler himself appeared as a dog in the Soviet circus ring, at the climax of a lengthy pantomime dramatizing the fate of a typical German soldier, who was played by a clown endowed with a pig's snout, a large belly, a flabby backside, and spindly legs. In the opening scene, the German soldier, called Fritz (the Soviets' derogatory name for all German soldiers), ran around the ring, chasing a dog that eventually sat down and refused to move. Fritz tugged on the dog, reminding his comrade in arms: "The Führer said to advance. If Moscow is taken, the war is over." The dog rebuffed the German soldier, who eventually thought to offer the dog a bottle of vodka that was hanging from his belt. The dog instantly stood up on its hind legs, reached toward the bottle, drank from it, and promptly sat down again. The puzzled soldier asked himself why the dog refused to budge and suddenly realized that, rightly enough, the dog was waiting for a bite of food to chase down its drink. He addressed the dog, "Comrade, if you only knew what kind of lunch awaits us in Moscow. We'll have *wurst* and *saurkraut*. Doesn't that entice you?" The dog remained unmoved, and the exasperated soldier cried out, "There is Moscow! Don't you see?" When he leaned forward to extend his hand, with his finger pointed toward Moscow, the binoculars that hung from his belt fell into a horizontal position, allowing the dog to stand up on his hind legs and look through them, fixing his view on Fritz's rear end. Fritz asked the dog whether he had caught sight of Moscow just as a shot resounded near the main entrance to the ring. The shot was followed by a voice shouting, "Here is your *wurst*," and, after a second shot rang out, "Here is your *saurkraut*!"

The startled soldier cried out, "The Russians! The Russians!" just as the dog broke free of the harness and began to run in circles around Fritz, who finally chased the dog offstage, bringing the first act to a close.

The ring was set for the second act with a single cannon standing behind a field of crosses that marked the graves of fallen soldiers and a single cannon. Beside one cross, which was adorned with a German helmet, stood a table, a chair, and a small stove. The scene began when an injured pig entered the ring at a run and began to jump over the crosses. Fritz chased the piglet, shouting "Halt! Halt!" and then approached the cannon, which, at his command, shot a dog across the length of the ring. Fritz, preoccupied by the piglet, took no notice of the dog, even when it climbed onto the table and hid inside a covered bowl. Fritz finally managed to quiet the piglet by shooting it. He gathered the fallen piglet into a pot and set it on the stove, but the instant he turned away, the piglet dashed across the arena. Fritz again gave chase, and the piglet eventually jumped back into the pot, which the soldier quickly sealed with the lid. Yet as soon as Fritz had finished setting the table for lunch, the piglet again escaped his fate, this time jumping out from the pot and onto the table, scattering the plates, and finally landing in the sugar bowl. When Fritz noticed that the piglet had thwarted his plans once again, he chased it out of the ring, shouting, "*Verflukhte Schweine!* Shoot them! Hang them! If they don't want to submit! Because of that damned sergeant-major piglet, the German army will end up eating some sort of day-old rubbish." The dejected soldier sat down at the table and took the cover off another dish, mute with fright as the dog jumped from the dish and ran out of the ring.

The succeeding acts dramatized Fritz's decline, until finally, in the climactic episode, the defeated soldier confronted his leader, a dog. The two stood beside a table, above which hung a horn of plenty that overflowed with sausages, hams, rolls, pretzels, and other victuals. Fritz turned to "Hitler," and said, "Tell me, Führer, what did you dream of when you invaded the Soviet Union?" The dog climbed onto a chair and rested his paws on the table, so that his nose approached the horn of plenty. "Ah," said Fritz, "You thought to feed yourself here." The dog barked affirmatively, and Fritz responded, "And do you think this is what awaits you in the Soviet Union?" The dog jumped down to the ground and, chastened, crawled under the table. The stagehands came to clear away the table, leaving in its place only a coffin—in which the dog, Hitler, lay.[14] This routine cast the Soviet citizen as a wily piglet who refused to submit, while representing Hitler as a dog and the home front as a horn of plenty. It presented viewers with an elaborate narrative plot employed to glorify the Soviet forces, stir up hatred for an enemy that threatened Soviet prosperity, and generate confidence in the inevitable defeat of a frail, inhuman enemy.

A skit titled "The March of Germany and Their Vassals to the U.S.S.R.," written by A. S. Rudini, conveyed this last message more succinctly. It featured a group of trained dogs that marched into the ring on their hind legs wearing Nazi uniforms and carrying weapons. The dogs proceeded to march up a hill that stood in the center of the ring and was adorned with a spherical map of the Soviet Union. The task, however, proved extremely difficult, as any dogs that succeeded in scrambling up the hill simply tumbled down the other side. They struggled up the hill again, and down again they fell. Finally, the dog wearing Hitler's uniform began to walk away from the hill, and the other dogs, tired and tattered from their tumbles, followed him on their hind legs. Hitler scanned the arena for a way out and eventually noticed a gallows that stood in the ring. He approached the gallows and put his head in a noose. All the while, the animal trainer read a monologue on the theme of the Germans' defeat.[15]

These comedic animal acts provoked the audience's fear of the Germans and then immediately relieved it. As Rosalinde Sartorti recounts, workers had used similar, if more literal, means to satirize enemy figures in the 1920s. Specifically, they created "effigies, models, and dummies" of kulaks, capitalists, and imperialists and engaged them in such recognizable positions as "'the Sick Englishman between the legs of a Chinese coolie'" and "'the imperialist puck who licks the feet of the bound kulak.'" Sartorti explains that, as papier-mâché figures, these "enemy powers were made ridiculous, and their actual power was at least symbolically dissolved." "Instead of causing fear or anxiety," she continues, "one could look at them and laugh." Sartorti concludes that these displays forecast the future defeat of popular enemies.[16] Similarly, laughter in the circus had long been recognized as a powerful if ambiguous weapon, capable of hastening the defeat of enemies that were, as objects of ridicule, already symbolically vanquished. Recall Lunacharskii's definition of laughter as a sharp weapon, as the "aspen stake that is driven into the recently slaughtered dark wizard, who is prepared to return from his coffin."[17] Durov echoed this sentiment in a wartime monologue, written by Dem'ian Bednyi, that explained how he and his troupe might serve the cause of national defense:

Prisvoennoe nam oruzhie nashe smekh.
Oruzhie ostroe, kak vsiakii eto znaet:
Smekh ubivaet!
Pust' ostaetsia vrag vse tem zhe zlym
vragom.
Pust' on eshche silen, svirep, i naglo
derzok.
No esli smekh zvenit krugom,
No esli vrag dlia nas uzhe ne tol'ko
merzok
No omerzitel'no smeshon
Pogibel'nyi konets zlodeia
predreshen![18]

[The weapon we've been issued is laughter.
It's a sharp weapon, as everybody knows:
Laughter kills!
Let the enemy be
as evil as ever.
Let him be even stronger, fiercer,
and more arrogant.
For if laughter rings all around him,
if the enemy is, for us,
not only sickening,
but sickeningly funny,
then the villain
is doomed!]

Bednyi and Durov explained that the audience's laughter signaled the enemy's eventual, inevitable defeat—a sentiment consistent with Aleksandrov's claim that "only people certain of their future, certain of their victory can laugh" like they did at the 1941 winter debut in Moscow.[19] As Vladimir Poliakov, a founder of the front-line miniature theater, later observed, wartime performers recognized that their "major weapon" was laughter, which helped the Soviet people overcome hunger, cold, and "at times even fear."[20] In 1943, the well-known and much beloved Pavel Alekseevich identified himself directly with another familiar source of relief from fear. He asked an audience of besieged Leningraders whether they wanted to hear "the most popular melody" in their city, and, in answer to their eager shouts, a trumpet played the tune of the all-clear signal after an air raid.

War is frightening, even on the home front, and wartime clown acts sought as much to relieve popular fears as to excite hatred for the enemy and to bolster confidence in the Soviet forces. Clowns were uniquely equipped to perform this function, given that their traditional role in the circus program was to allay fears. In his history of clowning, Sergei Makarov claims that early clowns chose to color their hair red in order to alleviate fears of redheads, who appeared in the folklore of many European cultures as crafty, cunning, devious, and dangerous figures.[21] Whether or not Makarov's account of the red-headed clown's origins is accurate, over the years, clowns did effectively mobilize laughter as an antidote to fear, particularly those fears aroused by other circus artists. In his history of the Moscow Circus School, Leon Harris explains that "clowns are important because the people at a circus are often frightened by a high wire or trapeze or wild animal act and must be made to laugh and relax by some expert clownery before they can enjoy another dare-devil act."[22]

Roaring

If Harris is correct, then clown acts became even more important during the war, when the anxiety aroused by animal acts was deliberately ex-aggerated by the performers themselves and by the press. For example, in February 1945, Ol'ga Pozdneva published a profile of Aleksandr Nikolaevich Aleksandrov, the first Soviet animal "tamer" to perform with leopards. Had her use of the appellation "tamer" not already signaled a departure from earlier celebrations of Soviet animal trainers as kind teachers, the opening lines of her homage to Aleksandrov certainly would have. She began by setting a treacherous scene: "The spectacle has concluded and the viewers have departed. . . . But, then, in the ensuing silence, a short, terrible [*groznyi*] roar resounds from somewhere in the distance. This is the terrifying growl to which Abys-sinian and Indian villagers awaken in the night. It is the voice of the master of the jungle, the handsome leopard." Pozdneva then promptly noted that just thirty minutes earlier, during the circus show, "this terrible [*groznyi*] predator . . . formed a pyramid in the ring, jumped through a hoop, and even stood on its hind legs, just like an ordinary dog." Pozdneva explained that Aleksandrov had bravely cowed the wild beasts, and she attributed his remarkable courage to his experience fighting through the "terrible [*groznyi*] years" of the civil war. She explained that Aleksandrov began to work in the circus only after his military demobilization and that he had performed for many years as a marksman until 1938, when he was commissioned to train a group of leopards. Since nobody in the Soviet Union had any experience training leopards, Aleksandrov relied on a book titled *The Life of Animals*, which explained, according to Pozdneva's citation, that "'the leopard is cunning, vicious, savage, blood-thirsty, and vindictive.' It 'kills any creature that it can,' and finally, 'its teeth are much stronger than a lion's.'" Yet Pozdneva reported that "the impending dangers did not deter this courageous person." She explained that Aleksandrov entered the leopards' cages alone and unarmed and that even though the animals "met him with hostility . . . the amazing courage and iron will of the tamer triumphed." Pozdneva's description cast Aleksandrov as a warrior, who conquered a beastly enemy by relying on his bravery, skill, and, patience—the latter was particularly significant, given the length of the war, which was then in its fourth year.[23]

The following month, Nikolai Strel'tsov recognized Aleksandrov as a leading practitioner of the "new methods" of animal training, which he claimed had become popular among Soviet trainers since the outbreak of war. Strel'tsov noted that four or five years earlier, Aleksandrov and the well-known lion tamer, Boris Eder, had both worked "according to the same principle," namely that the "beast is the human's friend." Strel'tsov explained somewhat snidely that as a result of their adherence to this principle, the performers maintained "genial, affectionate 'relations' with the wild animal." Yet Strel'tsov happily reported that, more recently, both trainers had adopted an "alternative method," which was first introduced by performers like Max Borisov, who lashed his whip, deliberately elicited the animals' roar, cracked wooden sticks in half, and generally did everything he could to reduce the "unruly beasts" to a "state of utter irritation and rage" before he placed his head into one of their mouths. Borisov's style proved to be influential, even among the veteran performers, and Strel'tsov reported that viewers of Aleksandrov's current act could now also sense "the victory of the human over the beast." Boris Eder, meanwhile, was preparing a tiger act in the same style.[24]

Strel'tsov also cited a lion act that was performed by Irina Bugrimova and Aleksandr Buslaev, who were married for a time, as an early example of this innovative approach, which "emphasized the instincts of the wild animals."[25] Bugrimova and Buslaev introduced their celebrated act, "The Sphere of Bravery," in January 1941. They performed their act on a motorcycle racing track that was enclosed in a massive lion cage. The artists mounted their motorcycles and raced the lions, which ran on foot alongside the track. At the climax of the act, Aleksandr placed a lion on the seat behind him. D. Rudnev reported that as the riders gained speed, "the lion calmly, majestically" rested his head on Buslaev's shoulder. It is hard to imagine a gesture more expressive of the friendly, affectionate "relations" that animals and humans enjoyed, and, in his review of the performance, Rudnev employed none of the more militant rhetoric that Pozdneva and Strel'tsov later used to describe wartime animal acts. In fact, Rudnev identified the act as an exceptional example of the art of the circus, which "more than any other" demanded not only agility and "muscles of steel" but also tremendous endurance and an "inexhaustible supply of cheerfulness." Rudnev similarly praised the Gavrilovs, an acrobatic troupe that performed in the same program, for performing the most difficult and dangerous tricks with such apparent ease. It was obvious to him that they performed these daredevil feats not "to frighten the viewer, but rather to delight him" or her by demonstrating that colossal obstacles can be overcome through training and hard work.[26] Rudnev's description of the 1941 program remained entirely consistent with the prevailing prewar interpretation of the circus as a space where cheerful, energetic, and dedicated young people surmounted nearly impossible obstacles for the pleasure of the spectator. It was only four years later, toward the war's end, that Bugrimova and Buslaev's routine came to be understood as a precursor of a new style of animal training that pitted a courageous tamer against a stronger, more savage, and bloodthirsty adversary.

In 1945, press reviewers did less to minimize than to exaggerate the fear that animal routines incited. In July, P. Venskii admitted that viewers, "seeing how easily A. Klichis's wild animals execute their number," initially "forget about the danger that constantly threatens the tamer." Yet Venskii went on to report that animal trainers "unanimously confirm that it is most dangerous to work in the arena with various wild animals."[27] Venskii implied that viewers might rightly fear for the gravely imperiled lives of animal trainers—an assertion that contrasted sharply with earlier interpretations of animal acts, including Iurii Dmitriev's 1938 description of Boris Eder's routines. At that time, Dmitriev admitted that Eder often performed highly risky tricks, but noted, proudly, that "he never emphasizes the danger." As a result, Dmitriev continued, "the viewer always feels that the tamer is significantly stronger than the animals and that nothing can happen to him." He admitted that Eder's act provoked some anxiety, but insisted that "this anxiety does not arise from fear for the life of the tamer, but from the tremendous emotional tension, with which any act of exceptional courage is viewed."[28]

If Strel'tsov was correct to claim that Boris Eder had adopted this new method by 1945, he clearly had abandoned it by March of 1946. In his review of Eder's program that year, D. Zaslavskii lavished praise upon the performer, who "demonstrated his wonderful school of calm and affectionate handling of wild animals."[29] By 1948, Eder and his animals had mended their friendship and could be seen breakfasting together in the ring. The routine "In the Ice-Fields of the Arctic" featured a group of polar bears who, according to Eder's description, "make friends with the explorers." A radio announced the arrival of the explorers as the two performers, Eder and his partner Tamara Eder, entered the ring, which had been set with arctic adornments. The polar bears welcomed them "warmly": one slipped a paw around Boris's waist while another embraced Tamara. After treating the bears to some fish, Boris addressed them kindly: "'Well, friends . . . tell us all about your life here.'" The bears proceeded to act out their daily routines, riding snowballs and walking along icicles. Boris then graciously invited the animals to join him and Tamara for breakfast, an invitation the "delighted" animals readily accepted. The bears fetched one large and two smaller blocks of ice to serve as a table and stools, and Tamara produced a bottle of wine "for our new friends." When one of the bears snatched the bottle from the table and quickly guzzled its contents, Tamara set off for another bottle and successfully evaded a second greedy bear who tried to steal it. When she finally returned, the bears and humans drank the bottle together. The scene concluded as the bears escorted their new friends to the nearby airfield. Two of the bears proved to be so well mannered that they harnessed themselves to a sleigh without Boris's having to lash a whip, fire a revolver, or even prod them slightly.[30]

That same year, Zaslavskii also commended the young trainer Ivan Ruban, an adherent of Eder's style of animal training, whose "play" with beasts evinced a "good-nature, behind which both will and courage could be discerned." Zaslavskii concluded his review by wondering whether the Soviet ring still had a place for old-fashioned, heart-stopping animal tricks, like the one in which a tamer placed his head in the mouth of a lion. He concluded that it did not.[31] Oddly, Ruban's repertoire did include the head-in-the-mouth-of-the-lion trick. Even more oddly, another witness to the creative review listed it among Ruban's "fresh and interesting" feats, which he performed according to the "best, long-standing traditions of popular Russian animal training," in which the "powerful wild animals" seemed to be Ruban's "old and trust-worthy friends." Ruban neither snapped his whip nor fired his pistol. Rather, he stood with his back to the animals, he danced a waltz with a huge brown bear, he fed a lioness pieces of meat from his own mouth, and he assembled them all into a complicated pyramid. The reviewer concluded by observing that the more dangerous the trick, the more Ruban executed it with "humor and ease."[32] It seemed to be Ruban's lighthearted, humorous style that made his performance of the very trick that dramatized the greatest danger a trainer would ever face—the danger of being eaten—seem like a merry game played between friends.

Humor had long been recognized as an effective antidote to fear, though it was an antidote administered almost exclusively by clowns during the war. At that time, animal trainers, along with their promoters in the press, deliberately provoked the audience's fears by playing up the dangers they faced in the ring. These routines provoked the audience's fears in order to allay them, and any lingering anxiety the audience might have felt was later diffused by the clowns, who also used animals—in this case, small, lumbering, inconsequent, and inane ones, even if they were flesh-eating—to represent an enemy that hardly seemed frightful. Wartime animal acts and clowning skits both cast Soviet foes as inhuman, man-eating beasts, and, like most Soviet por-trayals of Germans during the war, they alternately demonized and ridiculed the enemy.

The Fear of Fear Itself

While satirical clown acts and daring tricks with animals relied on the devices of metaphor and allegory alternately to summon and dispel spectators' anxieties, the so-called William Tell routines performed during this period spoke more explicitly to the themes of danger and fear. William Tell skits usually involved two clowns, one of whom would attempt to demonstrate his or her superior skills as a marksman by shooting at a target somewhere in the vicinity of a second clown, who, finding him- or herself in grave peril, would devise some cunning way to escape the dangerous situation. Teodor and Koko's "Balloon" skit, in which Koko repeatedly let go of the targeted balloon, claiming that "it flew away," exemplified this genre, as did a routine performed soon after the war's conclusion. In 1946, the *belyi-ryzhii* team Zhak and Morits received permission to perform a routine that began with Zhak's entrance into the ring, revolver in hand. Zhak scanned the arena, searching for an appropriate target, and decided to take aim at an electric lamp. He suddenly spotted Morits, took him by the arm, led him to the center of the arena, placed an apple on his head, and walked toward the edge of the ring. Before he could take aim, the apple "rolled off" Morits's head as he shouted "It fell!" His cry summoned Zhak, who again fixed the apple upon his partner's red head. Not surprisingly, the apple again fell to the floor to Morits's shout, "It fell," and Zhak again put the apple back in place. This time, he took great care to set the fruit securely upon Morits's head, yet the apple rolled off once more. Finally, it occurred to Zhak to take a bite from the apple before balancing it on Morits's head. This time, the apple remained in place. As Zhak again headed toward the edge of the ring, Morits retrieved the apple from his head and, mimicking Zhak's gesture, took a bite from it himself—and the unruly redhead proceeded to eat the whole thing. Morits's disobedience hardly fazed Zhak, who simply snatched the apple's core from Morits and attempted to stand it on his head. Morits tried to grab hold of the apple. Zhak swatted at Morits's hand, which failed to deter Morits's persistent efforts to consume the apple as soon as Zhak began to walk away. Each time that Zhak turned around to find Morits feasting on the fruit, Morits quickly placed the apple back on his head and swatted at his own hand, just as Zhak had. By the time Zhak reached the edge of the ring, Morits had eaten all but a tiny piece of the apple, which he then set back upon his head. Zhak turned around, took aim, and fired at it. Morits collapsed onto the floor, where he convulsed until his last breath was expelled. Startled by this result, the frightened shooter scanned the arena once again, this time in search of a target for the blame. Spotting the ringmaster, Zhak called out, "What have you done? Was it you who killed him?!" The ringmaster answered, "No, it was you," inciting an argument that concluded only when Morits stood up, pronounced that it was Zhak who killed him, and promptly lay back down.[33]

A number of wartime clowning duos introduced variations on the William Tell act that were unique for the explicit and repeated confessions of fear that some of the imperiled figures made and for the obvious fright that overcame even those who refused to admit that their loudly touted bravery had failed them. Moreover, whether they admitted their fear or not, it was, ultimately, the thing that always saved them. By depicting fear as a sensible response to a dangerous situation, these routines might have undermined the spectacle of bravery that animal trainers provided at the time. Or, they might have relieved another of the audience's fears: the fear of fear itself.

In one such routine, approved for production in 1943–44, a "rifleman," played by the clown Sim, entered the ring and asked the ringmaster, Aleksandr Aleksandrovich, whether he had heard of the renowned rifleman William Tell. The ringmaster answered that he had and informed any viewers who had not that William Tell was a "wonderful shot." Sim then boasted that he could shoot much better than William Tell and offered to prove it by extinguishing, with a single shot, the flame of a candle that he placed on the ringmaster's head. The clown took aim, counted to two, and was suddenly interrupted by the ringmaster, who stammered, "Excuse me, excuse me. You know, I am very scared." The clown assured him that his shot would hit only the candle's wick, but the ringmaster's fear was not allayed. He said, again, "Forgive me, but I am very scared," and recommended to the rifleman, in place of himself, "one brave young man who is absolutely afraid of nothing." The ringmaster then presented this young man, the clown Eilik, who responded to Sim's question as to whether he was truly a brave person by insisting that he was a very brave youth: "I am so brave that I am not even frightened of myself." Not to be outdone, Sim bragged that he was a wonderful shot, and his partner replied that he did not doubt it. "It wasn't so long ago that you arrived in town," Eilik explained, "and already you managed to shoot twelve young ladies with your glance." Impatient with his joking, the rifleman ordered Eilik to stand still, placed the candle on his head, took aim, and counted to two, at which point the young man of uncommon bravery politely interrupted the shooter's countdown to ask him to explain his intentions. Sim informed Eilik that he would extinguish the candle's flame in a single shot, to which the dubious clown replied, "And what if you don't put out the flame of that candle [pointing to the candle], but put out the flame of this candle [pointing to his forehead] instead?" The confident rifleman told him not to worry and instructed him not to fear for his life; literally, "to be calm regarding your life" (*bud' spokoen za svoiu zhizn'*). Suspecting that he misheard this entreaty, the frightened Eilik asked whether he had really been told that he would be a dead man for his entire life (*budu pokoinik na vsiu zhizn'*). In response, the former clown repeated his request for calm and began his count again. Eilik interrupted a second time and, after Sim once more resumed his count, Eilik interrupted him yet again, this time to ask why he was doing all of this. After explaining that his intention was to entertain the audience, Sim raised his rifle once again, prompting the once-brave clown to holler, "Oi, mama!" lift his wig, and sob. Sim rebuked Eilik for crying and asked him when he had ever known an artist to cry in front of the viewers. Then, finally, the ringmaster rescued the terrified clown by returning to the ring and offering him a tray of drinks. After instructing Eilik to repeat the toast, "I drink to your health," the ringmaster raised a glass to the clown's mouth, but then drained it himself and wiped Eilik's mouth with a napkin. This delighted Sim, who crowed: "He played a trick on you for real. He could only have done that to you. He couldn't have done that to me." Sim's boasting prompted the ringmaster to try his trick on Sim, but Sim brandished his revolver, relieved the ringmaster of his tray, and repeated, "You won't be able to do that to me. Now, I'll take it myself and drink to you!" The scene concluded with the two clowns, who apparently had been reconciled, raising their glasses in a toast, appropriately, "to health!"[34]

In a third William Tell skit, the frightened clown also escaped the dangerous situation by pretending he had been shot, but only after his first sly attempt to thwart his partner's plan had failed. In Albert Cherniak's routine "In Love," also approved for performance in 1943–44, a female *belyi* clown who claimed to be a master markswoman asked her partner, a male *ryzhii* clown, to help her demonstrate her talents. When she agreed to share the prize she would win in a shooting contest, he consented to serve as her assistant. Yet when she instructed him to place on his head an apple that she intended to shoot from ten paces away, he refused, explaining that his "heart [*serdtsevina* also means core] can't take it." When the *belyi* clown asked for an explanation, the *ryzhii* confessed his concern that she might ruin his hairdo. "You're just scared," she retorted, to which he responded, "Me, scared? Please, fire the pistol as you like." The happy markswoman then managed to place the apple on her assistant's head, load her gun, aim it, and count to one, before the ringmaster came to the *ryzhii*'s rescue by requesting the *belyi*'s presence backstage. The obedient clown quickly complied, setting the gun down in the ring before skipping behind the curtain. By the time she returned, the devious *ryzhii* had removed the pistol's cartridge, remarking to the audience, "It's better this way." When the *belyi* asked if he was ready, the newly emboldened redhead cried, "I'm ready.

Shoot! I've been shot at by cannons and even then I was not afraid." "So you mean you're not even a little scared?" the skeptical *belyi* responded. "What kind of a question is that?" the offended *ryzhii* demanded, prompting his partner to take a pistol from her pocket—this one loaded—and fire a shot toward the ceiling. The *ryzhii* moaned dramatically, fell to the floor, and, when asked to explain himself, said, "It appears to me that you murdered me outright. You know something, let's put off the shooting until next time." The markswoman agreed. "All right," she said, "I'm already convinced that you're a brave person." "Oi," replied the clown who, moments ago, had suspected her of murderous designs, "I'm in love!" In this case, the clown's fear, which inspired him to remove the bullets from the gun, saved him not only from death but also from any accusation of cowardice. It might also have gotten him a date.[35]

Conclusion

William Tell routines performed during the war obviously violated the standards for appropriate clowning set by Kuznetsov in February 1942. They neither glorified Soviet military achievements, nor forecast the enemy's eventual defeat, nor publicized the barbaric misdeeds of the hostile forces. They did, however, conspire with other clown acts and animal routines to relieve some of the fears that tormented both frontline and home front audiences. As Aleksandrov remarked, simply to go to the circus and laugh was to convince oneself and one's fellow revelers of the certainty of a Soviet victory. Aleksandrov recognized this effect as something new and he marshaled it as evidence for his claim that, despite all appearances, the circus had changed during the war. Aleksandrov was, of course, correct to insist that old routines, particularly clown acts, were invested with new content, while others, like animal acts, acquired new meanings in the context of war.

Yet, as Aleksandrov also noted, these wartime innovations did little to diminish viewers' sense that the war had not changed anything in the circus. The apparent constancy of the circus was precisely what allowed it to function as an effective antidote to wartime fears. By the war's end, the best thing about the circus seemed to be that it had hardly changed at all. In March 1945, just months before the Soviet victory, A. Roslavlev spoke of the circus as a place where everything was familiar, recognizable, unchanging, and, therefore, appealing. "When you go to the circus," he wrote, "a familiar, pleasant feeling seizes you. You know that now your old acquaintance [the ringmaster] Bushe will enter the ring and announce the first number. And after him a male or a female rider will appear, or a pair of acrobats, or, perhaps, Karandash himself. . . . You also know that you will see, too, aerial gymnasts on the trapeze, acrobatics on horseback, flips, and clowns' lively skits." Even the unusual technical words used only in the circus were comforting in their familiarity: "The mysterious circus terms do not bewilder you at all: you've long known that a *persh* is a long metallic pole and that *ekvilibr* is the maintenance of balance in an unstable position." Roslavlev concluded that "the charm of the circus lies entirely in its constant, unchanging, and everlasting tradition."[36] After the war, the circus continued to recommend itself as a vital participant in the return to normalcy as well as a formidable Cold War combatant. Paradoxically, but by this point not surprisingly, it fulfilled the new demands placed on it during the postwar period, and it did so by accommodating an entirely new set of meanings, not all of them officially endorsed.

Vladimir Leonidovich Durov (reproduced from Iu. Dmitriev, *Sovetskii tsirk, ocherk istorii, 1917–1941*)

Iurii Nikulin and Mikhail Shuidin (reproduced from Nikolai Krivenko, *Talant* [*sic*], *Daring, Beauty: The Soviet Circus*)

Iurii Nikulin greeting the circus crowd (reproduced from Nikolai Krivenko,
Talant [sic], *Daring, Beauty: The Soviet Circus*)

Vitalii Efimovich Lazarenko (reproduced from Iu. Dmitriev, *Sovetskii tsirk, ocherk istorii, 1917–1941*)

Mikhail Rumiantsev performing as Karandash (reproduced from Karandash, *Nad chem smeetsia kloun?*)

Mikhail Rumiantsev performing as Karandash on the highwire (reproduced from Karandash, *Nad chem smeetsia kloun?*)

Mikhail Rumiantsev performing as Karandash in "The Incident in the Park"
(reproduced from Karandash, *Nad chem smeetsia kloun?*)

Aleksandr Nikolaevich Buslaev (reproduced from Iu. Dmitriev, *Sovetskii tsirk,
ocherk istorii, 1917–1941*)

Irina Nikolaevna Bugrimova (reproduced from Iu. Dmitriev, *Sovetskii tsirk, ocherk istorii, 1917–1941*)

Margarita Nazarova (reproduced from I. Chernenko, *Zdravstvui, Tsirk!*)

Ali-Bek Kantemirov (reproduced from I. Chernenko, *Zdravstvui, Tsirk!*)

Oleg Popov performing on a slack wire (reproduced from V. Angarskii and L. Victorov, *Oleg Popov*)

Valentin Filatov (reproduced from Nikolai Krivenko, *Talant* [sic], *Daring,
Beauty: The Soviet Circus*)

Valentin Filatov performing with his "Bear Circus" (reproduced from Nikolai Krivenko, *Talant* [*sic*], *Daring, Beauty: The Soviet Circus*)

Leonid Engibarov (reproduced from Nikolai Krivenko, *Talant* [*sic*], *Daring, Beauty: The Soviet Circus*)

Soiuzgostsirk poster (courtesy of Circus World Museum, Baraboo, Wisconsin)

Soiuzgostsirk poster (courtesy of Circus World Museum, Baraboo, Wisconsin)

4

Home Front

Soviet Women and Western Menace
in the Postwar, Cold War Circus

The war finally did come to an end, but not everything went back to normal. More than twenty-six million Soviets had died during the war, more than three-quarters of whom were men. In 1946, there were nearly twenty-two million more women than men living in the Soviet Union. That year, 752,000 children were born to unmarried mothers and 393,000 orphans lived in Russian children's homes. As Elena Zubkova writes, "a whole generation of children grew up without fathers . . . without a home in the full sense of the word. They grew up in a truncated family or without any family."[1] Even children who did have a family still might have grown up without a home in the literal sense of the word, since housing remained in short supply, as did food and clothing. In 1945, only .38 pairs of shoes and .15 pairs of underwear were produced per person in the Soviet Union. Egg production had fallen to half its 1940 level, and less grain was harvested in the early 1950s than in 1929.

This was a problem for the Soviet state, which had promised both to secure the Soviet homeland and to provide Soviet families with well-appointed homes, common comforts, and even some rare and cherished luxuries.[2] Since the 1930s, material affluence had been offered as the Soviet people's reward for the hard work of building socialism, and personal prosperity became a mark of socialism's success. As a result, the legitimacy of the Soviet state, the relative merits of the socialist economic system, and the presumed political loyalty of the Soviet people all came to depend on the government's ability to ensure high living standards. In the postwar period, when domestic economies emerged as a primary arena of the Cold War competition, the state's imperative to provide a good life for all became even more pressing. For the Soviet Union, as for its adversaries, material goods, no less than armament stockpiles and atomic arsenals, provided the matériel with which the Cold War was waged. In this context, the security of the Soviet homeland became readily identified with the security of Soviet homes, whose security became, in turn, a critical indicator of the legitimacy of the Soviet state.

In the postwar period, the promise of universal prosperity provided a basis for the legitimacy of governments in both the east and the west. This was a problem for the Soviet state, whose ability to furnish the public with fashionable clothing, single-family apartments, culinary delicacies, lace doilies, and other bourgeois niceties encroached on its legitimacy as a socialist state. For much of the Soviet public, all these nice things, and the nuclear families that were meant to enjoy them, remained the stuff of fairy tales, or, increasingly, the stuff of Americans, their western European allies, and Soviet governing elites. It posed a particular problem for Soviet women, who were doubly burdened by the work they did as both domestic and wage laborers, first to produce all these happy families and then to provide for them.

The circus helped solve all of these problems, and in this it was unique among postwar Soviet cultural products. Like middlebrow novels and popular films, postwar circus programs encouraged the Soviet people to pursue their own private happiness and domestic comfort. Circus acts that advertised Soviet consumer goods, dramatized scenes from family life, and championed the benefits of cultured living contributed to the conversion of private values into public values that Vera Dunham describes in her study of postwar fiction.[3] At the same time, postwar clown acts, much like war rumors, political cartoons, and anti-cosmopolitan diatribes, exaggerated the threat that the western powers posed to the Soviet homeland. Many of these routines presented the United States and England as menacing aggressors whose economic imperialism specifically threatened the security of Soviet families and the sanctity of Soviet homes, just as their military ambitions threatened the Soviet homeland. Postwar circus acts implied that material prosperity was essential to national security and that the state's legitimacy rested, entirely legitimately, on its success in providing for them both.

The postwar circus thus offered a new defense of the so-called embourgeoisement of the Soviet system against the potential charge of ideological heresy. They told those few Soviet people who did receive postwar rewards that they were making life better in the Soviet homeland by enjoying the good life at home. The acts also offered an explanation as to why not all Soviets could yet enjoy the benefits of the embourgeoisement of the Soviet system: because the western menace required heavy investment in military defense at the expense of consumer goods. They told the many Soviet people who had not received postwar rewards that the state had failed to provide individual families with secure homes because it was devoting all its resources to providing the Soviet national family with a secure homeland. Finally, circus acts that equated a cozy home with a secure homeland offered a novel justification for the official and, from a socialist point of view, ideologically incorrect identification of the home as women's unique domain and exclusive responsibility. They told Soviet women that their service within their homes constituted a vital service to their homeland, for which they would be rewarded with ample homes inside of which to work.

Material Matters

Soon after the war ended, circus acts began to articulate the Soviet state's plainly paternal promise to provide Soviet families with food, clothing, and shelter, all of which was admittedly in short supply. Clowns found a rich subject for satire in the scarcity and poor quality of such basic provisions as eggs, shoes, and warm houses. For example, at a time when food shortages remained acute, the clown Karandash performed a skit in which he chased a hen around the ring and, when he finally caught the animal, announced his intention to beat it with a strap. When the ringmaster asked him why he planned to thrash the animal, Karandash replied by asking him what else could be done with a hen that laid only powdered eggs.[4] State clothing manufacturers also received a tongue-lashing in the circus. In 1949, a clown paraded across the circus ring in a pair of shoes that squeaked so badly that the sound echoed throughout the arena. The clown announced that he had decided to go on the radio so that the director of the shoe factory could hear how badly they squeaked.[5] In a similar act approved for performance the previous year, another clown had complained that he had fallen ill in his drafty room, whose broken window frames had not been repaired that year. Since all housing was publicly administered, maintenance of apartments was a government responsibility.

Although these acts admitted that Soviet living standards remained poor, they assured the audience that the government remained committed to improving them. This was a familiar promise, but one that acquired a new significance in the context of the Cold War, in which standards of living were emerging as a major battleground. It is for this reason, perhaps, that jokes about egg powder and squeaky shoes were actually exceptional for their frank acknowledgment of material shortages. Postwar clown routines more typically denied that any material privations persisted, and when the poverty of Soviet living conditions was acknowledged, they were said still to compare favorably with living conditions in the ideologically impoverished capitalist west. For example, the routine featuring the clown who lived in a drafty room did not end with his hoarse complaint. The healthy clown retorted that he knew of a house that was in a "much worse" state of repair. From the outside, this house appeared perfectly sturdy, but, in truth, its "foundation had rotted . . . the attic was not in order," and its inhabitants, who tended to play with fire, threatened to burn it to the ground. When his partner finally admitted that this was an outrageous state of affairs, especially in such a city as Moscow, the first clown explained that this house was located not in Moscow but in Washington: he was speaking of the White House. The clown's startled interlocutor was quick to ask why he thought the foundation of the White House had rotted, and he explained that "its foundation is capitalistic." "True," the other clown admitted, "but how could it be that the attic in this house was not in order?" "Very simply," his partner replied, pointing to his forehead, "there are some people there whose 'attic' is not in order." Finally, the clown explained that the White House's inhabitants "were happy to play with fire so long as it doesn't burn around their own heads." Impressed with his partner's expertise on these matters, the sickly clown finally asked him to account for the terrible state into which the White House had fallen. He replied, "The house manager there is not up to the job. He'll soon be replaced."[6]

This routine analogized the ideological decrepitude of the United States with the physical dilapidation of its seat of political power. It implied that viewers should sooner suffer a drafty room and a consequent sore throat than live a healthy life in an ideologically rotten state governed by dangerous and aggressive fools. This routine was typical of many postwar circus acts that asserted the superiority of the Soviet economy over those of capitalist nations, and deliberately presented indications of western political, diplomatic, and ideological infirmity as signs of its economic inferiority. For example, a 1947 monologue written in honor of the thirtieth anniversary of the Soviet Union celebrated all the good people who had "worked conscientiously and with love" to provide for the Soviet way of life. The narrator offered a toast to them all, beginning with the collective farm workers, whose labor succored the Soviet population. He then toasted "our dear builders." He asked, "How can we not raise a glass to our new home?" but then quickly corrected himself: "No, better yet to each floor! So that with each day and each year, we should have ever higher houses and ever lower costs . . . ever larger accommodations at an ever smaller expense." After announcing that he was prepared to drink all night to good housing, he raised his glass instead to the producers of new clothing: "The shirt is elegant, it even clings to the body. To your health, my friend, the silk maker. What a suit, the material has become more beautiful and delicate. To your health, comrade clothier! Boots are comfortable, lightweight, and sturdy. The shoemakers should be toasted!" After establishing the abundance of food, the quantity of housing, and the quality of clothing as the units by which socialism's achievement was to be measured, the narrator concluded that the Soviet Union was superior to the west. "We," he said, "the strong and healthy, are growing and getting stronger," while they, abroad, are ill again. Their illness, he continued, was psychological, and its symptoms included memory loss: they had forgotten Yalta and Potsdam, Stalingrad and the regions near Moscow. Obviously, no toast was made to them.[7] He implicitly claimed to contrast Soviet economic vitality with western economic frailty, although the signs of foreign infirmity that he noted were hardly economic.

Western Menace

This deliberate confusion of signs of economic and ideological failure is not surprising given that economic success, as evident particularly in the provision of food, clothing, and shelter, had become an accepted standard by which the relative merits of Communism versus capitalism would be judged. The Cold War had raised the stakes of the Soviet Union's longstanding promise to provide high living standards to its populace. At the same time, the official claim that the Soviet state would function as such a beneficent provider might have helped to raise the temperature of the Cold War, since the United States was readily identified as an economic menace as well as a menace to state security. It is, therefore, no wonder that circus performances dramatized the threat the United States purportedly posed to European and Soviet economic prosperity as much as they exaggerated the military threat the United States posed to the Soviet state.

For example, a routine approved for performance in 1948 explicitly identified American political aggression with the poor economic health of the United States, which was accused of nursing itself by bleeding the western European economies. Meanwhile, the Soviet economy remained robust. The routine began when two clowns announced that they had long known their tastes to differ. To prove it, one clown asked the other what he liked best of all. "Best of all?" the clown replied, "rice cereal with milk!" "Well, my dear," his partner cheerfully remarked, "now you can get as much rice as you'd like at any store, and milk, too. Eat to your heart's content and put on some weight." Then, turning to address the viewers, the clown continued: "Tastes really do differ! My partner likes rice cereal with milk, I like my partner, and, for example, Americans don't like to sit at home." When the other clown asked what Americans do like to do, he was informed that "they like to make themselves at home in other countries!" The clown added that as a result of this inclination, not everybody in America was home, explaining, when asked what he meant, that "very many Americans make themselves at home in Greece, in Turkey, in Korea, in Iran and therefore, not all of them are home, they are on business trips!" "Ah, that is another matter," his partner rejoined, bringing their exchange to an end.[8]

In another routine involving politicized comestibles, the clown Dubino, who played the part of a waiter at an Intourist restaurant, explained to Rolland, his partner, that "an Italian-style omelet" was prepared "by first taking the oil and sending it to America and then receiving from America oil for greasing guns, which was sent, purportedly, as 'relief aid.'" Dubino then took from his pocket a large can of machine oil and poured it into a frying pan. "And then you take the eggs," he began, and Rolland finished, "And send them to America." "That's right," replied Dubino, explaining that "egg powder" was received in exchange. He sprinkled sawdust onto the oil in the frying pan and with a shout of "Abra cadabra," he poured the "Italian-style omelet" onto the floor.[9]

The United States was now the hen that lay powdered eggs. It was also now responsible for the manufacture of squeaky shoes. A 1949 rhyming dialogue that noted a resemblance between the Voice of America and the voice of Goebbels opened with the following exchange between two clowns:

Parizhskim shikom moi znakomyi
uvlechen.
Na dniakh frantsuzskie kupil
botinki on.
Blestiat! Skripiat!
Nu, a nemnogo podgodia
ot nikh ostalsia posle pervogo dozhdia
Odin lish' zvuk! Odin lish' zvuk!
Podmetki proch'! Otstal kabluk!
I gvozdi vylezli vokrug!
Vse vydaet fal'shivyi zvuk![10]

[First: My friend has a passion for
Parisian chic.
The other day he bought
A pair of French boots.
Second: They shine! They squeak!
But a little later,
after the first rain, all that remained
was the squeak!
The soles came off! The heel detached!
And tacks fell out all around!
Everything makes a false sound!]

In their next exchange, which implicitly attributed the decline in quality of French consumer goods to American economic intervention, the clowns soundly thrashed the American bankers whose support for the Marshall plan exposed it as being a cunning trick:

Krichat v Amerike bankiry
vo vsiu moch'
Dolzhny Evrope my nemedlenno

pomoch'.
U nas gotov uzhe davno shirokii plan.
Poluchat porovnu ot nas
shestnadtsat' stran:
Odin lish' zvuk! Odin lish' zvuk!
Priduman lovko etot triuk!
No ne pomozhet lovkost' ruk
Vse vydaet fal'shivyi zvuk!

[First: In America, bankers shout
with all their might,
we should help Europe
immediately.
We prepared a broad plan long ago.
Second: Sixteen countries will receive
equal aid from us:
But that's nothing but a squeak!
That is a trick cunningly devised
But the sleight of hand won't work
Everything makes a false sound!]

Although circus acts did not blame the United States for Europe's
drafty rooms exactly, they did list broken dishes, shattered stools, and
general domestic disruption among the consequences of American
foreign policy. A skit that Karandash and his young protégé Iurii Nikulin
performed with some help from the ringmaster in 1950 began when
Karandash ran into the ring, stood on the elevated barrier that encircled
it, and shouted to the ringmaster, "Aleksandr Borisovich, I want to
show you how people live in the Marshallized countries." The ringmaster replied that he would be very interested to see this demonstration, and Karandash ran backstage to prepare it. While he was offstage, Nikulin entered the ring, mounted the barrier, and announced
his intention to show Aleksandr Borisovich how Americans "manage"
the Marshallized countries. The verb "to manage," *khozianichat'*, which
comes from the word for "host," can mean both to keep house and,
more figuratively, to boss people around. Nikulin then ran backstage
himself, right before Karandash returned with a table and chair that he
placed in the center of the ring. According to the stage directions, he
began to set the table "as if he were at home." Just then, Nikulin entered
the ring dressed as an American, carrying a tape measure and a flag.
Nikulin bent down to measure the ring and eventually "approached

the place where Karandash was occupied with his housekeeping [*khoziaistvo*]." The American surveyor hurled the table and chair out of his way and planted an American flag in their place: "There should be a base here," he announced. Greatly offended, Karandash returned the table and chair to their places and resumed his demonstration of life in the Marshallized countries. Nikulin, who continued to measure the ring, again approached Karandash's domestic display, but this time he sat down in the chair, put his feet on the table, and began to chuck objects from the table at Karandash. The exasperated clown ran off to fetch a saw, which he used to cut off one of the legs of Nikulin's chair. When Nikulin fell to the ground, Karandash hastened to gather up his belongings and move them to another spot in the ring. Nikulin sat back down at the table, Karandash sawed through another leg, and Nikulin again fell to the ground, but, this time, he rose to give chase to Karandash. Suddenly, Nikulin stopped running and stood, scared stiff, in the ring. Karandash, surveying the audience from a position on the barrier, noticed a Red Army soldier, smiled, and, with a nod of his head toward the soldier, directed Nikulin to flee backstage.[11]

In this routine, the distinction between the military and economic threats posed by the United States was entirely collapsed. According to Nikulin and Karandash, the expansion of the American military presence in Europe imperiled not only peace, freedom, and national sovereignty but also kitchen tables, fragile flatware, and pleasant meals at home. Postwar circus acts imagined the Soviet state to be the guardian of so many warm, prosperous, and carefully maintained homes, where real eggs were served on sturdy tables covered in domestically produced cloths that bore no holes, unless, of course, they were made of lace. They also implied that the security of Soviet domestic spaces could be preserved only if Soviet national security were ensured. This metaphor brought the threat of American intervention in Europe home to the Soviet people, and it also justified the Communist government's ideologically awkward offer to provide the Soviet people with material goods that were once condemned as petty-bourgeois—again, an offer intended both to appeal to popular loyalty and to establish the legitimacy of the regime. Since the legitimacy of any government rests, at least in part, on its ability to defend its territory, the sanctity of the cozy home, when taken as a metaphor for the homeland itself, became an ideologically sound source of legitimacy for the Soviet regime that had promised to secure it.

The Have-Nots

Yet for most Soviet people, the promise of material prosperity remained entirely unfulfilled. A 1947 routine lampooning the absurd prolifera- tion of small debts among acquaintances testified to the strained finances that many Soviets suffered after the war. In this skit, the clown Zhak asked his partner, Morits, whether he might repay the ten rubles that were owed him. Aghast, Morits accused his lender of attempting to shame him publicly, a ploy that he claimed would not succeed, since he had enough money to cover his debt. Morits searched his pockets for the sum, but he came up empty-handed and was forced to solicit the audience's aid. A young woman offered to help, but said she only had five rubles, which Morits graciously accepted. Then, just as Zhak had accepted the five rubles from Morits, the ringmaster approached Zhak and reminded him that he also owed him ten rubles. Zhak apologized for forgetting the debt and immediately handed the ringmaster the five rubles he had just received from Morits. The ringmaster began to leave with his money, but Morits stopped him to demand payment of ten rubles that the ringmaster owed him. The ringmaster immediately handed him the five rubles, which Morits offered to Zhak, in honor of the five rubles he still owed him. Zhak then passed the money to the ringmaster, who used it to pay off his own remaining five-ruble debt to Morits. Morits then returned the five rubles to the young woman who had first given it to him and happily pronounced all the debts settled.[12] By the end, though, the young woman was the only one with any money, and while some members of the audience surely identified with her, others might have related more readily to the penniless clowns. They, like many others in the Soviet Union, had yet to experience any improvement in their standard of living since the war's end.

Circus acts that identified the United States as both a military and economic menace served to reinforce one popular explanation for on- going material hardships: the Soviet government was preparing for an imminent war. As Elena Zubkova explains, some Soviets recognized harvest failures and the general wartime devastation of the countryside as satisfying explanations for the 1946 increase in ration prices. Yet Zubkova goes on to state that "the chief cause of the new sacrifices was seen, however, in something else"—a claim based on the remarks of a survey respondent: "'If our government decided to raise the price of food products, then it most likely means that the Soviet state is in danger.

It must be threatened by a new war.'" Zubkova explains that this assumption was "widespread among all sectors of the population," including the residents of Moscow, one of whom stated his conviction that "the price increase is related not only to the shortage of grain in the country but to the necessity of forming a reserve on account of the tense international climate. England and America are threatening us with war.'"[13]

It is for this reason, perhaps, that postwar circus acts also emphasized the purely military threat that western powers posed to Soviet security. In 1951, for example, an American "political boss" appeared in the Soviet circus. He was played by a clown who entered the arena with a cigar between his teeth, hurriedly checked the time, picked up the phone, and dialed a number. "Jim?" he called into the phone. "Yes, it's me. What's the deal? Where is your candidate for the Senate? I've already been waiting for him for five minutes. If this character doesn't understand what his election depends on, he can go to the devil. . . . You'd better remind him that I run politics in our state!" With that, the "political boss" hung up the phone, turned on the radio, and, singing the tune he heard playing, exited the ring. Suddenly, the music was interrupted with a report on the recent escape from a mental hospital of a "violent madman," who "imagines himself to be Hitler." As the announcer repeated his urgent report, a second clown crept into the ring and, addressing the radio, cried, "Your game is up, Mr. Conspirator!" This clown, playing "Hitler," continued, "And you declared me insane? We'll see who wins now! I will seize power again!" "Hitler" concluded his speech with a shout of "Heil!" and raised his arm in the Nazi salute.

The first clown, playing the American political boss, returned and addressed his visitor, whom he assumed to be the candidate he was expecting. The second clown greeted him with another shout of "Heil!" which prompted the first to glance about the room and, once he was assured that nobody had heard, scold the candidate for being "so blunt" about it. The latter accepted the rebuke without argument and informed the "boss" that he liked him. "That is not important," the clown replied. "The most important thing is whether I like you. And that depends on how you behave yourself." Then, as if he were auditioning for the job, the candidate shouted, "Be quiet!" which evidently met with the approval of the boss, who was even more delighted when his cohort shouted, "Don't argue with me! . . . Serve and obey!" After commending the eager candidate, the boss asked him to explain his political program. The candidate replied that it involved the "struggle against

Communism." He and his followers "stood for the old older," he continued, adding that their "natural element" was war. They promoted chemical war, bacteria, and atomic bombs, "all against Communism!" The first clown considered this quite sensible and enthusiastically offered his hand, stating, "My dear! You'll go far! For now, we'll elect you to the Senate." Yet the candidate suddenly interrupted him, stating that "fate has decreed that I be chancellor." Here ensued a lengthy squabble that nearly concluded with the candidate's departure from the ring. Yet unwilling to lose such a "suitable candidate," the boss conceded, promising that the Senate would be only the beginning of the candidate's political career. He communicated the particulars of his intention with a whisper into the candidate's ear. Thus appeased, the candidate proclaimed, "Heil! I said I would be chancellor once again! Heil!" This prompted the so-called boss to ask, "How do you say it?" and tentatively pronounce, "Heil." The candidate instructed him to say it more boldly, with his arm raised higher. The scene concluded with the two yelling "Heil!" again and again.[14]

Hitler was long since dead when this routine was approved for performance, but the Soviet circus continued to raise the specter of his aggressive, expansionist regime, which, according to the official rhetoric, was newly embodied in the United States and its allies. Not surprisingly, circus performers readily adapted many of the techniques they had developed during World War II to confront this new adversary. Karandash later explained that the war had equipped him with the skills and confidence to perform as a satirist, the comedic role on whose wartime conventions he and many other clowns continued to rely in the postwar period.[15]

After the war, clowns demonized America, Great Britain, West Germany, and France in much the same way they had demonized Hitler and the Nazis, only now they could identify the new enemies as a beastly, inhuman menace by associating them not only with such literally inhuman beasts as dogs and pigs but also by associating them with the old enemy, Nazi Germany, whose beastliness was already well established. The 1951 routine "A Suitable Candidate" was the most literal example of this strategy. Konstantin Berman's 1949 joke, which identified a radio broadcast of barking dogs as "The Voice of America" and a similarly transmitted cacophony of snorting pigs as "The BBC," not only cast British and American reporters as animals but, given the past association of Nazi propaganda with canine vocalization, it also identified them as particularly Nazi-like enemies.[16] So too did a skit performed the previous year, in which a dog started to bark when asked to demonstrate how Americans speak to smaller countries.[17] A rhyming ditty that was also approved for performance by the circus administration in 1948 dispensed with the animals altogether, simply stating that the Voice of America, which transmitted "everything that Uncle Sam orders" as well as American "threats, rage, and falsehood," resembled the voice of Goebbels.[18] Finally, in the same 1949 performance that featured Berman's jokes about the Voice of America and the BBC, the magician Emil' Kio conjured the ghost of Hitler to warn of the threat that the American and British states now posed to the working class, just as the Nazi regime had threatened it in the past. When Berman entered the ring to announce that he had just heard (naturally on the Voice of America) that a Nazi war criminal had been imprisoned, Kio offered to show the audience how this was done. A group of workmen wheeled a cage into the ring and watched as Hitler was escorted inside. Kio then placed "'not an iron curtain, just a silken one,'" over both the cage and the workmen. When he lifted the curtain, the cage enclosed not Hitler, who stood beside it, but the working men. Then, "to the audience's delight," according to *New York Times* correspondent Harrison Salisbury, Winston Churchill and an American capitalist entered the ring and greeted Hitler warmly. Kio asked the crowd, "'How much longer will this go on?" and then answered his own question: "Until the people's patience bursts, then it will end!'" The curtain fell over the cage once more and then rose again to reveal the three enemies of the people locked inside, while the liberated workers stood happily beside the cage.[19]

Kio's magic act, which triumphantly enacted and explicitly foretold the enemies' eventual defeat, did resemble wartime circus routines that heralded the inevitable conquest of a feeble and foolish enemy, from whom the Soviet people had little to fear. Yet while this routine doomed the antagonists to defeat, it still presented them as powerful and cunning conspirators. In this way, Kio's magic act departed significantly from wartime satirical conventions and adhered, instead, to a strategy that became prevalent during the Cold War period. Even those performances that did forecast the decline of the United States and its European allies did not attribute the enemy's collapse to any internal weakness, incompetence, or hubris. Rather, the enemy was defeated, often perfunctorily, in spite of its enduring strength and fearsome resolve. Postwar depictions of Soviet international rivals conspired, therefore, not to relieve popular fears of the enemy but rather to enliven them.

For example, a clown act approved for performance by the circus administration in 1948 metaphorically identified the Americans as dogs, but, unlike the silly, uncoordinated, and ineffectual dogs that represented Nazi soldiers during the war, these dogs, "wolfhounds and bloodhounds," were powerful and savage aggressors. The skit began with the entrance of the clown Kiro together with his companion, a *ryzhii* clown, who graciously asked after the dog that Kiro had recently taken with him to America. "He was so much trouble!" the pained pet owner replied, explaining that his dog had been completely corrupted in Washington, where, as a result of his prolonged exposure to American wolfhounds and bloodhounds, he had become completely beastly. "He simply went mad," the clown lamented, "rushing at everybody, growling and barking." The *ryzhii* clown asked Kiro how he planned to cure his dog, and Kiro explained that the doctors said he must be beaten. "Poor dog," sighed the *ryzhii* clown, who then asked his companion where the unfortunate animal might be found. "There he is," Kiro replied, pointing toward the edge of the ring. "Now you'll see for yourself." He commanded the dog, Trezor, to come but was not immediately obeyed. He offered the dog sugar, sausage, and lard, but none of these delicacies could move the animal. Finally, he called, "Trezor, come and get Europe!" and the dog promptly dashed across the ring, searching avidly for his quarry. "You see there," Kiro exclaimed, "he's an aggressor, with all the habits of one." After a rousing game of anti-American fetch—when asked to fetch a tablet with the word "America" printed on it, Trezor retrieved the ones labeled "Greece," "South Korea," and "West Germany"—Kiro finally succeeded in provoking the dog to lunge for his leg. After shouting, "Ugh, you accursed aggressor, you warmonger! Be quiet! Go to hell!" the clown donned a Red Army cap, thus causing the dog to tuck his tail between his legs and, squealing with fright, run straight away. The act concluded with the dog's retreat, but the real menace—the feral hounds that inhabit America—remained free to realize their threatening designs.[20]

American ambitions were also left largely unchecked in an act approved for performance in 1948 that featured two clowns, a *belyi* and a *ryzhii*, playing a life-sized game of chess. After the two clowns had unfurled an enormous black-and-white checked game board onto the floor of the ring, a stagehand entered carrying a gigantic knight set on a stand labeled "*ShAkhmaty*," or "Chess." The first two letters of the word, *Sh* and *A*, were capitalized. The *belyi* clown began to explain the rules of the game: "In chess there are sixteen pawns, and the most important figure is the king. Stand here, you will be the king." Unexpectedly, the *ryzhii* clown refused to be the king because "nowadays, kings are pawns," but when his partner explained that he would be not a real king, but a "chess king," the *ryzhii* agreed to play his part. The *belyi* clown then explained the rules for moving the king, the bishop, and the knight. When he had completed his lesson, he asked his partner whether he understood all of the rules. "I understand everything," the *ryzhii* clown assured him. "The king moves right, left, and backward, but never forward. The bishop runs abnormally. And the knight moves in a way that never gets him anywhere."

The *belyi* clown informed his inept pupil that it was a terrible shame that he understood so little of such a fascinating game. "Even the politics of a certain country across the ocean resemble the game of chess," he explained. "You know this country of course." "Of course I know," the *ryzhii* clown replied and, walking up to the knight, wrote a capital "*S*" in front of the word "*ShAkhmaty*," which was already inscribed on its base—S.Sh.A. is the Russian equivalent of the acronym U.S.A. "Exactly right," the *belyi* clown replied, since "people there are divided up, as in chess, into blacks and whites." "As in chess," the *ryzhii* continued, "there are kings: kings of finance, coal, and steel." "And of pigs too," the *belyi* clown added. "Those kings," the *ryzhii* clown remarked, "want, 'according to their plan,' to turn sixteen countries," the number of countries receiving Marshall aid, "into sixteen pawns," his partner concluded. The two clowns continued their joint recitation of the similarities between American politics and chess:

BELYI: Etot plan
RYZHII: Ikh "konek."
BELYI: Oni razoslali po vsem moriam
RYZHII: Svoi lad'i.
BELYI: Demokratii i nezavisimosti stran oni
RYZHII: Ob''iavliaiut shakh.
BELYI: I vsemu miru ugrozhaiut
RYZHII: Atomnoi bomboi!

[BELYI: This plan is
RYZHII: their "hobby horse."
BELYI: They've sent out across all the seas
RYZHII: their castles.
BELYI: Democracy and the independence of nations they
RYZHII: place in check.

BELYI: And they threaten the whole world
RYZHII: with the atomic bomb!]

"That's right," the white-faced clown concluded. "I see that you understand both politics and chess." "Yes, yes," the *ryzhii* clown replied, informing his partner of his intention to enter a tournament. "What for?" the *belyi* clown inquired. "I will beat everybody and be the champion of the world," he exclaimed as he mounted the knight, which promptly reared back, unseating the clown, and ran away. The scene concluded with the failed, buffoonish attempts of the two clowns to capture the knight.

Again, though the *ryzhii* clown's ambition to be crowned champion of the world was thwarted—if the *ryzhii*'s vague ambition can even be considered representative of the Americans' clearly specified aspirations—the Americans, according to the skit, continued to jeopardize democracy and national security in Europe, while their atomic strength remained a peril to the lives of all the world's inhabitants.[21] America's defeat was no more certain in "Fashions," a 1950 routine that called attention to the American menace and also predicted, with slight assurance, the ultimate deterrence of this threat. To open the sketch, the clown Golubtseva entered the ring carrying a magazine, which she, the ringmaster, and her partner, the *ryzhii* clown Koloshin, began to peruse. "What marvelous fashions we have, simple and at the same time elegant," the ringmaster remarked. Golubtseva replied, "At one time Paris was the arbiter of fashion," and Koloshin added, "Now, Paris fashions are 'the last word in fashion' [*V Parizhe i seichas mody 'poslednii krik'*]." "Why the last word [the idiom, in Russian, is literally "the last scream"]?" asked the ringmaster, who was told, in response, "You'll scream when the Americans take your last shirt!" Next, when Golubtseva "ironically" quipped, "Here's how they dress now in the Marshallized countries," the *ryzhii* clown produced a pair of pants that were loosely held together by rope, with cushions sewn onto the knees. The clown identified these pants as the "newly improved model" for clothing to be worn by the heads of the "Marshallized" countries. When Golubtseva protested that these pants would be unsuitable for walking, the *ryzhii* clown explained that the people for whom they were designed had forgotten how to walk "because they are always crawling on their knees before Wall Street." "I should tell you," he continued, "that in capitalist countries many people are wearing completely inappropriate suits." He proceeded to model these costumes, displaying a straitjacket, "in which the

American people will soon dress all of those who smother freedom in America," and donning a mask with the word "peace" painted on its lips. The clown identified this as an "American diplomatic mask" and, after Golubtseva observed that it smelled of something, he admitted that the mask stank of gunpowder. The *ryzhii* clown next offered to display "one outfit the warmongers have obviously forgotten, but which history dictates will fall on them to wear." He unfurled a striped prison uniform and added "a tie to go with it" in the form of a noose.[22] This routine did presage the eventual execution of the American "warmongers," but it was still far from the spectacle of a canine Hitler bowing his head into a noose. By even drawing a comparison between hypocritical American diplomats and the aggressors that history had found guilty of provoking wars, the routine implied that the American warmongers would succeed in igniting a military conflagration.

By repeatedly enacting the decisive defeat of an incapable and even ridiculous adversary, wartime performances had minimized the very threat that circus routines dramatized after the war. This contrast should come as no surprise, given that the American military threat was very different from the threat posed by the Nazi invaders. The war between the Soviet Union and the United States was not hot, and the Soviet government was less interested in relieving popular anxiety that it one day would be than in drumming up public distrust of the United States and, especially, its policy of postwar intervention in Western Europe. Circus performances exaggerated the American military threat at least in part to counter the more apparent threat that the United States, as the guarantor of Western European economic prosperity, presented to the Soviet state, which was struggling to fulfill its promise to provide for the material comforts and even some of the basic needs of its postwar population.

The idea that the United States and England presented a threat to Soviet security and therefore to popular prosperity provided an explanation for the Soviet government's continuing failure to endow every Soviet family with a cozy home and a well-stocked larder. It was a corollary to the idea that the western powers presented a threat to popular prosperity and therefore to Soviet security—an idea that legitimated the enjoyment of material benefits by those few who did receive them. Circus acts that figured the Soviet Union as a home whose comforts remained vulnerable to an external threat thus addressed two important constituencies in the postwar period: those for whom the promise of material prosperity was fulfilled, and those for whom it remained merely a promise. They also addressed another constituency entirely: Soviet women.

Soviet Women

As Susan Reid argues, the legitimacy claim implicit in the Soviet government's promise to provide for the material well-being of the Soviet people was directed largely toward women, who were assumed to be more concerned with their families, homes, and consumer products than with political events and ideological abstractions.[23] Happy Soviet homemakers, it was apparently thought, would make happy Soviet citizens, not only because material prosperity would secure women's loyalty, but also because women would be empowered to exercise their citizenship by acting "in their capacity as consumers and retailers . . . as the state's agents in reforming the material culture of everyday life."[24] Just as the identification of the Soviet Union as a cozy home legitimated the state's promise to provide for material prosperity while also explaining its failure to do so, the identification of the cozy home with the Soviet Union legitimated the official identification of the home as women's unique domain and exclusive responsibility.

For example, a monologue approved for performance in 1949 identified the acquisition of a private home, here presented as a uniquely feminine sphere, as an achievement commensurate with professional success. This routine recognized a young woman's anticipated move into a new apartment as a cause for celebration as significant as a factory director's fulfillment of the plan, a teacher's receipt of a commendation, and a student's graduation from school. The performer first congratulated a gentleman with a "bright tie" and a "shining face," whose portrait had appeared in the newspaper after his factory fulfilled the five-year plan. He next addressed another comrade, a teacher: "I can congratulate you all the more, and for that there's a very good reason— not long ago you received a decoration." The performer then turned to a young woman who wore a festive expression because "a house-warming party is in store for you, in the bright rooms of a new house." It was no coincidence that the figure associated with the bright new home was a young woman. The three honored professionals—the last was the student who recently graduated—were all male, whereas the only other woman to receive the narrator's congratulations was lost in happiness with her new husband, whom she had just married the day before. This monologue equated women's work within the home to men's work outside of it, since both provided for individually rewarding achievements and both, implicitly, constituted a public service.[25]

Circus routines written in honor of the eight hundredth anniversary of the city of Moscow in 1947 reinforced the identification of home-making as an exclusively feminine practice that served the public good. They did so by celebrating the many new homes that the young, beau-tiful, and grammatically feminine metropolis, Moskva, had bestowed upon the Soviet people. In a short exchange approved for performance that year, a clown marveled at the envy all women felt toward Moscow, who was eight hundred years old but became "younger and more beau-tiful with every year."[26] Another routine identified the city as a young beauty who provided a magnificent home for her children. To open the skit, one clown explained to another that he had gone for a walk in the forest and nearly gotten lost. The second clown asked whether he had walked very far, and the first clown replied that he had not walked far, but rather high, explaining that the forests were now fifty meters tall and still growing. The second clown asked where such tall forests grew, and the first replied that they were growing all across Moscow. When asked how he happened to have climbed up into these forests, the first clown explained that he had been promised an apartment on the thirty-first floor and, in the meantime, he was getting accustomed to the height. "Good! Good, it should be good to live in those houses!" his interlocutor cried. "And how! After I move onto the thirty-first floor I'll be able to look down on you," the first clown remarked, looking through the binoculars and spotting their friend Vasia, to whom he called, "Come on up, Vasia, to look at the pretty woman!" "What woman?" Vasia shouted back. "A young one!" "How old?" "She's just turned 800!" "How is she dressed?" "In granite and marble, encircled by a green belt" (referring to the boulevard known as the garden ring, which en-circles the center of Moscow). "I'm coming," Vasia finally cried, prompt-ing the first clown to conclude that "all of us here are in love with one beauty, and to one beauty we are all faithful!" The second continued, "And this beauty is visible to everybody from afar, and they call this beauty—Mother Moscow!"[27] By comparing "Mother Moscow" to a forest, this routine added an urban dimension to the largely pastoral idea of the motherland as a site of popular devotion.[28] It offered, as the rewards for loyalty, a new home in a high-rise building with a beautiful wife and mother to maintain it. At the same time, by presenting Mos-cow as a model Soviet woman, this routine also elevated the status of beautiful wives and generous mothers to a level commensurate with that of the nation's capital.

After the war, routines like these told Soviet women that by providing happy homes for happy families, they would be providing for the Soviet motherland, just as, during the war, they had served the motherland as mothers, wives, sisters, and homemakers. Women who served in World War II as snipers, sappers, pilots, and in many other roles once filled exclusively by men were publicly lauded as heroes who had fulfilled their duty to their families as much as to their motherland.[29] After the war, women again were urged to contribute to the Soviet Union's recovery by serving as mothers, wives, and homemakers, duties that entailed literally replenishing the Soviet population, caring for war orphans and wounded husbands, and provisioning their homes. The writer Il'ia Fink composed a series of circus monologues recognizing the wartime service and sacrifice of women, specifically of mothers and wives. One monologue, approved for performance in 1945, thanked mothers for everything they had done for "us," for hiding their fear as they sent their sons off to war, guarding their homes from enemy attack, living, believing, enduring, and waiting until victory was won before they tearfully embraced their sons.[30] Another monologue celebrated mothers whose sons perished before the victory was declared but who continued to serve as mothers to other women's orphaned sons. The monologue, titled "Someone Else's Mother," opened with a harrowing description of an apartment building the morning after it was bombed:

Eshche kruzhilis' iskry poutru
I dym kak voron
vilsia na vetru,
Eshche zenitki bili po vragu
Eshche tela cherneli na snegu . . .
I mal'chik plakal gliadia liudiam vsled
I mamu zval, kotoroi bol'she net.

[In the morning, the sparks still swirled
and the smoke, like a raven,
hovered in the wind,
the anti-aircraft guns still fired at the enemy,
bodies still turned black in the snow . . .
And a boy cried as he scanned the crowd
and he called for his mother,
who was no more.]

Into this scene entered another person's mother, who approached the child, offering him a "large and tender hand" to which he clung. This other person's mother—the child himself did not know whose mother she was—so warmed him with caresses that immediately he called her by the "joyous name" of mother. This mother took the boy into her home and helped him to feel that it was his own:

Chuzhie steny. Neznakomyi sad,
Tianula pamiat' mal'chika nazad
V tot dom, gde bol'she
mama ne zhivet
V tot dom, gde bol'she
klen ne rastsvetet,
Chuzhaia mama v zhizn' ego voshla,
Kogda ne spal on noch'iu—
ne spala,
Kogda igral—
delila igry s nim,
chtob novyi dom
stal mal'chiku rodnym.

[Someone else's walls. An unfamiliar garden,
the boy's memory drew him back
to the house where his mother
no longer lived,
to the garden where the maple tree
no longer grew,
someone else's mother had entered his life,
when he couldn't sleep at night—
she did not sleep,
when he played—
she shared in the games with him
so that the new house
would become the boy's own.]

In time, the child's loud and happy laughter rang ever more frequently across his new neighborhood. In his new home "he grew faster than green pines and birches, stronger than a poplar." He grew and, over the course of time, he came to call someone else's mother his own. He grew, and frequently his mother whispered, her brow furrowed in grief: "'My son perished . . . Grow quickly, my son.'" The monologue concluded with a final stanza that honored this mother, who would raise her son to be a "fearless, brave eaglet, a soldier proud of his motherland":

Chuzhaia mama,
ch'ia ne znal i sam on
Dorogu smozhet synu ukazat'
Nedarom syn svoiu chuzhuiu mamu
Zovet schastlivym, svetlym
slovom mat'![31]

[Someone else's mother,
he himself did not know whose
will direct her son along his way,
It's not for nothing that this son
calls someone else's mother
by the happy, joyous name of mother!]

As this monologue implied, women served the nation by raising generations of sons to defend it. It also implied that to be a mother was not
merely to fulfill a woman's patriotic duty but also to be happy. For
women after the war, motherhood was presented as being both a responsibility and a reward.

Another monologue composed in 1945 similarly recognized a happy
home, a loving marriage, and an orderly grocery store as women's rewards for the characteristically feminine strength and fidelity that they
demonstrated during the war. This monologue, prepared in honor of the
twenty-eighth anniversary of the October Revolution in 1945, rejoiced
with the Soviet people, who were celebrating a victory that women had
done much to secure and would do much more to preserve. The narrator
began by noting that, on this special night,

Tsarit vesel'e v kazhdom dome,
iz okon l'etsia iarkii svet,
khotia i tesno v Gastronome
nikakikh skandalov net!
Vino vsegda s vesel'em riadom
I raz moment takoi nastal—
za prazdnik nash, za nashu radost'
ia podnimaiu svoi bokal!

[Happiness reigns in every home,
bright light pours out from the windows,
although the grocery store is crowded,
There aren't any quarrels!
Alongside happiness there is always wine
And now the time has come—

To our holiday, to our happiness
I raise my glass!]

The narrator then proceeded to greet various members of the audience. He noted, first, the many pairs of lovers, admitting that even his experienced eye could not distinguish the newlyweds from those who had been married for twenty years. He then directed his remarks specifically to women:

Privet vam, devushki i zheny,
Vy zhdali mnogo-mnogo dnei,
S kakim volnen'em pochtal'ona
vy odzhidali u dverei!
Leteli k prazdniku podarki
v zemlianku tesnuiu boitsa,
i strochki pisem byli zharki,
kak vashi zhenskie serdtsa.
Za russkikh zhenshchin terpelivykh,
za tekh, kto veril, tekh, kto zhdal
za vsekh vliublennykh i schastlivykh
Ia podnimaiu svoi bokal![32]

[Hello to you, young women and wives,
you waited many, many days,
with such distress you waited by your doors
for the postman!
You sent holiday presents
to the crowded dug-outs,
and the lines of your letters were
as ardent as your feminine hearts.
To patient Russian women,
to those who believed, to those who waited,
to all those who are in love and happy
I raise my glass!]

Love, happiness, and a good marriage were publicly celebrated as the fruits of a military victory that faithful Soviet wives and mothers had helped to secure. As faithful wives and mothers, Soviet women would also help ensure that this victory remained secure from any threat that the new set of foreign aggressors might pose. A monologue recited by a female performer, O. Fadeeva, in 1951 explicitly proposed that women's marital and maternal fidelity made them able protectors of international peace and, therefore, of national security. Fadeeva began by describing a recurring daydream, in which she imagined herself entering the circus arena to find an audience of "hundreds of women—the daughters of Berlin, Prague, Warsaw, and Paris . . . women from India, Korea, and China." She would like to tell these women that "all of us are dear and close; I am a modest Soviet artist, a simple woman, a wife and mother." She claimed that they would understand her despite their national differences because "they have a house, a family, their own cares. . . . Their lovely children grow, their husbands come home from work in the evenings." According to her fantasy, Fadeeva would then ask the women to tell her, "Who among you would agree to send her son to the trenches? Who wants an exploding landmine to turn your comfortable home into ruins? Do you want that?" To her own question she replied that with one voice the women would cry "No!" She claimed to discern in that reply an unbending resistance to war: "'Our children do not grow up on the earth for war, people do not need war." Fadeeva, however, did not cast these women simply as pacifists, but rather as "heroic . . . noble fighters [*bortsov*] for peace and happiness, whose immortal image is crowned in glory and whose name is sung in popular legends." Yet, she continued, only some women numbered among these "dear sisters." Others deserved to be mercilessly denounced. These included Eleanor Roosevelt, who had lost the right to her husband's name when she so shamelessly betrayed him by joining the raving gang of bankers. "America will never forgive you," Fadeeva warned Roosevelt, at least not that segment of the American population that "desires a secure world." Fadeeva next advised the "inciters of war" to prepare to be judged "severely and fairly." "Neither a feminine first name nor a feminine skirt can save you from popular retribution," she announced:

Ne skryt' vashu podlost'
pod pyshnym nariadom,
vam bol'she podkhodit
zverninaia shkura.
I volchii oskal
ne zakrasit' pomadoi,
i kogti ne spriatat'
pod lak manikura.

[Don't hide your baseness beneath
magnificent attire,
an animal's pelt
suits you better.

And don't paint your wolf's maw
with lipstick,
and don't conceal your claws
with nail polish.]

Fadeeva explained that after pronouncing these "angry words" to
the "fascist rats" and the "well-dressed dolls," she would gaze at the
women assembled around her and become "warm, easy, and pleasant"
again. Her voice would again become strong and sure as she was reminded that "on the earth there are millions of us, simple women." In
this voice she would shout, "Comrades! We will struggle in unity, we
demand peace and peace we will receive!" Fadeeva concluded her
monologue by declaring that "war will not destroy our peaceful
hearth. . . . Our children do not grow up on the earth for war, people do
not need war!"[33]

Because they were good mothers, women would help win this new
struggle for peace, and, by doing so, they would help protect the Soviet
Union from foreign aggressors, just as they had helped defeat the army
of fascist rats by being good mothers in World War II. Yet, as the monologue itself demonstrates, Fadeeva promoted the cause of peace most
obviously in her capacity as a circus performer, just as women contributed to the defeat of the Nazis most obviously in their capacity as
military combatants, military support personnel, and workers on the
home front. Fadeeva was a mother, but she also had a job, as did most
women in the Soviet Union. Since the period of rapid industrialization,
the Soviet economy had depended upon women's labor, which remained
an essential resource during the postwar reconstruction. As Lynne
Attwood explains, Soviet women were required to work both inside
the home and outside of it, a double burden that found expression in a
peculiar gender norm: "The Soviet woman's new role as worker was
grafted onto her old role of homemaker, and female identity was meant
to encompass traditional male and female qualities and traits. She was
glorified for her capacity to work like a man, and at the same time celebrated for her nurturance and her willingness to sacrifice herself for
others."[34]

After the war, female circus performers were thought to embody this
ambiguous ideal. They did the same work as men, but they did it like
women: easily, gracefully, beautifully, elegantly, and cheerfully. Their
performances were taken as proof that women could work like men
and still work like women, which is precisely what Soviet women were

supposed to do. Fadeeva herself performed in the traditionally male role of the circus "conversationalist." Women rarely spoke in the circus ring, a gender division to which the performer Derval' attested in an introductory monologue she was authorized to recite in 1946. Derval' began by offering the audience a "heartfelt, friendly, and warm" greeting on behalf of all the Moscow State Circus performers, including herself, the master of ceremonies. Derval' presumed that the audience was "of course, slightly surprised that tonight a woman is serving as the master of ceremonies," but, she continued, "a woman's appearance as the master of ceremonies has now become a common occurrence." Whereas at one time, she continued, "arrogant men" were known to repeat the aphorism "as a chicken is not a bird, a woman is not a person," nowadays men often ceded to women their places at the workbench, behind the wheel of a car, and at the helm of an airplane. Derval' concluded that women could take the place of men in any occupation, which was why the circus troupe had promoted her to the post of master of ceremonies.[35]

Derval's sentiment contrasted obviously with Fadeeva's, but it was consistent with wartime assertions of gender equality in the circus ring. For example, a 1941 review of a Moscow circus performance in *Sovetskoe iskusstvo* praised female animal trainers, acrobats, and jugglers, who astonished the audience with their "endurance, training, and skill." The reviewer, Viktor Ermans, insisted that these women were not "those 'assistants' who typically hand 'bottles' and hoops to the juggler, participate in mass scenes, and support somebody who is doing something somewhere." Rather, they were "talented artists of the Soviet circus, who had achieved a terrific perfection of skill."[36] In a review of the 1946 creative revue in Moscow for *Trud* (*Labor*), D. Zaslavskii similarly noted that female trapeze artists were "not inferior to men," an assertion that, in later years, rarely went unqualified.[37]

Just as Fadeeva emphasized her maternal identity in order to justify her performance in the predominantly male role of circus "conversationalist," postwar circus reviewers, including those who did recognize female performers' strength, bravery, and skill, often called attention to their uniquely feminine virtues of beauty, kindness, and good mothering. For example, the program for a 1957 production featuring performers who had either performed internationally or received prizes at the First International Circus Festival touted the feats of four female trapeze artists. According to the program, these "girls [*devushki*]" performed a routine more difficult than any that had yet been seen by a female troupe. The "expressiveness, harmonious teamwork, and dynamism" of their various tricks were astounding, yet, the program claimed, audiences were amazed by the "ease" with which the young artists performed them. The program's description concluded with the observation that "one trick follows the next, each more interesting and complicated than the last, leaving the viewer with a grand impression from this cheerful and, in the full sense of the word, beautiful circus spectacle."[38]

Easy, cheerful, and beautiful were adjectives used solely to describe women's gymnastic performances, which, unlike men's routines, were only rarely characterized as agile, daring, or powerful. In his introduction to a memoir written in 1963 by the renowned acrobat Zoia Kokh, who performed with her two sisters, Iurii Dmitriev stated that the trio's tricks should "rightfully be considered achievements of the highest class, even had they belonged to men." "But," he continued, "the artists demonstrate these tricks with unusual ease and playfulness," a style that provided for the viewers' "aesthetic happiness." Dmitriev elaborated on this point further, noting that the sisters performed "easily, beautifully, freely, and elegantly." He concluded that the Kokh sisters entered the arena not only to demonstrate "several extremely complicated tricks" but also to enact their own theatrical transformations from earthly heroines into ethereal heroines: "They are three extraordinary beauties, three fantastical fairies, for whom any kind of magic is easy."[39] A 1970 profile of the acrobat Raisa Nemchinskaia similarly characterized the female performer as the embodiment of a feminine ideal. Although the commentator first praised Nemchinskaia's "wonderful figure," he or she interpreted the "content" of her routines to be "an assertion of a certain ideal of a woman, in whom grace, nobility, and elegance are combined with bravery and remarkable skill."[40] At least one female acrobat was thought to have achieved this ideal both inside the circus ring and in her everyday life outside of it. A pamphlet promoting the Soviet Circus that was published in 1968 included a description of Vladimir Doveiko's acrobatic troupe, which featured his wife, Lidiia. According to the pamphlet, Lidiia performed a "rare number" on two spinning wheels, an "effective entree" that Vladimir "staged . . . for her." The author went on to note that Lidiia was named the most beautiful circus artist at the international circus festival held in Brussels, an honor that did not, however, "prevent her from preparing tasty dinners, at which she is very adept and which is something she loves to do."[41]

Acrobats were not the only ideal women to appear in the circus ring. According to press descriptions, female animal trainers performed as bravely and skillfully as men, without forsaking any of their uniquely feminine charms or responsibilities. In 1958, M. Tartakovskii wrote a laudatory profile of the animal trainer Irina Bugrimova for *Sovetskii sport* (*Soviet Sport*). He did emphasize her "will to victory" and her courage, describing a bow she took with her back to ten lions as the "height of courage," a feat whose daring, in his view, even surpassed the trick in which she placed her head into the gaping mouth of a lion. Yet he also claimed that while viewers admired her courage, they also "loved the plasticity of her movements and her emotional expression."[42] In another profile of the "courageous and charming" animal trainer published for *Sovetskaia estrada i tsirk* in 1970, N. Lagina noted that "for some reason, as a rule, whenever we evaluate the performances of female circus artists who work with beasts, we note that they create an image of brave and daring women who are not afraid of any difficulties and who audaciously force their beasts to submit to their will." Lagina admitted that the image of the female animal trainer was unthinkable without courage and daring, but she insisted that these attributes alone did not suffice. In her view, female trainers were required to maintain a harmonious relationship with their animals, and it was in this that Irina Bugrimova distinguished herself. According to Lagina, Bugrimova, who had been called a "queen among kings," was a queen by virtue of her "warmth, charm, and femininity." "Her image," Lagina continued, was that of a "brave and willful woman. But of a woman [*Ee obraz—smelaia, volevaia zhenshchina. No—zhenshchina*]."[43]

Lagina and others considered female circus performers to be perfect exemplars of a feminine ideal in which women demonstrated their strength and bravery with ease, grace, beauty, and charm—an interpretation that was not inconsistent with the performances themselves. In 1972, for example, E. Ziskind was authorized to direct Val'ter and Maritsa Zapashnyi's performance of an animal routine of his own design. He attached a note to the written scenario explaining his intention to stage a routine divided into two contrasting segments, the first to be performed by Val'ter and the second by Maritsa. Val'ter's routine, which was based on the "best traditions of circus animal training," involved two lions, eight tigers, and one horse. According to Ziskind, it was meant to give expression to the "strong-willed, masculine origins of animal training." Zapashnyi's persona, he continued, was to be masculine, dynamic, and brave. Maritsa's segment, in contrast, was based on a "lyrical, musical, foundation," and was meant to be "calm, grand, and feminine." It featured white bears and black panthers. A third scene involved both performers and, as Ziskind explained, was choreographed so as to highlight the conflict between the two opposing styles.[44]

Though Ziskind neglected to describe the Zapashnyis' costumes, women's costumes often helped to distinguish them from men, and observers frequently drew attention to them. In his introduction to Kokh's memoir, for example, Dmitriev described the sisters' "effective" entrance into the ring. Their heads were covered in diamonds, their long trains trailed across the ring behind them, the sparkles on their costumes glittered and flashed beneath the spotlight, and all of it together created a "romantic, marvelous" effect.[45] Peta Tait also describes a practice that was common among Russian trapeze artists of wearing high heels into the ring, slipping out of them to perform, and then putting them back on to exit the ring—a practice that, in Tait's view, "suggests the extent to which the gendered consume becomes part of the act."[46] In at least one case, however, a woman performed in a costume that was less obviously feminine. In 1974, Tatiana Kokh performed an equestrian routine wearing a golden top hat and high riding boots, even though, as Natalia Rumiantseva noted in her review, "anything would have suited her—a miniskirt, a splendid dress flowing down in tender tones." Nonetheless, Rumiantseva approved of the "amazon costume from the variety theater" since it even further emphasized "this graceful girl's slimness and youth.[47]

By interpreting Kokh's masculine attire as a feminizing accoutrement, Rumiantseva reinforced the gender ambiguity that Kokh's performance introduced into the ring. According to Rumiantseva, Kokh was a strong and daring rider as well as a slim and graceful girl. Like other female circus performers, she was an ideal Soviet woman, capable of doing anything a man could do, but without compromising her uniquely female identity as an object of beauty and charm or her uniquely female responsibilities as a wife, mother, and homemaker. The circus proved to be a perfect arena for the propagation of a Soviet gender norm that doubly burdened women. At the same time, postwar circus performances reminded women of the rewards they would receive if they adhered to this norm: a well-dressed, well-fed family that lived in a comfortable home within the secure borders of a prosperous nation. They also reminded all viewers that Soviet women were working hard to secure the homes and the homeland of the Soviet Union from any threat that the militarily and economically aggressive western war-mongers posed.

Non-Russian Brothers

Although mothers and wives were uniquely burdened with both of these tasks, they did have some help with them from their brothers in the non-Russian republics. Like mothers and wives, inhabitants of the so-called brother republics came together in postwar circus rings, where they offered proof of the strength of the Soviet family and the security of the Soviet multinational homeland, which they purportedly had so valiantly defended during the war. The Soviet circus had begun to showcase "national" performers even before the war had ended. As Iu. S. Iurskii, the artistic director of the Moscow circus, reported in a 1946 meeting of the artistic council of the Main Administration of State Circuses (GUTs), in 1944 the Moscow circus had invented a new tradition of staging a "national spectacle." The Uzbek national circus collective staged the inaugural show, and performers from the Baltics were invited to appear the following year. Members of the Azerbaijan circus collective greeted audiences in 1946,[48] and in 1947, the Moscow circus organized a program that featured representatives of all the Soviet republics in honor of the Soviet Union's thirtieth anniversary. The highlight of its 1948–49 season was the production of "Our Guests," which, according to the program, showcased "artists of the circus of the brother republics." The performers' printed biographies emphasized their wartime service. Viewers learned, for example, that M. Gismatulin, the leader of the Ukrainian acrobatic troupe, "defended the motherland from within the ranks of the Soviet Army" and fought in the battle of Stalingrad, where he suffered from shellshock. It was only after his demobilization that Gismatulin began to train acrobats at the Tashkent Circus's national circus studio. Similarly, the two Azerbaijani acrobats, Ismail Mirzoev and Manuchar Manucharov, who performed among "our guests," also served as riflemen in the Soviet Army. Before they were called up, they had practiced gymnastics in their free time; once they were demobilized they joined the newly formed Azerbaijani national circus collective, to which they contributed a "new, complicated demonstration of strength."[49] Russian nationals were also lauded for their wartime service, but the patriotism of their brothers in the non-Russian republics stood as proof that the Soviet family was varied, that its homeland was vast, and that, therefore, both would remain safe. This point was made explicitly by the artist O. Fadeeva in the monologue she composed to open the 1949 performance of the Uzbek national circus troupe in Moscow:

Iz dalekikh kraev my speshili siuda
Tam tsvetut kishlaki i rastut goroda,
Solntse shchedroe l'et zolotye luchi,
Tam zemlia goriacha
i serdtsa goriachi! . . .
Pust' na nashi kraia
zdeshnii krai ne pokhozh,
Vyzrevaet v poliakh zdes'
ne khlopok, a rozh',
No pod solntsem odnim
my rastem i zhivem,
I bogat, i krasiv,
i prostoren nash dom.

[From distant lands we rushed here,
There, villages blossom and cities grow,
and the sun generously spills golden beams,
there the land is hot
and hearts are ardent! . . .
Though the land here
does not resemble ours,
here cotton and not rye
grows in the fields,
we grow and live
beneath the same sun,
and our home is rich,
beautiful, and spacious.]

Yet according to Fadeeva, it was not only the sunshine that the residents of the rich, beautiful, and spacious Soviet home shared, and it certainly was not only the sunshine that made this home so rich, beautiful, spacious, and secure:

Vse my pesni poem o svobodnom trude,
O rodimoi strane,
o liubimom vozhde,

O tverdyne Moskvy—krasnozvezdnom
Kremle,
O schastlivoi, bol'shoi,
vsenarodnoi sem'e.

[All of us sing about free labor,
about our native motherland,
about our beloved leader,
about the stronghold of Moscow—
the Kremlin with its red star,
about the happy, big,
multinational family.]

Fadeeva explained, in conclusion, that this family was born of the union between the Soviet motherland and Stalin:

Vse my vmeste
idem po doroge pobed,
Vsem nam Rodina—mat',
vsem nam Stalin—otets,
Tak primite poklon i primite privet
Ot goriachei strany,
ot goriachikh serdets![50]

[All of us together march
along the path to victory,
The motherland is mother to us all,
Stalin is father to us all
So accept the greeting and the warm regards
From a hot country
and from ardent hearts!

Like the fantastical image of the "daughters of Berlin, Prague, Warsaw, and Paris . . . women from India, Korea, and China" united in their maternal pursuit of national security that Fadeeva conjured in 1951, her greeting from Uzbekistan imagined the Soviet people to be a family that resided in a home that was spacious and secure, bright and beautiful. The Soviet home was also well-stocked with the cotton clothing and rye bread that the Stalinist state and Soviet motherland provided and that all Soviet brothers continued to secure. Fadeeva's act helped bring the Soviet family together, under the generous golden sun and, more literally, under the circus dome. Like postwar routines that identified the Soviet home with the Soviet homeland and that identified Soviet women as mothers to all the children of the Soviet Union, programs that recognized non-Russian minorities as brothers helped to reconstitute the Soviet national family and to situate it in a safe and well-provisioned home.

Conclusion

The postwar circus told viewers the same story that was implied by Mikhail Kalatozov's 1957 film, *The Cranes Are Flying*. The film ends as Veronika, hoping that her beloved, Boris, has survived the war, searches for him at the train station among the soldiers returning from the front. When she learns from another soldier that he has died, she weeps and runs frantically through the crowd. She is soon stilled by the speech of this soldier, who addresses the crowd not as "comrades" but as "mothers, fathers, sisters, and brothers." Veronika hears him say that "we share the grief of those who cannot meet their loved ones today and we will do everything to insure that sweethearts are never again parted by war, that mothers need never again fear for their children's lives, that fathers need never again choke back hidden tears." As Veronika's own tears begin to dry, the soldier concludes with the cry, "We have won and we shall live not to destroy, but to build a new life!" An old man, who stands beside Veronika, asks her, "Why are you just standing there? Give your flowers to whomever they're for." Veronika gives a sprig of flowers to him and begins to smile as she hands the flowers she has brought for Boris to other soldiers. She gives flowers to a woman in uniform, who embraces her and says, "Thank you, sister." She gives flowers to a man who stands holding his "beautiful granddaughter" up to the sky. She gives away all of the flowers and then stands alone, until Boris's father, who took her in after her own parents died in a bombing, comes to guide her away. Veronika's family was now the Soviet family, and together they would build a new life. This was a story the circus told in the immediate postwar period, but without explicitly acknowledging the psychological devastation experienced by the aggrieved family member, a topic that remained taboo until after Stalin's death.

The postwar circus brought families together, and some viewers might have been comforted to see themselves surrounded by other Soviet families whose sacrifice and sadness they shared. They might have been proud to know that it was their sacrifice and sadness that ensured the safety and material security of all the other families that surrounded them in the arena. Some might have been pleased to learn that their own family's prosperity helped to support the extended Soviet family, while others might have been relieved to learn that their own family's privation did so too. They all might have been inspired to work as hard to provide for the one as for the other, since, as women especially learned in the circus, the best way to provide for the Soviet family was to provide for one's own family, just as the best way to secure one's homeland was to secure one's own home.

Yet the circus could not really bring families back together again, and it certainly could not provide them with real homes, secure borders, cotton clothes, and rye bread. Some circus viewers might not have been comforted to see themselves surrounded by the Soviet families that stepped on their toes, whispered too loudly, and whose children would not stop crying. They might not have been proud to know that their sacrifice and their sadness had ensured the safety of these strangers. They might not have been reassured to realize that their family members had been replaced by juggling Uzbeks, Azerbaijani acrobats, and other people's mothers. Some might have been disheartened to see families that were more prosperous than their own, while others might have felt guilty to realize that other families still suffered privations.

Instead, circus viewers might have liked the circus simply because it provided a respite from their sadness and required no additional sacrifice. They might have liked it because it provided their families with a break from the nearly constant work of providing for their families. As always, some viewers might have liked the juggling Uzbeks and Azerbaijani acrobats because these performances had nothing to do with their own lives outside of the circus. Children especially might have liked Nikulin and Karandash's physical comedy, whatever it was meant to mean, just as they might have liked to see a life-size chess game, regardless of how *Shakhmaty* was spelled. Even those viewers who did not at all like couplets about other people's mothers could easily have ignored them, since there was, after all, always some other person's mother to watch, behaving strangely, in the crowd.

Once again, there was more than one reason to like the circus, and these reasons were not necessarily shared by the many different members of the Soviet family who came together to see the show. Yet whether circus viewers really did constitute one big, happy, national family hardly mattered. When Soviet adults sat beside Soviet children, laughing as they watched the mothers, brothers, fathers, and wives on display in the arena, they certainly did appear to belong to the same big, happy family. And, as with all families, keeping up this appearance might have been what mattered most.

5

In Defense of Offensive Peace
The Soviet Circus Finds Itself Abroad

The Cold War remained a constant feature of international politics for much of the latter half of the twentieth century, but the Soviet government did not wage it consistently. Both Nikita Khrushchev and Leonid Brezhnev claimed to be committed to the pursuit of peace, and at times they did initiate periods of "thaw," or detente, in Soviet foreign policy. Yet they both remained committed, or at least claimed to be committed, to promoting socialism internationally, building up the Soviet nuclear arsenal, maintaining the Soviet Union's position in Eastern Europe, and advancing its influence in the developing world, none of which made peace a very likely prospect. This was a contradictory and inconsistent foreign policy, which is why the circus was so well-suited to promoting it between 1953 and 1985. Even as the Soviet state suppressed Polish and Hungarian revolts in 1956, smothered the Czechoslovakian experiment in "socialism with a human face" in 1968, expanded its own nuclear arsenal, and armed Communist groups in Asia, Africa, and Latin America, Soviet circus performers unfurled their carpets of good cheer in cities around the world. They offered tidings of peace, friendship, and goodwill to international audiences, whom they addressed in the universal language of movement, gesture, kind smiles, white doves, and big fake flowers. Marquee performances by grateful Central Asians and friendly Eastern Europeans portrayed the Soviet Union as a multinational, anti-imperialist state whose exportation of socialism promoted economic development and posed no threat to world peace.

The warm reception that the Soviet circus received abroad was presented as proof that westerners liked the Soviet Union as much as they liked the peace that the Soviet Union claimed to be pursuing. At the same time, magic tricks and "cosmic" aerial flights celebrated the Soviet Union's superior scientific, technological, and military achievements, implying that the Soviet Union might be a good friend but certainly would not be a very kind enemy. The friendly, universally admired, multinational, space-age circus was presented as proof that the Soviet Union was the world's only exporter of the humane, anti-imperialist, and progressive socialist ideology and, therefore, its best guarantor of international peace. Circus performances and the rhetoric surrounding them also told viewers everywhere that the Soviet Union was the world's best-equipped combatant, should international peace prove elusive.

International Friendships

In the mid-1950s, the Soviet state mobilized the circus to help strengthen the friendships that it claimed already to enjoy with its Eastern European satellites, its own national republics, and its many sympathizers across the globe. In 1954, for example, the Soviet Ministry of Culture invited a troupe of Czechoslovakian performers to tour the Soviet Union for three months. The animal trainer Irina Bugrimova publicly thanked "our friends" for offering performances that "further strengthened the friendship between our peoples and served our mutual cultural enrichment."[1] The following year, East German circus artists entered the Moscow circus, some with flags of the GDR and others carrying flags emblazoned with doves of peace. They greeted a troupe of Soviet performers, who handed them flowers when they entered the ring. According to Vladimir Durov's review in *Trud*, more than two thousand viewers energetically "applauded this demonstration of friendship between the Soviet and German peoples." Durov went on to attribute the success of the German tour to the "broad development and strengthening of the cultural relations between the peoples of the USSR and the German Democratic Republic." Durov's claim was not that viewers simply liked the circus show, the way they might have liked an exhibit of East German monumental painting or an evening of German folk music and dancing. In his view, the circus's warm reception testified so reliably to the friendship maintained between the Soviet and East German peoples because circus performers, like no others, "sustained close contact and engaged in lively intercourse with viewers."[2] As Durov explained, the intimate bond established between circus performers and viewers both relied on and further reinforced the close ties between them.

The following year, Soviet circus performers were sent to make new friends with the peoples of western Europe, who, according to the official press, welcomed them warmly. In 1956, circus performers embarked on a two-month tour of Belgium, and to meet demand in Brussels, where the Soviets consistently sold out the Cirque Royal, ten performances were added to the itinerary.[3] From Brussels, the performers traveled to Marseilles, Saint-Etienne, and finally to Paris, where an estimated 18,000 viewers attended circus performances.[4] That same year, the Soviet circus made its first appearance in England, where audiences attended a total of fifty performances of the Soviet circus in London and Manchester, despite the declining popularity the English circus had experienced since the turn of the century.[5] Performers also made appearances in Hungary, East Germany, and Poland that year.

The Soviet press attended closely to the remarkable triumph of the Soviet tour, reporting that the emissaries of peace were received warmly by audiences who clearly considered the Soviet people their friends. Zhorzh Soria reported in *Sovetskaia kul'tura* (*Soviet Culture*) that thousands of Parisians attended the daily performances of the Soviet circus, which received "exceptionally benevolent and friendly reviews" in the French press. He insisted that this response was not only a testament to the high quality of the performances but also "an expression of friendship to the Soviet people." According to Soria, the Soviet performers were lauded by circus professionals no less than laypeople, "whose hearts beat in unison with the hearts of the performers." He noted that Soviet circus artists were "met in Paris as envoys of peace, envoys of a great country, with which French men and women want to establish friendly and stable relations."[6] The animal trainer Valentin Filatov shared Soria's view. Upon returning from the European tour, he reported in *Sovetskaia kul'tura* that "of course we understand very well, that the first and fundamental reason for the success of our performances in Belgium, France, and England is the feeling of friendliness toward and interest in the Soviet people that the popular masses of these countries experience."[7] Filatov's opinion was shared by the equestrian performer Ali-Bek Kantemirov, who performed in Budapest in 1956 and appeared in France in 1958. Droves of fans assembled to receive him at his hotel in Montmartre, according to a 1960 biography. He addressed the crowd, to whom he described his encounters with Parisians as having been "simply miraculous." He went on to explain that "we were met so happily, so warmly not only because we achieved something in our art, but most importantly, because we are Soviet people, people of peace, labor, and happiness."[8]

Soria, Filatov, and Ali-Bek seem not to have exaggerated the warmth with which the Soviet circus was welcomed in France, Belgium, and England. Kennett Love, writing for the *New York Times*, also made note of it, though he attributed Londoners' appreciation for the show to the absence of any overt propaganda from its repertoire:

Unlike the Soviet officials—Georgi M. Malenkov, who came in March, or Premier Nikolai A. Bulganina and Nikita S. Khrushchev, who came last month—the bear and the clown had no trouble communicating with the British public. Their language was pantomime. Ten thousand Londoners roared in delight at their antics yesterday. . . . It looked as if the bears and the clown, the acrobats, aerialists, equestrians and jugglers would be by far the most welcome Soviet delegation of the year. . . . The circus did not contain a trace of propaganda. This was clearly just what the customers wanted.[9]

Love might have been right, and although Soviet readers would not have known his view, some might have doubted whether the pleasure European audiences took in watching a foreign circus performance indicated that they experienced anything other than curiosity about the Soviet people and respect for the talent of Soviet circus performers.

Yet other readers might have been convinced that foreign viewers, who were as easy to idealize as domestic circus audiences, really did like the circus for the reasons they were supposed to. There was certainly no shortage of articles, statements, and reviews in the Soviet press claiming that foreign viewers liked the circus because they liked their Soviet friends, that Soviet viewers liked foreign circuses because they liked their foreign friends, and that Soviet and non-Soviet performers liked to perform together because Soviets and non-Soviets liked each other, as all friends do. An article published in *Sovetskii tsirk* (*Soviet Circus*) documented the series of performances held during the 1961 season in which circus artists from different nations performed together.

The article offered these international programs, and their success with Soviet audiences, as an indication that "the striving for peace and friendship has entered the flesh and blood of the Soviet people." Specifically, the Moscow Circus's production of a new version of the "Arena of Friendship," which featured Russian artists "united in a single collective" with artists from Ukraine, Georgia, Uzbekistan, Latvia, Lithuania, Tuva, Dagestan, and North Osetia, revealed that "our epoch is characterized by friendship not only among different people but also between peoples and countries." The "large international presentation" of East German, Polish, Romanian, Czech, and Soviet republican performers offered by the Leningrad Circus told the same story.[10]

Even those Soviets who continued to doubt that foreigners harbored any feelings of friendship for them might still have recognized the circus's ability to inspire those feelings in its more hostile foreign viewers. Some might have agreed with B. Galich, whose description of the appearances by a medley of circus performers at the 1957 International Festival of Youth and Students in Moscow began with the assertion that "this circus is a most ancient art, understandable to and beloved by all peoples." He explained that because "its language needs no translation," the circus was "by its very essence international" and had connected people "with bright threads of mutual goodwill from time immemorial." Galich argued that because the circus was "truly accessible to all, understandable and pleasing to each of these young men and women" who represented 131 countries, it was to "serve the great cause of peace, which is now the most important, the most urgent cause."[11] Vladimir Poliakov credited one performer in particular with promoting this cause. In his history of Russian clowning, which was published in English and intended for foreign consumption, Poliakov described Oleg Popov's performances at the Moscow Festival: "During the VI Youth Festival . . . I watched many different people laughing at the antics of Oleg Popov—a teacher from Rome, a serious-looking Norwegian docker, a thoughtful Chilean, a schoolgirl from wind-swept Iceland, an Indian from Surinam, and a negro from Puerto Rico. They were all enjoying the performance and they all understood Popov's jokes. Each of them enthusiastically applauded the clown."[12] Poliakov concluded, "Popov has a superb mastery of the art of laughter, the comic art that brings people closer together and helps to establish friendship between people of different nationalities."[13]

Galich and Poliakov's insistence that the circus helped promote peace and international friendship probably proved more convincing than claims that its popularity offered proof that peace and international friendship had already been secured. The latter claim was hardly credible in the immediate aftermath of the uprisings in Poland and Hungary in 1956. It was perhaps for this reason that Galich's interpretation of the circus as an international form of art, capable of promoting peace and expressing the Soviet Union's good will to foreigners, so closely described the circus that the Soviet state demanded in the late 1950s.

The director of the Leningrad Circus, Vladimir Andreevich Tsvetkov, shared Galich's conviction that the circus's universal appeal made it an effective weapon in the Soviet Union's struggle for peace. Tsvetkov opened his speech to a 1958 meeting of circus directors by stating that "the central question of our state, which is the question of peace, the question of the softening of the international situation, and the establishment of contact not only with leading figures in various countries but also between people, is pertinent to the task set by the party and state in the sphere of widening our cultural ties with foreign nations." He congratulated the circus administration for its recent achievements abroad and concluded that "the small, modest paths that have been laid by separate artists, have already been transformed . . . into the wide main roads of cultural connections thanks to the popularity, the intelligence, and the rich content of the Soviet circus."[14] The idea that circus performances fostered international friendships became so commonplace that even a critical review of a Parisian circus's 1961 performance in Leningrad, which noted that France had nurtured many of the rudest and most naive circus traditions, concluded that "this did not prevent us from watching with great interest the presentation by the talented French artists, whose performance contributes to the further cultural rapprochement [*sblizheniiu*] of our peoples."[15] That summer's performance by Hungarian, East German, Romanian, Czech, and Soviet artists at Moscow's Gorky Park was also celebrated for its contribution to the "great matter of the strengthening of the friendship of the peoples." E. Semenov reported in *Sovetskii tsirk* that he did not know which scene was more interesting: "the stands, where Muscovites warmly applauded the first-class numbers, or the artists' foyer, where exclamations of greeting and good wishes offered in various languages never fell silent." Semenov considered the "circus of friendship" to be a "good thing" and noted that forty thousand Muscovites joined the artists in this friendship.[16]

Those viewers, both foreign and Soviet, who had not experienced this effect still might have been convinced of the circus's potential to promote peace and international friendship in later years, when performances began to champion these causes more explicitly, in a manner that foreign observers readily recognized as propagandistic. Some might have counted themselves among the viewers whose friendly feelings toward foreign Communists were stirred, for example, by the 1957 production of "The Arena of Friendship," which featured performers from among "our loyal friends—circus artists of the democratic republics of Europe and Asia." According to I. Tumanov's review in *Sovetskii tsirk*, the show began with spotlights shining on Lenin's portrait and the Soviet flag. The "guests of Moscow" entered the arena carrying the flags of their own nations: "How many friends we have! . . . How many friendly smiles are directed toward the audience and how many brotherly answering glances meet the guests of our arena."[17] Viewers were greeted with more than mere smiles during the opening parade, which concluded with V. Uspenskii's recital of a monologue on the themes of "peace, friendship, and happiness," according to Viktor Ermans's description in *Sovetskaia kul'tura*. Ermans noted that these themes were also expressed at the end of the production, when doves were released into the arena. This created, in his view, "an especially touching mood in the hearts of viewers, who recall the words of the prologue: 'for lasting peace on earth!' 'for friendship.'" For the benefit of any readers who might have been confused, Ermans explained that "white doves are a symbol of peace, friendship, and brotherhood."[18] Ermans's description hinted at the conclusion drawn explicitly by Timonov, who maintained that this meeting between "guests and hosts" confirmed "the inviolable friendship of our peoples and their will for peace and happiness."[19]

Soviet artists further extended offerings of peace, brotherhood, and friendship to the international audience that attended their performance at London's Wembley Stadium in 1961. Vladimir Durov concluded his routine by asking that "the sun, not concealing itself in haze, bring happiness on earth to all people beneath the blue firmament and peace and friendship to all peoples." As he recited the final line, four hundred white doves were released into the arena, prompting the audience to burst into applause, according to the performer's own account. A. Gryaznov also described the enthusiastic reception that Durov received among European audiences. He reported that Durov's performances even convinced some viewers that the Soviets were a humane and peace-loving people:

> There were many words of praise and gratitude for the truly humane, artistic performances which Durov and his colleagues gave in France and Luxembourg. They were besieged by fans backstage and in the streets of Paris and Marseilles, Turin, Lyon, and Liege, for the language of the circus is indeed international. A gentleman came up to Durov after a press conference in Italy and confessed: "Senor Durov, I was really prejudiced against the Russians. I'll have to change my opinions now." . . . No member of the Durov dynasty has ever been seen brandishing a stick or a whip. The "actors" perform freely, mischievously and even with obvious pleasure. Herein lies not only the "secret" of their training, which is based on encouraging their natural instincts and habits, but of the humane nature of our art. The Soviet circus is known as "the arena of friendship," "the arena of peace."[20]

Durov himself considered his act to be a demonstration of "art's power to bring people together," and he was understandably proud to know that his homeland was the "most active and steadfast champion of the friendship of the peoples, their mutual understanding, and peace." He was, therefore, naturally troubled to read a review of his performance that accused him of concluding it with the recitation of a "Russian propaganda text."[21] Audiences, both foreign and Soviet, might also have considered the bright smiles, warm greetings, doves, and flowers to be only so much propagandistic packaging, meant to obscure the Soviet government's true intentions toward non-Soviet nations and the authentic feelings of enmity that existed between them. It is for this reason, perhaps, throughout the post-Stalin period, circus administrators and official commentators directed viewers' attention to the oldest and most loyal friendships the Soviet Union claimed to enjoy: those among the multinational peoples who lived peaceably within its borders.

Multinational Friendships

The Soviet circus frequently featured performers of different nationalities who worked together to produce a single, harmonious spectacle that celebrated the differences between them as much as their ability to transcend them. The multinational circus demonstrated that the expansion of socialism threatened neither national interests nor world peace, and it told those Soviets who might have doubted it that friendships need not be secured at the expense of socialism's expansion internationally. As A. Georgiev wrote in 1961, "Circus art in our country, like all forms of Soviet culture, is national in form and socialist in content. The development of national traditions and the specificity of national forms serves the ideas of proletarian internationalism and guarantees the further flowering of Soviet circus art." The peaceful coexistence of Russians, Uzbeks, Tuvans, Ukrainians, Armenians, and all their other brothers was offered as the most credible evidence that the Soviet Union could promote international friendships at the same time it exported socialism to different nations.

The Soviet circus celebrated multiple nationalities and commentators celebrated the Soviet circus for its multinationality, which offered proof that national groups' interests were served by their participation in the Soviet Union. In 1957, for example, Iurii Dmitriev argued that the circus was "an ancient art that was born and formed on market squares, in popular fetes, in popular fairground theaters." In his view, the circus was, as it had always been, a national form of art. While Dmitriev admitted that, with time, some circus acts had lost their national specificity, he insisted that many more had retained it, particularly in the Soviet Union, where national circus traditions had been intentionally enriched.[22] As he explained in another article he published that year, "our circus strives toward the utilization of national [*narodnykh*] traditions so that numbers which develop the national particularities of circus art will appear more frequently in the ring. . . . The originality of the Soviet circus also arises from the combination of these qualities."[23] The Ukrainian performer P. Maiatskii made this point more elaborately the following year. He disagreed with those who refused to recognize the circus as being a national form of art because it was "accessible to all peoples regardless of their race and the color of their skin." He found this view to be "fundamentally faulty" and insisted that the circus was a national art form that "reflected the life and characteristic features of its people." He explained that the development of national Russian circus traditions had been impeded before the Revolution and in its immediate aftermath (he was referring, presumably, to the NEP era, when foreign performers populated Russian rings). He claimed that the "Europeanization" of the circus arrested the development of national circus traditions, which were revived only after the "October revolution caused the national cultures of all the peoples of our country to blossom." Maiatskii noted that national circus forms had continued to develop in recent years, as the circus administration endorsed the establishment of national circus collectives, whose members strove to express the cultures of their peoples.[24]

National circus collectives proliferated in the post-Stalinist period, although the Uzbek circus collective was the first to be created, in 1942. In 1956, a Ukrainian collective was formed at the Kiev circus, and two years later, Georgian and Belorussian collectives were also founded. In 1959, the Azerbaijani circus collective made its debut in the Moscow circus, and the next decade witnessed the establishment of Armenian, Latvian, and Lithuanian collectives. In 1969, the collective Young Kirgizia began to perform. The Kazakh national circus collective was founded the following year, and a Tadjik circus collective took shape soon after that. As Dmitriev explained in his history of the Russian circus, the "national essence" of these collectives was expressed through the participation of artists of a given nationality and through the music, costumes, set decorations, and opening and closing monologues, which gave their performances a "national coloring." Dmitriev recalled that the national circus collectives took on such a "special meaning" because they "provided for the mutual enrichment of national cultures."[25] National circus performances implied, at the time, that the Soviet state had strengthened the cultural traditions of national groups whose cultural traditions had strengthened the Soviet Union.

For example, Ali-Bek Kantemirov was hailed as an exemplary representative of his native Osetia who had enriched his own national traditions by integrating them into a multinational and therefore uniquely Soviet equestrian demonstration. In his 1961 biography of Kantemirov, B. Fedorov explained that from his earliest days as a performer in prerevolutionary Russian circuses, "the young rider had nurtured the dream of creating a noble image of the proud rider, brave, agile, and energetic, who scorned danger and death . . . that would contain the best characteristics of his people."[26] Yet, Fedorov continued, Ali-Bek also scorned "national narrow-mindedness," and studied the national equestrian traditions of Central Asian riders, Spanish matadors, ancient horsemen, and European equestrian acrobats. Although "the idea of the brotherly friendship among national performers was close to his heart," he was able to realize this dream only after the October Revolution, when he began to perform his multinational riding routine in rings across the Soviet Union and, eventually, over half of the world.[27] According to his biography, Kantemirov served the Soviet motherland — Fedorov quoted a letter Kantemirov addressed to the young men and women of the Soviet circus, admonishing them to "work for the glory of your beloved Soviet Motherland"—without ever forgetting that his Osetian motherland was always watching him, as his own mother reminded him when he first "set off on his horse in search of happiness."[28] Ali-Bek's biography, like his equestrian performances, implied that dreams of brotherly friendship among nations were nurtured in the Soviet Union, whose glory relied on their realization.

Another circus artist who was often applauded for expressing his nation's cultural traditions while still serving the Soviet motherland was the Tuvan juggler Vladimir Oskal-Ool. According to the biographical statement included in the program for the 1948 Moscow Circus's production of "Our Guests," which featured "artists of the circuses of the brother republics," Oskal-Ool had been inspired to become the first Tuvan professional circus performer after attending a performance of circus artists held at his local Pioneer camp. Since he had already proven himself to be an exceptional athlete, he was readily admitted to study at the Moscow Circus School in 1936.[29] As a 1972 profile of the performer noted, the first thing Oskal-Ool did upon arriving in Moscow was to take the name Vladimir, in honor of Lenin and in place of his given name, Sat.[30] When he completed his training in 1939, he returned to his "motherland" and selected fifteen young men and women from across the Tuvan autonomous region to participate in a circus troupe.[31] The performers made their debut in the summer of 1946 in Omsk and then embarked on a tour of the Soviet Union.

Tuvan circus troupes performed under Oskal-Ool's direction for thirty years, treating audiences around the world to spectacular displays of Tuvan national culture. For example, in "Naadym," a program named after a Mongolian national festival that was celebrated on August 15, the date that had become Tuvan Republic Day, members of the troupe wore "bright national Tuvan costumes and robes" and appeared in a ring adorned with a "a colorful carpet and a runner that featured bright national designs," according to the description of the program that was approved in 1963. The orchestra played "national Tuvan music" as the artists entered the ring through a "beautiful, nationally bright, colorful curtain" to greet the audience. They surrounded a single artist, who stood on a pedestal holding the Tuvan national flag and read an introductory text that concluded with the troupe's collective cry of "hello" in their native language. The Tuvans' program featured gymnastics, acrobatics, balancing acts, a traditional pantomimed battle, and national dances on the wire rope, but was best known for its signature routine, a juggling act that dramatized Tuvan national chores. The routine began immediately after the opening parade, when a group of artists produced a series of domestic objects, including mortars, pestles, and washtubs, and began to "demonstrate to the viewer their nationally specific everyday labor in precisely choreographed physical movements."[32] The program notes for the troupe's 1968 performance in Australia described this labor in greater detail: "Sitting in a circle the artistes 'pound the millet' and 'beat the wool.' With flashing speed, long thin poles pass from hand to hand flying in complete synchronization." The program explained that unlike most jugglers, who performed with bright balls and traditional clubs, the Tuvan jugglers worked "with their own national equipment," in order to "show us the working process of Tuvinian peasants who, not so many years ago, were still leading a nomadic existence."[33] The following year, Nikolai Krivenko described the routine in remarkably similar terms. A caption accompanying his photographs of the jugglers noted that "national traits add a picturesque touch to the performance of a group of jugglers and rope-walkers from Tuva, headed by Vladimir Oskal-Ool. Seated in a circle, these jugglers use the medium of their art to depict the labour of Tuva peasants, who have only recently relinquished their traditional nomad form of life."[34]

The Tuvan juggling act celebrated the brightest traditions of Tuvan culture as well as the bright future the Tuvans had been granted under socialism. This act told viewers that the Tuvans had become modern Soviets while still remaining Tuvan. It offered proof that national groups had benefited from their inclusion in the multinational Soviet state, which hardly resembled the aggressively expansionist empire that western governments accused it of being and, of course, exemplified themselves. The Tuvan juggling routine implied, finally, that while the Soviet Union was the sum of its multiple national cultural parts, it was also something more: it was modern. As V. Nikulin, the director of the Kiev Circus, explained in his instructions for the Ukrainian collective's 1963 program, "the creative capturing of national traditions in a contemporary refraction is the task that has been set before producers." He went on to describe Ukraine as a country of "powerful industry, a country of unprecedented abundance, plenty, and beauty" and thought that "the greatness of the republic is best characterized by smokestacks and the ceaseless roar of tractors, by electronic machines and the concrete bunkers of grain elevators." Nikulin acknowledged that national traditions remained preserved in the hearts of the people and he did believe that the circus program should include elements of popular Ukrainian humor, music, and decoration in order to give it a "national coloration." Yet he insisted that the "features of the new Soviet Ukraine" also find expression in the Ukrainian circus program.[35] Nikulin hoped that the circus would celebrate the industrialization of Ukraine, just as it celebrated the Tuvans' own recent development, and all of modernity's many other triumphs within the Soviet Union.

The Space Age Circus

Throughout the post-Stalin period, the circus continued to introduce viewers to new technologies and assure them of the superiority of Soviet science. In the first years of the Cold War, circus performers, administrators, and observers generally agreed that one of the most pressing tasks of the circus was to propagandize Soviet technological achievements. As early as 1945, for example, at a discussion of the 1947 artistic production plan for GUTs, the head of the organization, Nikolai Strel'tsov, encouraged illusionists to incorporate "our achievements in science and technology" into their performances.[36] He suggested that they cooperate with technical and scientific specialists, a recommendation that was reiterated two years later by a member of the GUTs artistic council who encouraged his colleagues to propagandize technological achievements by demonstrating them in the circus.[37] It seemed that this challenge had not yet been met by 1950. At a meeting of circus workers that year, the Ukrainian performer P. Maiatskii criticized illusionists for performing anachronistic tricks that failed to meet the ideological demands of the party and state. He encouraged them to improve their repertoire by developing routines whose "ideological content" would be the "propaganda and unveiling of the latest achievements in science and technology."[38]

Two years later, the illusionist A. Sokol finally met the challenge. His program "Miracles without Miracles," debuted in 1952, appeared in a 1954 production of the best routines of the past year, and was widely celebrated as an innovative departure from the traditions of the illusionist genre. In the words of Iurii Dmitriev, Sokol "bravely turned to technology, which he used as the foundation for a series of wonderful tricks," including one that allowed any member of the audience to make a call to his or her home without using any apparatus. Another made it possible to fry an omelet over a frying pan that Sokol held over a refrigerator instead of a stove, and another still featured cordless, plugless, switchless lamps that lit up in viewers' hands at the magician's command.[39] When Sokol then submerged those same lamps in an aquarium, they began to glow in various colors, just as "all the colors of the spectrum began to flow through absolutely transparent bracelets upon the magician's wish," according to the description provided in Iurii Blagov's history of illusionism in the Soviet Union. The program also included a "prank," in which the viewers were given empty wine glasses that were suddenly "lit up with liquids of the most appealing hues; but one had merely to raise the glass to one's mouth for it to become empty once more."[40]

For the benefit of any viewers who might have wondered whether any of these acts were actually magical, Sokol explained that they, in fact, were miracles of science. According to a script for his routine that was approved in 1973, one version of his performance featured a clown who reacted skeptically to Sokol's claim that a glowing, multicolored crystal, which also produced a loud busy signal, was "a very curious scientific technical invention" that he had received from his friends at the Telemechanics Institute. "A telephone?" the clown asked incredulously. "If that is a telephone," he continued, taking off his shoe, "then this is a motorcycle with a sidecar." Sokol offered to prove that his device was a telephone, and as soon as the clown recited his home telephone number, the crystal began to ring, until it was answered by a woman, who identified herself as the clown's mother. After a lengthy, occasionally comedic exchange, the clown hung up the phone and implored Sokol to explain how he did it. "It is very simple," Sokol replied. "With the help of contemporary science and technology and, of course, circus art."[41]

Sokol's routine was credited with bringing the "circus closer to contemporary times," and it stood, itself, as proof of the Soviet Union's modernity. In 1961, for example, his routine was included in a program produced by the Leningrad Circus in honor of the Twenty-Second Communist Party Congress. The production, which "demonstrated the creative cooperation of circus artists from the people's democracies and from the Soviet Union," featured performances by the Soviet Union's "guests" in the first act, while the second showcased "Soviet masters," including A. Sokol's attraction.[42] The juxtaposition of performers from non-Soviet nations, friendly as they might have been, with Sokol's routine, which lacked any national brightness, coloring, music, or traditional forms of labor, identified the Soviet Union with modernity itself.

Like Sokol, Zinaida Tarasova was another illusionist praised for having forsaken everything "mysterious," everything reminiscent of those "traditional" magicians who hid doves up their sleeves and pierced beautiful women with swords. According to S. Zinin's profile in *Moskovskii komsomolets*, Tarasova rid her routines of any mystery at all, and viewers were never left guessing how her tricks were done. This was because it was "clear to everyone that these are miracles of acoustics, electronics, optics, and physics." For example, nobody had to wonder how Tarasova installed a water line into a piano that spouted forth multicolored streams of water to the music of a waltz she was playing. According to the review, the trick was so obviously the product of science that, in this case, viewers were free to marvel at the spectacle's beauty, rather than its mystery.[43]

Illusionists were not the only circus performers who celebrated Soviet scientific achievements at the time. Aerialists were particularly well equipped to propagandize Soviet advances in rocketry, aeronautics, and space flight, and some even incorporated technologically advanced mechanisms into their acts. Sokol himself considered trapeze acts that dramatized humans' striving to reach the cosmos to be among the circus's most modern routines. Sokol made this appraisal in 1976, only five years after he announced his own plans to "create a picture of the cosmos, with stars igniting, a nebula forming, and planets soaring,"[44] though circus performers had been celebrating Soviet cosmonautics since its earliest years.[45] Within one month of the Soviet's successful launching of Sputnik I, on October 4, 1957, and just days after the dog Laika flew into space on Sputnik II, the clown Karandash announced that the balloon he had just been holding, until it popped, was a "Sputnik." When the viewers burst into laughter, the clown explained, "'You do not understand. . . . That is the American Sputnik.'"[46] Karandash's joke proved prophetic: on December 6, the United States' first attempt to launch a satellite into space failed when Vanguard I lifted four feet into the air before falling back in flames onto the launch pad. The aerial gymnasts P. Chernega and S. Razumov similarly celebrated the Soviet Union's cosmonautic achievements. In 1961, they unveiled their plans to create a routine in honor of the Twenty-Second Party Congress, in recognition that "we live in an epoch in which the most audacious dreams come true," and in anticipation of the imminent departure of "the ingenious creation of Soviet science, a wonderful spaceship operated by our compatriots" to faraway planets. Using a set of wings constructed by the engineer D. Il'in, the performers planned to fly through "our skies, beneath the circus cupola." They admitted that their flight would be considerably more modest than a cosmonaut's, but confessed that they would be happy if their flight, by so much as the slightest hint, "reminds viewers of the amazing achievements of Soviet science and technology in the opening up of outer space."[47]

Viktor Lisin also performed an aerial routine that he thought bore "some relationship to the flights" of the two communists who had completed the first group flight into space, in August 1962. As Lisin explained in an article published in the September 1962 issue of *Sovetskii tsirk*, his performance featured a large model rocket that hung suspended from the top of the arena and from which Lisin and his partner, Elena Sin'kovskaia, hung suspended. Lisin was proud that his routine had anticipated the cosmonauts' flight, which was, in his view, "yet another victory in the name of science and progress, in the name of Communism!" He also confessed that it pleased him to realize that "there is something in common between the circus profession and the heroic work of cosmonauts." Lisin explained that a significant part of the cosmonauts' training was based on circus exercises and that one of the cosmonauts, Adrian Grigor'evich Nikolaev, loved to jump on the trampoline.[48] The next month's issue of *Sovetskii tsirk* featured an article by B. I. Rossinskii, the so-called grandfather of Russian aviation, who recognized additional similarities between aviators and circus performers, including their strength, agility, bravery, and audacity.[49] In November, Adrian Nikolaev and his comrade Pavel Popovich made their own contribution to the discussion, claiming that the example set by circus performers, especially their "tireless toiling, their constant training at rehearsal, and their nightly demonstrations of their bright and brave art," inspired their own commitment to completing the first group flight.[50]

Over the next two decades, circus performers continued to ally themselves with aviators and cosmonauts and to remind circus viewers of Soviet advances in aeronautics and rocket science. In 1967, for example, the animal trainer Valentin Filatov taught neither his pig, nor his rat, but rather his bear how to fly: "I made use of Herman Reznikov's aerial torpedo and later Boris Levadovsky's special apparatus. I then began rehearsing a rather complex and effective trick, a flight under the Big Top. There were two participants, my bear Malchik and a gymnast. The man and Malchik would both hang by their teeth as they were raised to the top of the circus. The torpedo would then begin to circle over the area. During this act Malchik would do four difficult acrobatic tricks."[51]

More often, circus programs featured flying humans. As Richard F. Janssen noted in his 1974 account of the Soviet circus for the *Wall Street Journal*, "the space exploits of Soviet cosmonauts are symbolized at the circus. Lest anyone fail to make the connection the aerialists are in space attire, and the dome of the darkened arena is suddenly transformed into starry heavens by planetarium-type projectors; the aerialists soar and plunge great distances to the audience's gasps."[52] A program typical of this trend had debuted two years earlier at the newly built Moscow Circus on Vernadskii Prospect. "Time, Forward!" according to the director P. F. Abolimov, was "saturated with the theme of modernity, with the striving of the human being toward the conquest of the cosmic heights." Abolimov explained to his fellow members of the party planning committee that the show, which featured the Volzhanskiis' "Ascent to the Stars," was "permeated by the theme of peace and the progress of the Soviet state."[53] This program, like Mstislav Zapashnyi's 1973 acrobatic routine, which, according to one review, "compelled viewers to perceive the poetic image of a cosmic flight," won praise from the board of the Ministry of Culture, which passed a decree that year recognizing the "artistically significant circus numbers that reflect . . . the theme of space exploration."[54] Nikolai Krivenko agreed that these routines were among the best the Soviet circuses had to offer. In his 1975 pamphlet documenting the achievements of the Soviet circus over the previous four years, Krivenko concluded that "no other artistic spectacle is capable of recounting, so brightly and affectingly, the story of the conquest of space." He described an aerial act titled "Cosmic Fantasy," whose evocation of a flight through space was, in his view, "characteristic" of the 1970s circus repertoire. "It is very effective," he explained, "when the gymnasts, who are dressed in fluorescent costumes that are covered in luminescent paint, float in the air as if they were in zero-gravity conditions, flying from one trapeze to the next, swiftly falling down and then soaring once again beneath the big top."[55]

Like magic acts that demonstrated the latest advances in Soviet science and technology, athletic routines that evoked space flight also advertised the Soviet Union as a modern, technologically advanced state that was capable of winning the space race and, implicitly, the associated arms race. The association between the two was made explicitly in routines that actually involved model rockets. Yet these routines were also bright, colorful, warm-hearted, and, at times, even funny. They were, in other words, typical of the many circus acts that continued to champion the causes of peaceful coexistence and, later,

180

In Defense of Offensive Peace

detente. The Volzhanskiis' 1972 production of "Ascent to the Stars" was not the only circus routine that was permeated by the themes of both "peace and the progress of the Soviet state." In 1972, for example, Nina Velekhova analyzed a trapeze act titled "Galactica," which, in her view, "was founded on the idea of the high moral and aesthetic relationships between human beings: the flight, which relies so heavily on the *lovitor*, especially clearly manifests [*vystupaet*] the ideas of help and friendship, the idea that any one person's success depends on the help of another, on the participation of all." Thus, although the routine's name, as well as the "unusual technical attributes" of its lighting, obviously identified it as one of the many aerial routines that evoked the exploration of space, "Galactica" also implied that technological advances and scientific discoveries were not only driven by geopolitical conflicts and international competition but also relied on and might reinforce friendship, mutual aid, and cooperation.[56]

This same story was told by the most celebrated of all space-age routines, Vladimir Volzhanskii's "Prometheus," which premiered on March 20, 1977, in the Moscow Circus on Vernadskii Prospect. The one-act pantomime involved several high wires and several high-wire walkers, who together demonstrated how "man conquered fire and became the master of the world" and showed "how people have conquered the atmosphere and reached the cosmos," according to Iurii Dmitriev's ecstatic description in *Sovetskaia kul'tura*.[57] The Volzhanskiis' routine implied that conquering fire and conquering the cosmos were simply two steps along the same line of human progress, which is why stars, being both cosmic and fiery, played a prominent role in their performance. The red velvet curtain that hung in front of the artists' entrance was covered with golden, five-pointed stars that gradually grew smaller toward the top of the curtain, "as if they were receding into space." During the overture, the blue, white, and light-blue lights shone on the stars, illuminating them brightly. When the overture concluded, the lighting changed, and the silhouette of a sculpture symbolizing "Labor and Heroic Feats" was cast across the curtain. This image served as the visual accompaniment to the verses that introduced the program:

Gori, ogon', zazhennyi Prometeem
V sto tysiach solnts gori, ogon'
Tepla dlia cheloveka ne zhaleia,
Gori, ogon'!
Gori, ogon' dobra,

derzanii zharkikh
Ogon', vedushchii v Kosmos korabli.
Gori, ogon',
v bessmertnom serdtse Danko
Dlia schast'ia vsekh liudei zemli.

[Burn, fire, that was lit by Prometheus
Burn in one hundred thousand suns, fire,
Not begrudging warmth for the human being
Burn, fire!
Burn, fire of kindness
and daring achievements
Fire that guides spaceships into the cosmos.
Burn, fire,
in the immortal heart of Danko
for the happiness of all people on earth.]

The poem's recognition that "all people on Earth" were the happy bene-
ficiaries of scientific progress immediately indicated that this routine,
like "Ascent to the Stars," would be permeated by the theme of peace
and not only Soviet progress. Any viewers who missed the signal might
have been alerted to it in the program's next vignette, which featured
"two enormous flying doves" and a "dove of peace," performed by the
gymnast L. Pisarenkova, who now appeared in front of the curtain. A
collection of artists then burst into the ring with rainbow-colored flags,
which they held in a circle, as another set of verses was recited:

Gori zhe, sozidaiushchee plamia
Liudskogo razuma, gori ogon'
Vo imia
neba mirnogo nad nami.
Gori ogon'.[58]

[Burn, creative flame
of the human mind,
burn, fire, in the name
of the peaceful sky above us.
Burn, fire.]

Pisarenkova's aerial act then commenced, and, much like other flights
that circus viewers had witnessed over the past two decades, it evoked
the human triumph over the law of gravity. Yet because Pisarenkova

played the part of a dove, the symbol of peace, her flight, like Prometheus's gift, was meant to remind viewers that the benefits of Soviet progress were shared equally among all people of Earth.

Conclusion

Those who both produced and praised "Prometheus" seemed not to have recognized any contradiction in the program's simultaneous celebration of science and its promotion of peace. This might have been because the Soviet Union was preparing its population for war at the same time that it encouraged foreign people to accept its public overture of peace. Or it might have been because by the late 1970s most people on Earth had long been hoping that the scientific advances that propelled the nuclear arms race would also preserve world peace by assuring the mutual destruction of the Soviet Union and the United States, should either launch a nuclear strike. In either case, this war remained a possibility, which is why the Soviet Union cultivated means of both diverting and preparing for it. Technologically advanced magic acts and cosmic aerial routines, like the space race they promoted, were peaceful means of advertising the Soviet Union's eagerness to avoid a war that it was nevertheless ready to wage. So, too, were circus programs that showcased national minorities. They congratulated the Soviet Union for maintaining peaceful relations among the many different national groups that resided within its borders and implied that the Soviet state might further expand its influence without threatening world peace. Yet during World War II, for a decade after, and throughout the post-Stalin period as well, the presence of national groups in the Soviet circus, as in the Soviet Union itself, had also offered proof of the Soviet Union's martial strength. Even Ali-Bek Kantemirov's 1961 biography quoted a Red Army commander, who told Kantemirov on the eve of World War II that his art, which he had just displayed before a regiment of soldiers, "served the Red Army, it teaches Soviet young people to be agile, strong, and fearless soldiers. We know that, if it becomes necessary, Osetian horse riders will stand with us in the ranks of defenders of the Motherland."[59]

It seems likely, therefore, that these multinational and space-age circus productions were the result of measures the circus administration instituted to "realize the decisions" of the Twenty-Third Party Congress in 1966, which included developing programs on the themes of "socialist internationalism, Soviet patriotism, and the friendship of the peoples."[60] The Party reiterated its demand for works of art that promoted "Soviet patriotism and socialist internationalism" at the Twenty-Fourth Party Congress in 1970,[61] and any doubts that Soviet or foreign observers might have entertained as to the compatibility of these two principles might have been allayed by circus productions that simultaneously advanced the causes of world peace and international friendship, and demonstrated the Soviet Union's technological superiority.

Some viewers, both foreign and domestic, might have been convinced by the story the circus told during the Cold War. Some might have liked the circus because it assured them that the Soviet Union remained committed to promoting peace and human progress even as it continued to export socialism internationally. Some Soviet viewers might have been relieved to learn that the principles of peaceful coexistence and, later, detente, advanced rather than impeded the cause of international revolution.[62] Some might have liked it because it assured them that Soviet technological progress would help secure world peace and some might have liked it because it assured them that, if a nuclear war were to be waged, Soviet technological progress would help keep them secure.

Yet not all foreigners received the circus warmly, which perhaps should not be surprising. These viewers seemed to consider the Soviet circus's offering of peace to be merely a cover for the Soviet state's aggressive imperialism. Soviet performers appearing at Madison Square Garden in 1963 were greeted by angry protesters who picketed the show, chanting slogans against Communism and Castro. Although the protest remained orderly, seven Cuban Americans did disrupt the performance once it had begun. According to Richard F. Shepard's account in the *New York Times*, they "marched quietly across the unoccupied end arena behind the band and unfurled a banner that proclaimed, 'Communism is the destruction of freemen. Wake up, America.'"[63] Although this incident went unreported in the Soviet press, some Soviet viewers might still have doubted whether foreign viewers applauded the circus because they felt friendly toward the humane, progressive, anti-imperialist, and peace-loving Soviets. Some viewers, foreign and Soviet alike, might have wondered whether the Soviet state really was humane, progressive, anti-imperialist, and peace-loving. They might have liked the circus because it confirmed their view of the Soviet state's hypocrisy and of socialism's malevolence. Once again, there was more than one reason to like the circus. Yet whether viewers applauded the

Soviet circus for all the same reasons or not, all different peoples did applaud it all the same. They might not have liked each other, but they did appear, at least, to like some of the same things, which might not have provided the basis for an intimate friendship, but might at least have kept them from coming to blows.

6

Courting Jesters

The Clown as Everyman
in the Late Soviet Circus

Just as the post-Stalinist circus was presented as proof that peaceable relations might be maintained among the coldly warring states, circus producers, performers, and reviewers also implied that harmonious relations might be enjoyed among all the different and not always entirely friendly members of the Soviet domestic collective. Beginning in the so-called Thaw era, proceeding through the so-called era of stagnation, and culminating finally with *perestroika*, Soviet subcultural groups proliferated, dissidents demanded personal freedoms, political consensus collapsed, and all sorts of people gave expression to their individuality through their choices in clothing, music, magazines, cigarettes, poetry, and films, some of which they consumed illegally. Not surprisingly, the official demands placed on the circus changed along with everything else, and the circus was remade once again. This time it was turned into a showcase for the achievements of exceptional individuals whose original, innovative, and idiosyncratic performances were harmoniously integrated into artistically consistent, thematically coherent spectacles that were, according to the official rhetoric, always fresh and new. The term most often used to describe this quality of consistency, coherence, or unity was "wholeness," or *tselnost'* in Russian, and while "wholeness" was the ideal to which all circus programs were required to aspire at the time, individual performers were rarely encouraged to sacrifice their own interests in order to attain it. To the contrary, the late socialist circus was presented as proof that individuals' personal interests were always, and always only, fulfilled through their collective pursuit of the common good.

The New Individuals

In the post-Stalin period, most commentators agreed that the "search for the new" was the definitive characteristic of the Soviet circus.[1] They also agreed that the best place to find "the new" was in "the old." For them, the circus was stable and at the same time perpetually self-renewing, just like the Soviet Union as a whole, or so, at least, this line of reasoning seemed to imply. For example, in 1957, Viktor Ermans praised Oleg Popov for introducing new details into a routine he had performed many times before, and congratulated Aleksandr Kiss, a juggler who was so talented that his tricks, paradoxically, "always seem to be new."[2] In 1970, Il'ia Simvolokov, "an authentic innovator," was applauded for executing familiar magic tricks in an original way, as, the following year, was Zinaida Tarasova, another magician whose "traditional tricks" acquired "a completely new character" when performed in her own unique style.[3] In 1986, the magician Emil' Emil'evich Kio, son of the original magician Kio, Emil' Teodorovich, and brother of the more famous magician Kio, Igor' Emil'evich, won particular acclaim for undertaking a "leisurely search" for the new: "gradually, step by step he renewed his program, without rejecting the past achievements of his father, which have endured the test of time. On the contrary, he attempted to prevent the old from aging. He sought his place in the traditions of the circus, but not at all in its traditionalism."[4]

Some commentators even revealed how this trick was done. They claimed that innovative performers made old tricks new by making them their own. In other words, the secret of a trick's novelty lay in the performer's individuality. For example, at an "All-Union Conference on the Question of the Development of Clowning" organized in 1959, the general director of Soiuzgostsirk, F. G. Bardian, stated that, for every circus artist, "creative individuality is something to strive toward," and he encouraged clowns, in particular, "to seek and find their own character . . . even those remaining within the bounds of traditional circus masks." It was important for clowns to develop individual personas because, in his view, it was extremely difficult to develop new and original routines for so many clowns who were all the same.[5] Similarly, in a 1972 meeting of the Ministry of Culture, the circus director Nikolai Barzilovich seconded Iurii Dmitriev's conclusion that some circus numbers had grown repetitive because "in these numbers creative individuality is lacking." Barzilovich agreed that in order to find "the new" it was necessary to "seek out individuality."[6]

According to some, certain exceptional performers had already sought out and found their individuality and put it on display in the ring. In 1968, Michael Zarin, writing for *Sovetskaia kul'tura*, praised contemporary clowns who developed unique personas that painted a "consistent, creative portrait, especially individualized, alien to everything clichéd." He thought that a clown's most important task was "to introduce the viewer to the inner world of a person, of his 'lyrical hero,' of his 'mask.'" Zarin was thrilled that this task was already being accomplished by Soviet clowns,[7] as was Nikolai Krivenko, who celebrated the achievements of innovative individual clowns in a 1977 article, "The Delight of Novelty," which also appeared in *Sovetskaia kul'tura*. Krivenko defended the circus against the frequent criticism that its performances hardly ever changed, that jugglers almost always tossed the same old pins and rings, that acrobats almost always performed the same old flips and leaps, and that animal trainers almost always made their beasts demonstrate the same old tricks. He admitted that there was some truth to this criticism, but insisted that it only pertained to mediocre performers, "who do not possess the gift of creative searching, fantasy, and experiment." He considered it entirely unfair to direct this judgment against "talented people, who are able to interpret a familiar genre in their own way, to widen its boundaries, and bring something new and original to it."[8] Exceptional individuals brought something new to the circus by bringing something of themselves into otherwise generic routines.

Karandash agreed, and added that Soviet clowns were among the most individualistic of all circus performers. In 1979, he observed that "clowns do not at all resemble each other, but rather are each interesting by virtue of their individuality," which he considered a "characteristic peculiarity of contemporary clowning."[9] Oleg Popov thought so too. As early as 1957, he wrote that "one of the most significant creative achievements of the Soviet circus is undoubtedly the style and character of the work of its comics," each of whom "strives to find and reveal his individuality, to create his own repertoire that is peculiar precisely to him."[10] Karandash and Popov's repertoires were each peculiar to them, but Popov's was also individualized in the sense that it championed individual self-determination itself. Routines such as "The Ray," for example, dramatized the human capacity to take possession of one's own self and conquer intrusions into one's own private space. As the routine began, the auditorium lights were dim and a spotlight shone in the center of the ring. Popov entered the arena carrying a small bag and a bouquet of flowers. He walked cautiously into the spotlight, where he warmed his hands and face in the light before settling down on the ground. He took a bottle of milk out of his bag and raised it to his smiling lips. But just as he was about to drink, the ray of light moved away from him, and he was left in the dark. Popov gathered up his bottle, bag, and flowers and ran into the circle of light again. Once more, he warmed his hands and sat down to drink, and once more, the light stole away. Popov stood up uneasily and approached the light again. Afraid to enter the circle of light, he gently stroked the beam and began to push it in different directions, making the light obey him. He directed the ray of light back to its original place and again stretched his legs and assumed his place in the sun. As Popov began to raise the bottle of milk to his lips, he hesitated, wary of the ray's caprice. He stroked the beam, as if trying to soothe it. The circle remained steady, and Popov finally gulped down his milk. Suddenly, an alarm signal sounded, and the circle of light contracted sharply. The clown quickly gathered the circle into a tiny, shining spot, which he folded up and put into his shopping bag. He got up and scurried out of the ring, clasping his glowing bag. Popov wrote of this skit, "Everyone understood that the ray of light did not symbolize only the sun but everything that can warm a man. The ray represented rest after work, peace and calm, which are broken by the alarm signal. The spectator sees the latter as a menace: to the rest and work of a man, and to peace."[11] He left it to the viewer's imagination to determine the specific nature of that menace.

A reprise Popov performed at the 1957 World Festival of Youth and Students further warned viewers to guard their individual identities vigilantly. At the climax of the routine, in which Popov was cruelly spurned by his sweetheart Lilia, the clown placed a noose, with a heavy stone tied to its end, around the neck of his partner, another male clown. Popov heaved the stone into the water, and the unfortunate clown fell in after it, as Popov solemnly bid farewell to Lilia. In this routine, Popov killed his partner in an act of suicide. He confused his "self" with his partner's, whose failure to defend his own "self" resulted in his death. Popov similarly dramatized the danger of relinquishing control over one's own self in "The Pasha," a routine in which Popov sat cross-legged as a troupe of concubines danced around him. When he tried to move, he realized that his legs would not obey him (they were made of papier-mâché and the clown stood upright behind them). The clown's failure to control his own willful legs resulted in his immobilization. The routine dramatized the frightening consequences of losing command over oneself, just as "The Ray" presented a positive object lesson in self-possession. Popov's clowning marked the "re-examination of the meaning and place" of circus clowning, to which Nikulin attested in 1969. Nikulin explained that "today it is already possible to speak of a new type of Soviet clown," whose "interest in the human individual" was characteristic of all current Soviet art. He contrasted the new Soviet clown with western clowns, who still lacked "any hint of what we would call a soul."[12]

Clowns, however, were not the only circus performers thought to have sought, found, and given expression to their individuality by this time. In 1983, a review congratulated students of the circus training school for offering many routines that were "not only filled with interesting tricks, but that also bore the imprint of the creative individuality of those who performed them." The review went on to criticize a number of performers who had failed to develop a unique artistic "image" and therefore could not "demonstrate their individuality, their distinctiveness."[13] These were the mediocrities described by Krivenko, and few observers denied that they could occasionally be seen in Soviet circus rings. Yet viewers might have easily overlooked them, since their attention was drawn consistently, and more explicitly than ever before, to the exceptionally talented individuals whose star performances were showcased in circus productions and celebrated in the press.

In 1988, for example, the "new" Moscow Circus on Vernadskii Prospect offered the program "When Stars Blaze," which featured performers who might not have been among the better-known stars of the Soviet circus but who had all won prizes at recent circus competitions and, according to V. Il'in's review, should therefore be considered stars.[14] With this production, the revival of the star system, which had been rejected after the revolution as the epitome of bourgeois individualism, was complete. The return of the star system had also been marked by the proliferation of artists' biographies, memoirs, and profiles in the post-Stalinist press and by explicit calls for its return, congratulations on its return, and complaints that it had not yet returned.[15] For example, in an article covering a 1974 meeting of the Soiuzgostsirk party cell, *Sovetskaia kul'tura* reported Iurii Dmitriev's recommendation that the administration be bolder in its creation of "new circus 'stars.'"[16] Dmitriev made this point more elaborately the following year, when he complained that circus producers either had not learned or had forgotten how to "kindle stars." In order to attract viewers to performances by young, lesser-known artists, it was necessary, in his view, "to surround them with attention, not to be afraid to advertise and to construct programs so that an artist's debut appears especially striking."[17] His point appears to have been a persuasive one. In 1979, Evgenii Milaev, the General Director of the new Moscow Circus, described the recent performance by members of the Kazakh circus collective as a "joyful holiday," in which the viewers were introduced to "new talents" and "circus stars."[18] Yet in 1986, Vladimir Shakhidzhanian attributed a recent decline in the circus's prestige to its failure to "make stars."[19] Shakhidzhanian might have been pleased that the 1988 program "When Stars Blaze" featured newborn stars, or he might have considered this too little too late.[20] Either way, the production gave expression to the new value that he had already placed on individual stars, whose stardom was secured by their individuality as much as their individuality was secured by their stardom. The program thus reinforced the gradual shift in public values that had been made with the help of the circus, as well as other forms of Soviet culture.[21]

The New Collective

Individual expression seemed to be a powerful source of innovation within the circus, and the circus itself thus offered proof that individuals might renew Soviet society. Yet this was only part of the story. Individuals alone could not always create new and original circus productions, but according to the official rhetoric, they could do it together. Cooperation was considered no less essential to innovation than individualism. For example, a 1969 editorial in *Sovetskaia estrada i tsirk* began with the observation that "the birth of a new, authentically original work of circus art is almost always the result of the collective labor of a performer, director, scriptwriter, artist, and composer." The editorial went on to report that "frequently, even very good ideas go unrealized simply because an artist has been working alone."[22] Mstislav Zapashnyi made the same point in an article he wrote for *Sovetskaia kul'tura* in 1977. He began by criticizing Soiuzgostsirk for failing to produce a sufficient number of innovative routines annually. He hastened to add, however, that this did not mean that "stagnation has set in in the circus," and he named a number of individual artists who continued to devise new and original routines. Yet, according to Zapashnyi, their efforts to innovate meant nothing without "the corresponding material-technological resources needed to bring them into fruition." He complained that the administration withheld equipment and rehearsal space from artists, which he took as evidence that "our system still lacks collective responsibility for the general concern [*kollektivnaia otvetstvennost' za obshchee delo*]."[23] Two years later, the General Director of Soiuzgostsirk, A. Kolevatov, also recognized creative collaboration as the best method for producing original circus routines. In a 1979 *Pravda* article, he announced his intention to create three permanent experimental groups, each composed of performers, scene writers, directors, ballet masters, engineers, artists, composers, and designers, who would work together to develop "new solutions" for the various genres.[24]

Individual expression and collective labor were considered complementary sources of renewal in the circus. This may seem contradictory, but it was completely consistent with the idea, maintained throughout the post-Stalinist period, that individuals would strengthen the collective and that the collective would strengthen individuals. Viktor Shklovskii was convinced, for example, that "in recent times the collective spirit of the country has matured the Soviet clown. . . . He plays the part of an ordinary man who seems to have forgotten for several long moments that people are watching him, and he lives for himself, he is a simple, touching person."[25] For Shklovskii, living for oneself was an expression of the collective spirit, a view that many commentators shared. Even as the press lionized individual performers, observers continued to celebrate the circus for maintaining a spirit of collectivism among its performers as well as its audiences. In 1961, for example, a *Sovetskii tsirk* editorial titled "Communism Begins Today!" announced that "in the past year, a spirit of collectivism has emerged among artists of the Soviet circus." This spirit was manifest in the daily life of the circus, and it involved "unselfish assistance to comrades, suggestions to improve the circus across the country, and the voluntary transfer of one's own equipment to the state," all of which "have become norms of behavior."[26] The author of this editorial confirmed the observation made the previous year by A. Barten, writing for *Literatura i zhizn'* (*Literature and Life*), that on a recent tour of provincial circuses he had discovered "that the constant, persistent, and unseen work that occurs behind the scenes of the circus . . . cultivates the feeling of collectiveness, a collective spirit, the ability to live by the interests of the entire collective and the ability to subordinate one's own personal, private interests to it." He exclaimed that "today the circus does not belong to kulaks, egotists, or pilferers. No, it belongs to the collective, to collective responsibility for the general concern [*kollectivnaia otvetsvennost' za obshchee delo*]!" Barten explained, further, that the collective spirit facilitated the production of artistically unified shows, which was extremely important given that, in his view, this was what distinguished the Soviet circus from foreign circuses: "It seems to me, that the principal difference between our circus and the foreign, western circus lies precisely here. For our circus, the understanding of the performance as a unified artistic whole is becoming ever more natural and obligatory."[27]

Barten, it seemed, was right. The idea that the Soviet circus was new, different, and better than other circuses because it incorporated individual acts into a unified whole had become canonical in the 1960s. By then it seemed that circus producers had addressed the criticism leveled in 1947 by Iurii Olesha, who complained that while the Moscow Circus debut featured a number of strong numbers, "as a whole it was a failure." He explained that "the law of art is in its wholeness. When the proper arrangement of all of its parts has been achieved, then . . . one receives a general impression of delight." He had not received that impression from that year's debut, but Olesha hoped "that the next circus program will be better integrated [*bolee tselostnoi*] and thus richer and more artistic."[28] Three years later, the director of the Moscow Circus assured N. N. Bespalov, the assistant director of the Committee for Cultural Affairs, that the "first and most important task" of the Moscow Circus was "to gain experience organizing thematic presentations." In the past, circus productions had been created by artificially combining various numbers, but now, he insisted, "it is necessary more and more to introduce a system into the program."[29]

In the early 1950s, the Moscow Circus did offer a series of programs organized according to various themes. In 1950, *Izvestiia* published a review of the previous year's circus repertoire praising the presentations that were "unified by a general idea and a thematic prologue," which addressed such topics as the "flowering of circus art in the national brother republics," "the significant place that women's skill has in the Soviet circus," and "the rich fruits borne by the training of young artists."[30] In addition to "the struggle for peace," the valor of minority nationalities, women, and youth became frequent themes of circus programs,[31] which were also unified by the monologues and prologues, carpet clowns, consistent costumes, constant lighting, and uniform stage settings that helped integrate the individual circus acts into a harmonious whole.

Iurii Dmitriev agreed with Barten's claim that it was the "wholeness" of Soviet circus productions that distinguished them from western variants, which continued to resemble variety shows rather than artistic spectacles. In his review of a Parisian circus troupe's 1961 performance in Moscow, Dmitriev praised the French artists' skill but criticized their program, which lacked "a unified artistic approach." This, he claimed, is what distinguished it from Soviet spectacles, which were framed by prologues and epilogues that identified their dominant themes and were held together by the appearance of carpet clowns during the pauses between the acts.[32] In a 1969 interview, Bardian claimed explicitly that the Soviet circus had become a "circus of dramaturgy" that presented "a unified [*edinyi*] spectacle with a beginning, climax, and denouement, with lyrical and comical digressions." By "unified" spectacle he meant both mass, narrative pantomimes and the "traditional variety show in its new, contemporary form, in which the fantasy, taste, and artistic feeling of the director unites seemingly heterogeneous numbers into an organic, compositionally complete whole." The viewer of such spectacles was meant not only to admire the fragments but also to see the "entire authorial design as a whole," which, in Bardian's view, was part of what made the Soviet circus unique.[33]

While many observers might have shared Barten's conviction that the "wholeness" of Soviet circus programs relied on the "collective spirit" maintained by circus performers, few endorsed his claim that individual performers were required to subordinate their own personal, private interests to achieve it. In 1960, for example, V. Ardov argued that, at least as far as clowns were concerned, a thematically unified repertoire actually promoted artistic individuality: "our authors have, in practice, turned to the thematic unity of clowning, and that unity does not kill, but rather sustains the creative individuality of the performer."[34] Later critics claimed, more generally, that thematically consistent and artistically integrated productions actually helped to cultivate the

individualism of the performers who participated in them.[35] In a glowing review of the Moscow Circus's 1984 production of "On the Wings
of Time," V. Gorokhov praised its authors for attempting "to create a
spectacle where the essential wholeness would be achieved not by the
progress of an external plot or by the consistent [*skvoznym*] appearance
of a solo clown, but by the unity of its artistic intonation and the stylistic
tendency of its numbers." Gorokhov claimed that the "intonational
resemblance [*obshchnost'* — literally, the community] of numbers" did
not result in monotony precisely because "the design of the spectacle
allows various individualities [*razlichnym individual'nostiam*] to more
fully reveal themselves."[36] In the circus, innovative individuals helped,
in turn, to renew the collective that helped them to renew their innovative selves.

As Gorokhov and Bardian's statements reveal, the production of
unified, artistically integrated circus programs relied on the work of
one individual in particular: the artistic director of the show. Commentators and circus administrators had paid little attention to the role of
directors until the early 1950s, when the movement to produce compositionally complete shows elevated their function. In 1954, for example,
an editorial in *Sovetskaia kul'tura* asserted that "the role of the director in
the organization of the circus presentation is great. . . . The director is
called upon to create a harmonious and well-conceived composition
for the entire presentation, to add high artistry to every number." The
editorial lamented the absence of capable directors, whose training had
been neglected, and concluded that "the circus cannot exist without
good and talented directors, who know and love the circus."[37] In 1961,
B. Kalmanovskii, writing for *Sovetskii tsirk*, claimed that the director's
influence over the content of Soviet circus productions was precisely
what distinguished them from their western capitalist counterparts.
The work of Soviet directors, "whose hand can be felt in the programs
of the Soviet circus and nearly all of their separate numbers,"[38] satisfied
Kalmanovskii more than it did the author of the 1954 editorial, but both
did agree that directors were essential to the production of "whole"
programs. Most reviewers agreed, and they began to credit individual
directors for successfully "creating a whole, cheerful presentation out
of diverse numbers," as A. Arnol'd and A. Aronov were said to have
done in their 1953 production of "Greetings to the Capital," which featured performances by representatives of various Soviet nationalities.[39]
Nearly twenty-five years later, Mark Mestechkin was similarly praised
for "uniting uncoordinated [*razroznennye*] appearances into a whole

spectacle,"[40] and in her review of the Moscow Circus's 1981 program "Brave People and Kind Animals," Irina Bugrimova congratulated the director for endowing the spectacle with a "single spirit." According to Bugrimova, each routine followed the next, seemingly without interruption, thanks in part to the carpet clowns, who performed in the intervals between acts, and thanks also to the "directorial 'bridges' that cement all the numbers, transforming a variety show into a whole spectacle." The reviewer concluded that "the creative signature of the director-producer lies in the ability to subordinate all circus actions to a single goal, to thoroughly reveal a theme."[41]

Directors were the leaders of the collective, and without their leadership there would have been no collective. They took a group of individuals whose performances had little in common and gave each of them something—a costume of a certain color, a particular style of background music, a specific lighting scheme, or a common theme—that they all could share. Directors were supposed to rely on their artistic vision as well as their managerial talent to produce consistent, harmonious, and unified circus performances that did not imperil the individuality of the performers. Ideally, the circus became a model community, in which the parts were greater than the whole, which was also greater than its parts. During the post-Stalin period, the circus told the Soviet people that social cohesion could be achieved if an able leader organized, coordinated, and directed a strong collective by attending to, rather than suppressing, the individuality of its members.

Trained animal acts told the same story during this period. The relationship between trainers and their charges had always provided a model for human relationships, and after Stalin's death, a handful of animal trainers began to play the part not of teachers, warriors, friends, or parents but of circus directors, with their animals appearing in the roles of the various and very talented circus performers. Like all good circus directors, these trainers appreciated performers' individual idiosyncrasies and managed to induce them to cooperate with each other, in spite of all their differences—or so they claimed.

One of the most popular of these acts debuted in 1956. It was Valentin Filatov's "Bear Circus," which featured a group of trained bears who performed variously as jugglers, gymnasts, acrobats, bicyclists, roller skaters, boxers, and motorcyclists. The troupe even had its own carpet clown, Maks, who performed tricks with a dog, appeared as the second in a comedic boxing match, and played the role of a firefighter, "who ran into the ring to extinguish the burning torches that his friend,

the bear Potap, was juggling."[42] Though Maks disrupted Potap's performance, the two bears actually worked together to achieve the scene's
comedic effect. The bears cooperated with each other, not only with
Filatov, who participated only peripherally in the scene to which he
was nevertheless integral. Filatov was, himself, an individual whose
work was essential to the success of the "Bear Circus," and his performance as a circus director helped elevate the status of circus directors at
the time. It also helped explain their function to viewers who might not
have recognized the "wholeness" of thematically unified and artistically integrated circus spectacles as the achievement of an individual
director.

The same message was also conveyed that year by the young animal
trainer V. Volkovoi, who developed a "Monkey Circus" that featured
monkey-acrobats, monkey-balancers, monkey-aerialists, and monkey-
antipodists, who juggled people and things with their feet.[43] Twenty
years later, tigers made their debut: as balancers, gymnasts, dancing
parodists, solo ballerinas, strongmen, and even as actual wild beasts in
the ring. Their trainer, V. Tikhonov, played the parts of both director
and ringmaster, and he introduced the act by announcing the entrance
of each animal. According to Durova's review of the performances, he
called each of them by name and described "the abilities and individuality of each one." She explained that "it became clear to everyone that
these are not countless clones of the same tiger, but rather a constella-
tion of 'talented tigers.'" Tikhonov made this point most clearly when
he "forgot" to acquaint the public with its favorite tiger, Fatima, who
"expressed her offense with a fierce roar and knocked the stick out of
the trainer's hand with her paw."[44] Tikhonov had failed to accord the
proper respect to the biggest of all his "Striped Stars," as the program
was named. Fatima was offended, and rightfully so. By 1976, trained
animals, like the circus performers they aped in the ring, had come to
expect some individual recognition, though only a few were granted
the star status that Fatima enjoyed.

Animal trainers were themselves among the individual circus performers who were feted in the post-Stalinist press, and their success
was often attributed to their sensitivity to the individuality of their
animals, a point to which the trainer Boris Eder testified himself in his
1958 memoir. He explained that "every animal has a personality of its
own. The trainer owes his success to his ability to understand the differences in animal characteristics and to utilize these differences in

the elaboration of a varied circus programme." He explained that some animals were smart while others were slow, some had a sharp memory while others were dim, some are dull, some are lively, and others lazy, all of which "goes to show that the tamer must ascertain the character, memory, and temperament of the animal before he begins training it."[45] Boris Eder was apparently one of those "masters of the Soviet circus," who were "least of all animal 'tamers,' if by this world [*sic*] we mean harsh suppression of the animal's psychic state," as Nikolai Krivenko put it in his 1968 paean to the Soviet circus.[46] Eder was a committed adherent to the Durov school of animal training, a method of training based on the humane treatment of animals, which was popularized by Vladimir and Iurii Durov, both grandsons of the original Durov, Anatolii. According to Iurii Dmitriev's 1963 profile of the Durovs, their technique required trainers to recognize that "each animal has its own way of life, character and habits," which meant that "training methods which bring the desired results when working with a seal prove futile when working with an elephant."[47] Eder further explained that the Soviet school of animal training was based on a thorough knowledge of the behavior and disposition of individual animals, even when they are members of the same species: "Soviet animal trainers always take into account the 'individuality' of a beast, including his manners and his memory."[48] Eder accordingly attributed Filatov's success to "his skill and patience in discovering the individual 'talents' of his four-legged performers."[49] The trainer Tamara Iur'evna also followed this approach, which, as she explained it, was really not one approach at all but rather a variety of different approaches, each tailored to the individual animals, which in this case were monkeys. As she explained in an interview published in *Sovetskaia kul'tura* in 1983, "for each of them I take a particular approach: you see, they are so different!" She even named each of the monkeys "according to their characters: Dik is wild [*dikii*], Ves is eccentric [*vzbalmoshnyi*], and Boks assumes a boxer's pose when you approach him. There's also Intik, who is intelligent, and Trus," which means "coward."[50] It was animal trainers' appreciation for the individuality of their wards rather than their suppression of it that enabled them to integrate the various animals into a unified collective, which was then able to produce a coherent spectacle or, in some cases, a model circus. Trained animal acts and the rhetoric used to describe them thus reinforced the story of social cohesion told by the "whole" circus at the time.

Courting Jesters

So far, the only people left out of this harmonious community of individuals were the circus viewers. This is where the clowns came in. Like circus directors and the animal trainers who played their roles, carpet clowns also helped integrate the various parts of the circus into a whole; only they included the audience among those parts. Carpet clowns such as Karandash, Popov, and Nikulin had always entertained the crowd between the acts while stagehands cleared away the apparatus from the last act and prepared the set for the next routine. In the post-Stalinist period, they were also directed to make use of their unique position within the circus program "to cement" the various discrete acts into a "whole" spectacle. Unfortunately, according to Comrade Kudriavtsev, a manager of the state circus administration who participated in a discussion of "the development of circus art," by 1950 many carpet clowns had not yet recognized the significance of their role. He claimed that "instead of participating organically in the program, instead of cementing the comedic foundation of the entire circus presentation," carpet clowns present "nothing general, nothing connected with the program."[51]

The situation seemed to have improved by the following decade. In his review of the Moscow Circus's 1961 production of "The Arena of Friendship," a production "that united the artistic forces of three generations, of six brother republics," P. Bernatskii explained that Oleg Popov "'cements' the entire program" with his performance of lyrical etudes in the intervals between acts.[52] Yet it was Karandash and not Popov who was recognized as being the first clown to have achieved this task, though he received credit for it only in 1971. In his biography of Karandash, A. Viktorov wrote that in the 1930s "the carpet clowns became the central figure, who cemented all of the numbers into a single whole [*edinoe tseloe*] and set the tone for the entire circus spectacle." Viktorov explained that he used the word "spectacle" deliberately to refer to circus programs that adhered to a new style, which emerged in the 1930s and sought to "avoid the eclectic collection of numbers and to unite them so that the viewer perceived acrobatics, and juggling, and the other routines as parts of an artistic whole."[53]

While it is true that calls for the production of unified artistic spectacles were voiced in the 1930s, Viktorov's account speaks more closely to the aspirations of his contemporaries than their predecessors. Circus producers in the 1930s considered these "spectacles" to be products of collective labor and, perhaps for that reason, they made no reference to the individual contributions that carpet clowns might have made.[54] In 1973, Iurii Nikulin further maintained that carpet clowns had only recently been directed to cement circus programs. He wrote, "In my lifetime the role of the clown in the circus presentation has changed significantly." He explained that twenty years earlier, most carpet clowns performed short parodic skits or purely entertaining reprises, whose only purpose was to fill the time between acts. Now, however, carpet clowns offered lengthy attractions "that cement all of the activity in the ring, that connect its separate elements into a whole spectacle."[55] Like directors, carpet clowns were responsible for uniting the individual parts of the circus program into a coherent whole. They secured the integrity of the community without sacrificing their individuality, which was also a quality for which they were widely celebrated.

Yet clowns also joined an entirely different set of parts into a whole: they helped integrate each individual viewer into a "whole" community by developing clowning personas that were said to typify all Soviet individuals. Carpet clowns claimed to have transformed their characters into the image of an ordinary Soviet individual, with whom viewers were meant to identify. Their acts invited viewers to recognize themselves as participants in the circus program and in the larger Soviet community that it incarnated. Yet unlike portrait artists, for example, clowns were not working from real, living models. Rather, the characters they portrayed were ideal distillations of the average Soviet individual—an imagined figure. The ideal personas created by carpet clowns thus advertised the particular characteristics that individuals were supposed to embody in order to participate in the Soviet community. These were the characteristics of the "ideal" Soviet individual, and they were often confused with the "real" characteristics that both clowns and viewers were said to evince. Yet once again, this contradiction hardly gave anyone pause because it allowed Soviet clowns to claim that they had invested Soviet viewers with collective authority over the clowns' own creative personas, while the clowns' own creative personas actually authorized Soviet viewers to embody only certain ideal characteristics, habits, and practices. Carpet clowns rhetorically empowered Soviet individuals to dictate the criteria for membership in the Soviet community while exhorting them to submit to Soviet communal norms, which was one way they sought to contribute to the renewal of the Soviet Union.

The idea that clowns were "drawn from the crowd" was not new to this period. After the revolution, clowns and their critics advocated the abandonment of the traditional, buffoon-like *ryzhii* clown that had indulged the baser tastes of the audience with slapstick humor. Instead, they developed more naturalistic clowning personas, which were meant to realistically reflect the healthy, happy, decidedly unfoolish Soviet person. This remained the predominant conception of Soviet clowning after the war and throughout the post-Stalinist period. In 1950, for example, Bespalov insisted in a meeting of circus performers and administrators that practitioners of the so-called conversational genre develop personas that "reflect, reveal the features of the bare Soviet individual with his contemporary, characteristic particularities" and that "reflect the ideas and feelings, the habits and manners of our Soviet person."[56] Yet clowns were also charged with the task of reflecting the ideas and feelings, the habits and manners of an ideal Soviet person—a figure that would become real, once clowns incarnated it and viewers imitated it. The performer N. El'shevskii explained this process in an article he wrote for *Sovetskii tsirk* in 1959. He began by identifying the "content" of circus art as being "those qualities and features of the social person [*obshchestvennogo cheloveka*] that are indissolubly connected to the presentation of the harmonious person, of the ideal of the human being." El'shevskii admitted that clowns often manifest human qualities that were far from ideal, but he insisted that they did so in order to ridicule them and was convinced that "the comedic circus image" could "assert the same positive ideal as a heroic image."[57] Popov agreed. In 1977, he explained that clowns presented realistic images of ideal human beings, which was how they helped bring those ideal individuals into real being. This was also how they "establish the future: the norms of our Soviet morals and way of life, new relations between people and their best qualities—bravery, resourcefulness, and kindness."[58]

Like Lazarenko and Karandash before him, Popov claimed to have developed a realistic persona that represented the ideal Soviet man. He purged from his costume the traditional red wig, garish makeup, oversized shoes, and "in fact everything which hid, be it only to a small extent, the ordinary human features."[59] The clown affectionately portrayed this everyday character in his memoirs: "He is not a 'sentimental' antique. His tenderness would seem today to make him real. He is a completely modern man, full of moderation, interest in current affairs, sometimes equipped with a certain cold humor, not lacking in know-how, a characteristic of our technical age."[60] Commentators agreed that Popov had succeeded in creating a realistic persona, an achievement that represented the "victory of the realistic tendency in clowning," according to A. Viktorov's 1961 profile of the clown.[61]

Iurii Nikulin also presented himself as the Soviet everyman. His 1987 memoir, *Pochti ser'ezno*, opened with a series of photographs that juxtaposed images of the smiling clown performing tricks in the ring with everyday snapshots of Nikulin walking his dog, relaxing at home, and preparing a meal in his kitchen. The oddly assorted images illustrated one of the first passages in Nikulin's autobiographical account: "Without any hesitation, I can list what I like and what I don't like. For example, I like: to read books at night, play solitaire, visit friends, drive a car. . . . I love witty people, songs (listening and singing), jokes, days off, dogs, Moscow streets lit by the setting sun, cutlets with macaroni. I don't like: to wake up early, to stand in line, to walk on foot. . . . I don't like (probably, many don't like this) when I'm pestered on the streets, when I'm cheated. I don't like autumn."[62] The photographs, like the text they illustrated, portrayed Nikulin as an ordinary man, with a typical character and familiar tastes. Nikulin fashioned himself as an everyday man, qualifying the single reference to his celebrity with a parenthetical statement that identified the throngs of adoring fans who pester him in the streets as just another commonplace annoyance. Yet Nikulin's introduction was more than a memoirist's necessary gesture toward modesty, and more than a sincere attempt to make himself, the zany clown, recognizable to a common reader. Nikulin's portrait of the clown as an ordinary man was, rather, the rhetorical realization of one of his primary aspirations as a circus artist: to represent, realistically, the average Soviet man. Like Lazarenko, Karandash, and Popov before them, Nikulin and his partner, Mikhail Shuidin, adopted more naturalistic guises, abandoning the wigs and false noses in which they first performed in the late 1950s.[63] Leonid Engibarov also performed without any makeup or oversized clothing and received frequent praise for appearing "as himself" in the ring.[64] Anatolii Marchevskii was another Soviet clown who did "not resemble a clown." According to N. Khalatov's description, Marchevskii performed without a fat nose, wig, or funny costume, and resembled "only himself," a skinny, charming fellow dressed in short-sleeved shirt and fringed bell-bottom pants. As Khalatov remarked, "you could walk down any street looking like him and nobody would turn their head."[65]

Yet it was not only clowns' appearances that made them recognizably Soviet everymen. According to the official rhetoric, they also expressed a uniquely Soviet sensibility. Their tenderness, cheerfulness,

peacelovingness, resourcefulness, interest in current events, and especially their optimism were understood to be typical characteristics of
the ideal Soviet individual. In 1970, for example, Viktor Ardov described Popov's official reception in the Soviet Union, noting that critics
"write about how optimism and clarity, kindness and cheerfulness are
characteristic of the clown." Ardov also contributed his own opinion.
He considered Popov a "clear example of a sanguine clown, an opti-
mist by temperament," a type of comedic persona devised in the Soviet
Union precisely because "for us, pessimism has no place." It was no
surprise, he continued, that the majority of western clowns were gloomy
"melancholics and phlegmatics," since "the life of the little person under
capitalism is fraught with difficulties and subject to unavoidable catas-
trophes, . . . anxiety is a constant sensation," and the poor vastly out-
number the rich. Foreign clowns, just like their Soviet colleagues, aspired
to be recognizable to viewers as one of their own, which is why they
avoided "irritating" them with any of Popov's "wild optimism."[66]

Soviet clowns were, by contrast, noted optimists. Like Popov, Karandash and Leonid Engibarov were celebrated for their optimism, which
seemed to have pleased the Soviet viewers, since, in the critics' view,
they naturally identified with the optimistic clowns. In his 1971 biography of Karandash, for example, Viktorov identified "optimism" as the
"main element" of Karandash's character,[67] and, the following year,
Iurii Dmitriev contrasted Engibarov's clowning with Chaplin's on the
basis of the former's "more optimistic view of life, of the surrounding
world." Dmitriev explained that Engibarov was a "Soviet artist and
could not but understand and sense, by means of his very existence, the
general optimistic mood of our reality."[68] In a 1985 profile of Engibarov, V. Ivashkovskii described the clown as a person who "believed in
happy endings," which he allowed his viewers to experience as well.
Ivashkovskii recalled that Engibarov traveled from city to city, "compelling people to believe in beauty and goodness."[69] Ivashkovskii
had good reason to consider Engibarov an optimistic clown, since his
routines very often did end happily. In 1971, Vladimir Poliakov described one of Engibarov's most famous routines and perhaps his most
optimistic:

In this scene a boxer who is incomparably stronger and more experienced
that [sic] Engibarov gets in one blow after another until it seems that the
weaker of the two is ready to drop, without the strength to get to his feet
again. Just then a girl, who is a stranger to him, rises from her seat in the circus

and throws Engibarov a flower. He is touched, bows to the girl and thanks her for the unexpected gift. The other boxer rudely steps on the flower, crushing it. You should see Engibarov's reaction! He takes it as the deepest insult, both to the girl and himself. The feelings aroused by the boxer's rudeness fill Engibarov with almost superhuman strength. He begins to fight back fiercely, determined to get the better of his opponent. He is now the cavalier of the rose tossed to him, the knight of his fair lady. He is fighting for his honour. And he downs his opponent. The circus roars with laughter and applauds the victor. A clown who is a gallant knight—such is the title I should give this boxing duel.[70]

This routine, like Popov's "The Ray," ended happily, as did another contemporary skit performed by the clowns Gennadii Rotman and Gennadii Makovskii, in which an individual, in this case a gardener, successfully defended his private allotment of beauty, goodness, and future happiness. Their skit began as Rotman stood watering a bed of flowers and Makovskii, dressed as a reckless "Iron King," with his crown aslant, burst into the ring, dragging a cannon and a cannonball behind him. He pitilessly trampled the flowers. Rotman reacted to this offense by taking a stick in his hand, placing a bucket on his head, and, "having turned himself into a scarecrow," rushing at the King. An explosion resounded. When the smoke finally cleared, the King had disappeared and there remained only the "peace-loving gardener," who planted a flower in the exploded shell casing.[71] The king fell before a figure whose authority was entirely moral.

Anatolii Marchevskii also performed a long skit that ended with the clown's successful defense of his right to happiness, according to Khalatov's interpretation. It began with Marchevskii happily skipping rope, until the ringmaster abruptly interrupted him to explain that rope skipping was prohibited in the circus. The ringmaster confiscated Marchevskii's rope and left the arena. The clown's happy smile faded but was soon replaced by the "crafty smile" that appeared on his face as he glanced "mischievously" around the ring and produced from his pocket another skipping rope. Just then the inspector returned, and the "rascal" hurried to turn over his "ill-fated" rope. Yet as soon as the inspector turned his back again, Marchevskii pulled a "whole tangle of ropes" from his pocket. "This is so unexpected," Khalatov wrote, "that the audience laughs involuntarily." Marchevskii also began to laugh, which attracted the attention of the ringmaster, who turned around to discover and immediately take possession of the ropes. In Khalatov's view, "Of course the viewers do not sympathize with the ringmaster. Although the ringmaster, from his point of view, is absolutely correct. The viewers see how obediently the skipping ropes are given up. They see and they understand: it's not only the skipping ropes that are being given up, something more is being given up. Happiness is being given up. The riches of childhood are being given up." Yet Marchevskii was not so easily defeated. If he could not skip over a rope, then the silk ribbon adorning the performers' entrance to the ring would have to do. When that was taken away, Marchevskii skipped across his jacket, and when the jacket was taken away, he skipped across his pants, and when his pants were taken away, he skipped across his shoelaces, all of which conveyed a "very simple idea," according to Khalatov: "It is forbidden to take away happiness. The conflict between the rules of behavior and the right to happiness, the right to childlike spontaneity, is not only staged but resolved: the little person defended his rights with all his strength. He could not but defend them!"[72]

Things ended just as happily for the character in the title role of Nikulin and Shuidin's famous skit "The Big Doings of Little Pierre [*Bol'shie dela mal'enkogo P'era*], A Scene from Life in Contemporary France," in which a resourceful young Frenchman thwarted the efforts of two bumbling police officers to restrict his freedom of political expression. The scene was a satire of French political repression, which stood in implicit contrast to the protections that the Soviet Union purportedly afforded to political agitators. The action occurred in a city square at night. An unemployed man, who, according to Nikulin's description, helped Pierre make a fool of the police officers, lay sleeping on a bench beside a statue of a lion. The young Frenchman was covertly posting leaflets when he was approached by two officers, played by Nikulin and Shuidin. Nikulin recalled that as the officers crept up to the young delinquent, the children in the audience screamed, "Police! Police! Run!" In the ensuing confusion, the lion's head cracked off, and Pierre disguised himself by placing the broken head onto his own. The lion then "came to life," startling Nikulin, who had been abandoned by his partner and had since sat down on the glue-covered brush that the boy had used to post his leaflets. The orchestra then came to young Pierre's aid, alarming the police officer with a series of disarming notes. Nikulin described the scene in which "every sharp, unexpected, sinister chord scared me and I began to tremble."[73] In this scene, the audience voiced its sympathy for the criminal, who eluded the inept police officer by assuming the lion's appearance. This transformation allowed Pierre to swap roles with the originally menacing figure of authority, who was frightened away by the animated statue. In another famous routine, which they performed for the Leningrad Circus in 1975, the two clowns eluded another oppressive foreign agent. Christopher Wren provided an account of it in the *New York Times*:

Nikulin and his partner, Mikhail Shuidin, shuffle into the ring. A director modeled on the Hollywood stereotype, complete with beret and dark glasses, bounds in with his camera crew and offers Nikulin and Shuidin a chance to make some quick money by acting in a movie. When they agree, the director's crew brings in a huge log. "Just pick up the log and carry it from here to there," the director says to Nikulin and Shuidin. They strain at the log. Pulling, panting, they manage to move it a few feet while the camera is rolling. "No, no, no!" the director yells. "Like this!" And he places an imaginary log on his shoulder, prancing, dancing happily.

The two clowns try. Nikulin, the bigger man, gets his end of the log up on his shoulder, but he cannot straighten up. He struggles along, his knees bent, until the director shouts, "No! Smile! Smile!" Nikulin manages a painful grimace that brings down the house. Then he and Shuidin, wielding a knife and a brick, chase the nattily dressed director out of the ring.[74]

While endings like this one became commonplace in the post-Stalin circus, they did not entirely account for the noted optimism of the clown routines, some of which did not end happily at all. For example, Engibarov's circus adaptation of the French film *The Red Balloon* ended when the "touching friendship" between the balloon and the boy was cut short by a rude street-sweeper's broom that turned the balloon into a "lifeless red smudge" on the floor of the ring. Engibarov himself said that his repertoire included a number of sad interludes, and this was certainly one of them. Yet the optimism of these routines—the promise of a brighter future that they not only offered but fulfilled—might have lain, at least in part, in the new life that Engibarov seemed to give them. R. Slavskii wrote in his 1972 biography of Engibarov that even old routines acquired "a new coloration, both touching and heartfelt," as a result of "having passed through the bright individuality of the actor." According to Slavskii, "clown acts that had aged considerably, seemed to have become young. A spring freshness suddenly blew off of them."[75] Like other innovative circus performers, Engibarov made old acts new by making them his own, a claim with which Ivashkovskii agreed. He wrote that Engibarov was constantly creating new scenes—"every night he was able to offer the new and the new"—and always "played himself, his own life." Ivashkovskii explained, further, that by being himself, Engibarov brought the viewers together: "they laughed together with him, they grieved together with him, and together with him they took joy from the circus, which is what helps one to live [*i vmeste s nim unosili iz tsirka svetloe, to, chto pomogaet zhit'*]." Engibarov's individuality, which enabled him to establish a connection both with and between the viewers, was another source for his optimism. What viewers took away from his performance might have been the knowledge that even grief could bring joy because grief could bring everybody together. The joyous experience of belonging to a community was another of the happy endings that Engibarov's repertoire offered. Like Popov, Engibarov sought to "establish the future" by offering viewers proof that a beautiful, good, joyous, and new future would be had by anybody who believed that a beautiful, good, joyous, and new future could be had.

The Bad Apples

According to the clowns, the belief in a better, brighter future was something that all individual members of the Soviet community necessarily shared. Like other circus performers, clowns also sought to bring that ideal future into being by demonstrating "the best characteristics of the developing Soviet person," as Bardian described their task in a 1961 meeting of leading circus artists and administrators. He explained that, in accordance with the instructions of the Communist Party, "the workers of the Soviet circus are called upon to raise the ideological-artistic level of circus art, to create routines and attractions that demonstrate the best characteristics of the developing Soviet person, the inexhaustible potential of his physical and spiritual qualities, and to achieve the greatest mastery of artistic skill." He urged practitioners of the so-called conversational genre to develop monologues, interludes, and reprises that glorified "the great accomplishments of the Soviet people under the leadership of the Communist party, to display the heroic deeds of simple Soviet people." This demand was already a familiar one. Yet Bardian had more to say, specifically to the clowns, whom he ordered to "struggle against everything that impedes our swift movement forward" by satirizing idleness, drunkenness, hooliganism, bureaucratism, and "other horrific qualities" that were "manifestations of bourgeois ideology and the vestiges of capitalism in the consciousness of the people."

During the post-Stalin period, many Soviet clowns met Bardian's challenge to celebrate the best individuals and malign the worst by embodying all of them in the ring.[76] Clowns ridiculed the idlers, drunkards, hooligans, and bureaucrats identified by Bardian, as well as the swindlers, sycophants, and "all those who," in Boris Eder's view, "interfere with the construction of the new life." Eder also included bureaucrats and idlers among them.[77] Soiuzgostsirk's plan of basic measures to be taken in 1963 also numbered "spongers, bribery, drunkenness, hooliganism, and religious prejudices," among the "remnants of capitalism in the consciousness and behavior of people" that should be satirized in the circus.[78] The plan for 1967 added to the list "apoliticism, the remnants of private ownership and petty-bourgeois inclinations, and against manifestations of a nihilistic relationship to the ideals and achievements of socialism."[79]

Soviet clowns combated cynicism, nihilism, and apoliticism by presenting optimistic routines that staged the defeat of officially designated impediments to the renewal of the Soviet Union. Sometimes they even did it in a funny way. Clowns used their old bag of tricks—visual gags, verbal puns, physical slapstick, unpredictable reversals, and pyrotechnics—to make topical routines entertaining and to make jokes about current events amusing. In 1956, for example, *New York Times* correspondent Jack Raymond described the satirical skits performed at the Moscow Circus, the first of which relied on slapstick and a visual pun to lampoon an idle repairman who was too lazy, disinterested, and dim to do his job but not to evade reprisal for his failure:

Two customers come in[to a state operated repair shop] with broken music records they want repaired. Another customer comes with a pair of boots to be soled. The repairman cuts the side of one boot in the shape of a sole to place on the other boot. When the infuriated customer complains, he is thrown out of the shop, his ruined boots after him, and he is advised to go elsewhere. In the meantime, the repairman places one of the repaired records on a turn-table. It begins to play, but first one tune and then another. The angry customers wail that their records have been combined. But the records are strong, the repairman insists, and will not break again. The customers smash the records on the head of the repairman. After they rush off he takes off his cap and reveals a tin pot underneath. To be a repairman, one must be hard-headed, he explains, while the crowd roars its approval.[80]

Another joke performed that night, about an idle girl who graduated from an institute and "having taken all that the government has to

offer ... got married so she would not have to work," also delighted the
audience, though Raymond offered no explanation for its appeal, other
than the apparent truth of it.[81]

Alcoholism was a common companion to idleness—both its cause
and its consequence—according to the circus clowns who warned of
the harm the combustible substance could cause those who abused it.
Popov often peppered his satirical entrées against alcohol with fiery
displays. In one routine, he played a doctor who suspected his patient
of feigning an illness. The doctor began to suspect that the ailing man
was drunk after he asked him to say "aah" and was met with a current
of breath so stiff with alcohol that he was forced to chase it back by
chomping on a pickle. To prove that his patient was drunk, the doctor
held a flaming torch in front of the patient, whom he again asked to say
"aah." When the patient did, the torch instantly burst into flame.[82]
Another routine featured Popov and his partner Shekhtman's comedic
attempt to make "jam." The two clowns entered the ring carrying a
large sack labeled "sugar," a gas stove, and a large cauldron with a glass
coil poking out from beneath its lid. As they explained to a curious
bystander, they planned to use all of this equipment to cook jam. Popov
lit a fire beneath the cauldron, placed a bucket beneath the coil's spout,
and sat down beside Shekhtman, who already held a mug and a cucum-
ber in his hands. Drops of liquid dripped from the coil with increasing
frequency, until a steady stream of liquid began to flow into the bucket.
The artists filled their mugs from the bucket and drank the home brew,
which they each chased down with a pickle. Then they did it again. At
this point, Popov's nose turned bright red and began to shine. Shekhtman burst into laughter, as did Popov when his partner's nose also began
to shine. The two clowns continued to stumble and laugh drunkenly
until they became startled by the appearance of what seemed to be a
green snake slithering out from under the lid of the cauldron. The
boiling liquid continued to pour out from the snake's mouth, and Shekhtman collected it into his mug. As he lifted his mug to drink, Popov
shouted, "Don't drink, you'll get burned," but Shekhtman ignored the
warning and, draining his cup, reported that he was not burned. Popov
was unconvinced. He lit a match in order to examine his partner's
mouth for any sign of injury, and when he lifted the match to Shekhtman's mouth, the dim arena was "cut through with a huge curl of fire"
and then suddenly plunged into darkness. When the lights came on
again, the ring was empty, and all that remained of the clowns were

two hats, four shoes, and a pile of charred clothing, all of which was carried out of the ring in a funeral procession.[83] In another act, titled "Vodka," Nikulin and his partner Mikhail Shuidin also satirized idle drinkers, though without any pyrotechnic display. According to Joel Schechter's description, "[Nikulin] and Shuidin are about to drink when a clean-cut official . . . enters and stares in disapproval at their glasses. The clowns proceed to wash their hands with the clear liquid, as if that is what they planned all along. Nikulin gargles briefly, then spits out his mouthful, as if he is simply fighting a cold. The two men eat bread and exit."

Alongside idlers and alcoholics, speculators and thieves also stood in the way of the more perfect Soviet future, and they were ridiculed for it in the circus. Speculators were the target of a joke told in 1958 by the celebrated math whiz Ostrin and his quizzer, the carpet clown, who presented him with a "difficult problem": "At the department store Aunt Masha bought a pair of shoes for two hundred rubles. . . . Aunt Masha sold them to Aunt Dasha for two hundred and twenty-five rubles. Aunt Dasha sold them to Aunt Pasha for two hundred and fifty rubles. Aunt Pasha sold them to Aunt Glasha for two hundred and seventy-five rubles and Aunt Glasha sold them to some unknown female citizen for three hundred rubles. How much did they earn?" Ostrin replied that each earned twenty-five, but the clown corrected him, shouting, "Mistake! Each earned fifteen nights [in jail]." When the ringmaster remarked that "none of this pertains to quick calculations," the carpet clown replied, 'But it pertains to the laws of petty speculation."[84] This routine seems not to have been an effective deterrent for speculators, since it was reapproved for performance in 1965. It is unlikely that any greater impact was made by Nikulin and Shuidin's 1962 skit satirizing speculators, one of whom forced Nikulin to give up his pants to purchase a bouquet of flowers for his sweetheart, despite Iurii Dmitriev's praise for their active participation "in the struggle against everything stagnant and moribund, everything that disturbs the construction of the new life."[85] In another routine, Nikulin played the part of a successful cheat rather than his victim. Both clowns appeared as apple vendors who had devised a scheme to cheat their customers. Nikulin was supposed to weigh the apples, holding a tray with the fruit in one hand and a tray with weights in the other. According to the plan, Nikulin would overload the weights so that the customer would be overcharged. The two fools cheated the ringmaster in this way, but when the second

customer approached and asked for 100 grams of apples for thirty kopeks, Nikulin measured out three kilograms worth of produce. Shuidin
was appalled until Nikulin explained that the customer was his wife.[86]

Popov also ridiculed an individual willing to enrich himself at the
expense of the collective in 1960, just days after the government implored Soviets to conserve electricity. According to Max Frankel's description in the *New York Times*, Popov roamed "the arena searching for
something, demanding more and more light until the house is flooded.
'Aha!' he announces. 'What did you find, Oleg?' 'Five kopeks.' 'Five kopeks? But, Oleg, we spent many times that in electricity to help you find
it!' 'Aha! But the five kopeks are mine.'"[87] The following year a joke that
held a local committee responsible for the shortage of light made a play
on the phrase *"konets sveta,"* which can mean both "the end of the
world" and literally "the end of light." The joke began when one clown
asked the other clown to tell him where the end of the world (*konets
sveta*) could be found. When the second clown began to explain that the
end of the world did not exist, the first clown interrupted him and,
"condescendingly" patting him on the shoulder, said, "The end of the
world is on Mel'nichnaia Street. Gorkomkhoz still cannot light it!" According to the viewer I. Makharov, who encouraged circus performers
to write more jokes on local subjects, the routine received the applause
not only of residents living on that particular street.[88] Nikulin also satirized the poor state of public space, in this case the entryway to his apartment, where he happened to have dropped his keys while he was trying
to unlock his door. He crouched down on the floor and began to search
for the key. Thinking he had found it, he lifted something up into the
air, but soon realized it was not his key but a gob of phlegm. Nikulin
squeamishly cleaned off his hand.[89]

The individuals who received the most blame for impeding the development of the Soviet Union were those most responsible for ensuring
its development—that is, state officials. Bad bureaucrats were offered
as the explanation for the Soviet Union's failure to thrive, which, according to the clowns, could not be attributed publicly to any flaw in
either the structure or the ideological foundation of the institutions that
employed them. Bureaucrats were model targets of approved satire,
and Soviet clowns attacked them accordingly. As Laurens van der Post
observed, "in the Moscow circus . . . the bureaucrat is just a pompous,
cigar-smoking, overnourished, hard-drinking man at a desk, a facsimile
of the classic Soviet caricature of the capitalist."[90] One of the most celebrated anti-bureaucratic routines was performed by Akram Iusupov,

another clown, in whose appearance "there is nothing of a clown." He was a rotund Uzbek of medium height who, according to Poliakov, wore "a national Uzbek costume without the slightest touch of the grotesque, and that's all." Poliakov described a routine he performed in the middle of the Tashkenbaiev's highwire act, which was "probably Yusupov's best":

The Tashkenbayevs are performing on the rope. . . . All of a sudden Akram Yusupov rushes into the ring, although the attendants try to stop him, in the middle of the act. He says he has to see the chairman of the local trade-union committee. He is told that the chairman is a rope-walker and right now he is up there, performing on the rope.

"And how do you get up there?" Akram asks. "Is there a lift?"

This question is asked with such sincere simplicity, with such assurance that everyone is anxious to help him and with such winning naiveté that the audience literally roars with laughter.

Climbing up the pole is not a very easy job, but after some puffing and panting, Akram reaches the platform at the top. It turns out that the chairman is on the platform at the other end of the rope.

Akram looks at the rope and in a serious voice asks, "Why is that rope so thin?"

He is handed a balancing pole and starts out to cross over to the other end where the chairman is standing. . . . When he comes to the place where the cables holding the rope fan out in different directions he stops for a moment, as though at an intersection, and asks, "And where does that road go?" Then, when he finally reaches the middle of the rope, he announces, with obvious satisfaction in his prowess: "Not much left now." Once on the opposite platform he sighs with satisfaction and asks, "Are you the chairman? I have to have my sick-leave certificate signed and stamped."

And he begins to look for the certificate, having forgotten where he put it. . . . He looks for that paper for about three minutes, which is a long time in the theatre of the circus. The audience, however, never notices this. They never stop laughing for an instant. Finally he extricates the paper from some part of his attire. The chairman signs it but informs Akram that the secretary has the rubber stamp—and the secretary is at the opposite end of the rope. Yusupov must go through that ordeal once more! He cannot suppress a deep sigh at what lies ahead of him but it is lost in the laughter of the audience. And so he starts back. "I'm getting used to this," and the spectators continue to laugh.

Poliakov concluded his account with a commonplace commendation for the clown, who "presents the oft-repeated theme of bureaucracy, interpreting it through the techniques of the circus and his own original talent."[91] In other words, Iusupov made the tired critique of bureaucracy new by making it his own. His routine, as read by Poliakov, told viewers that individuals were responsible for both impeding and securing the future of the Soviet Union.

Nikulin and Shuidin also satirized a typical Soviet bureaucrat, though their routine ended more happily, with the bureaucrat's demise. According to Van der Post's description,

A timid citizen [played by Nikulin] comes to apply for a post and is kept hanging about for no reason except that the bureaucrat [played by Shuidin] wants to have several more swigs in secret at his bottle of vodka. When he condescends to see the common little man at last, he fires questions at him like bullets from a machine gun. Has he got his card of identification, photograph of himself, his wife, his children, parents and parents-in-law, all their marriage and birth certificates, references from previous places of employment, legal certificates of discharge, school certificates, certificate of national service, and so on and on? At each request the little man slapped the relevant document on the desk while the bureaucrat got obviously more and more perturbed that he might in the end have no excuse for turning down the applicant. The final despairing question was: "Have you got your mother-in-law's fingerprints?" When these too were triumphantly produced the bureaucrat pulled out a pistol from the desk and shot himself.[92]

In Van der Post's view, the realism of this scene made it a funny and therefore effective satire: "So much did this simple pantomime reflect the private world of all that the audience long roared its delight." Yet what made it realistic was not its depiction of the public world, in which such scenes never ended so happily, but rather its realization of a fantasy held privately, in Van der Post's view, by all Soviet viewers. That a simple citizen might bring down the bureaucracy was a fairy tale that Nikulin and Shuidin's routine made real. Yet their routine did not sanction any overt resistance to the bureaucratic system, since the bad bureaucrat's demise came as a result of the citizen's obedience to his demands. The bureaucrat brought ruin upon himself, and the lesson to be learned from his story was that the system was self-renewing, that it would rid itself of deviant elements all by itself—or with the help of state-sponsored satires of them.

Not all of these routines ended so unambiguously. This particular idle, drunken bureaucrat did shoot himself, just as the idle, drunken makers of home brew blew themselves up, and Aunts Masha, Dasha, Pasha, Glasha, and some unknown female citizen landed themselves in jail for fifteen days. These skits were optimistic. The bad guys lost in the end, and the community was restored. But the bureaucrat who tormented Iusupov won. He never shot himself. The idle repairman also won in the end, as did the idle, recently wed girl; the idle, drunken, fire-breathing shirker; the idle, drunken picnickers; the speculator in his new pair of pants; the speculator whose wife made off with one hundred grams of apples; and the squanderer of electricity who found his five kopeks. These routines ended happily for the bad guys. All they did was identify the bad guys as such, which was not insignificant given that their villainization in the circus set them in league with capitalists, agents of the Imperial Russian state, White officers, Nazis, and executors of the Marshall Plan, all of whom threatened the future of the Soviet Union. Perhaps the authors of these routines refused to dramatize the villains' defeat for the same reason that Maiakovskii refused to dramatize the victory of the revolution in *Championship*: in order to mobilize viewers to participate in the defeat of these enemies. Viewers might have been persuaded that idlers, alcoholics, speculators, swindlers, bad bureaucrats, and people who spit in entryways were to blame for the Soviet Union's failure to have established a better future. Yet even if viewers were so persuaded, there remained little for them to do about it. They could stop loafing, drinking, speculating, and spitting, while trusting the state to stop everyone else who was doing it, and the prevalence of satires against these behaviors in the state circuses did seem to imply an official commitment to doing just that.

Yet, at times, the supposed targets of a satirical routine appeared to be the good guys. Nikulin and Shuidin's skit with the apples might have been meant to mock thieving speculators—this is certainly why it won official approval—but the ordinary, everyday, realistic clowns, with whom the viewers were meant to identify, might have appeared to be sympathetic characters. Technically, they were more than honest with the young customer, though admittedly to their own advantage. Viewers might have recognized the routine less as a satire against speculators than as an endorsement of the everyday rule-breaking and networks of pull on which most real Soviet people relied. They might have viewed it as an acknowledgment that it was impossible to stop speculating themselves, and that it was impossible for the state to stop everyone else from doing it, not only because anti-speculation laws were unenforceable, but also because the shadow economy had become an essential bulwark to the legitimate economy. In other words, the routine might have sanctioned the very behavior that it professed to stigmatize.

"Vodka" was a similarly ambiguous routine, although Joel Schechter has interpreted it as a straightforward satire of alcoholics. Schechter concludes that "the looks of loss and regret in their eyes, as the vodka is poured away, say more about the clowns' and (Moscow citizens') sad states than any words could."[93] Yet Nikulin and Shuidin did not endow the characters they were supposedly satirizing with grossly exaggerated negative traits. They appeared, rather, to be ordinary Soviet friends preparing to enjoy a rest and a drink. The clowns most likely won the audience's sympathy by outwitting the official and avoiding punishment, just as they had in *The Big Doings of Little Pierre* and the sketch satirizing the Hollywood film director. The clowns' triumph over authority was not complete—they were forced to discard the vodka and forego their revelry—yet the official who disrupted their pleasant afternoon did appear to be a villainous adherent to the rules. Viewers might have recognized Nikulin and Shuidin as a menace to the Soviet community, or they might have seen them as two little people defending their right to happiness with all their strength.

Conclusion

These ordinary, everyday, realistic clowns were also irreverent, disorderly, and cunning. Viewers were thus encouraged to spurn rulebreakers, while at the same time they were invited to identify with the ordinary Soviet clowns, who were simply going about the ordinary business of being Soviet, which seemed to involve breaking some of the rules. Yet clowns' apparent endorsement of unruliness was itself ambiguous. Spectators might have laughed at the clowns' jolly rulebreaking because they delighted in a fleeting moment of vicarious transgression, or because they suddenly recognized the frailty of systems that ordered their world, or because they recognized in it something familiar—an echo, amplified perhaps, of their own daily evasions, inversions, and violations of the rules. For their part, state officials might have appreciated these routines because they appeared to be satires of approved targets, or because idle, drunken, spitting bureaucrats also enjoyed a laugh at their own expense, or because the official endorsement of such routines implied that the Soviet state could tolerate certain disorderly, unruly behaviors, just as it could tolerate the free expression of individuality and the unfettered pursuit of private happiness. Officially licensed violations of the official rules might have strengthened the Soviet system by offering proof of the government's commitment to self-renewal. Or, it might have weakened it by exposing its persistent failure to have renewed itself, an effect that would only have bred the very cynicism that the circus was charged to combat. The state's willingness to suffer violations of its rules might have been a source of its strength or of its weakness, since, if the rules could be broken without consequence, then there was little reason not to dispense with them—which is eventually what happened.

Some viewers might have liked the circus because it bound them more securely to the Soviet state and to each other. Some might have liked it because it allowed them to remain alienated from the Soviet state and from each other. The circus might have helped to reinforce the difference between those who were bound and those who were alienated, or it might have helped to erase this difference, since everyone liked the circus, regardless of their relationship to the Soviet state and to each other. In this sense, the circus really might have helped cement individual Soviets into a whole, harmonious community and a cohesive body politic. Of course, it could not do it alone and it did not do it for long. The circus might have been a place where pigs could fly and bears could dance, where the rules were broken and an individual could be the star of the show, but, in the end, it was still only the circus, and it could not secure the future of the Soviet Union.

Conclusion

A Peculiar Institution

The story of the circus in the Soviet Union is, in some ways, a familiar one. It comes as no surprise that the Soviet circus, like circuses everywhere, was an indeterminate, flexible, and polyvalent form of art that satisfied the diverse demands of the Soviet people who consumed it. It also comes as no surprise that the Soviet circus, like most every Soviet cultural product, propagated political messages, ideological lessons, and legitimating myths to the consistent satisfaction of the succeeding regimes that produced it. What is surprising, though, is that the circus in the Soviet Union satisfied the diverse demands of both state and society by remaining an indeterminate, flexible, and polyvalent form of art that consistently propagated political messages, ideological lessons, and legitimating myths.

The circus was already an anomaly among the revolutionary cultural products created after 1917, when "political and aesthetic revolutionaries tried to suppress the allegedly dangerous old world of commercial popular culture."[1] After the revolution, Soviet cultural officials preferred to give "the people what they thought was good for them and not what they wanted."[2] Both Bolshevik and non-Bolshevik revolutionary intellectuals favored cultural policy that condemned "what would now be called urban popular culture . . . as 'vulgar,' 'trivial,' and 'petty-bourgeois.'"[3] There certainly were some among the makers of Soviet revolutionary culture who objected to the inclusion of the circus for those very reasons, but they failed to convince those officials, including Lenin himself, who chose to produce the circus largely because it was what the Soviet people wanted. It was precisely the popularity of the entertainment among workers, peasants, and Red Army soldiers that, according to the Bolsheviks, justified their incorporation of an old-world commercial entertainment into the Soviet cultural administration.

The circus was hardly the only prerevolutionary popular entertainment that the Soviet government continued to produce, and yet even among those, the circus remained exceptional. Like other "popular forms once consigned to the periphery of Russian culture," such as festivals, folk songs and dances, wood carvings, and fairground diversions, the circus was "moved to the center" after the Bolshevik Revolution and "given new responsibilities."[4] Throughout its history in the Soviet Union, the circus was "infused" with "revolutionary content" just like everything else was.[5] It did propagate political messages, it did help to establish legitimating myths, and it did offer proof that the Soviet people were eager to receive them both. Yet unlike other forms of popular culture, such as Bolshevik festivals, which were subjected to "structural changes" so that they might meet these new responsibilities, the circus retained, throughout much of its history, the "element of play that had been the essence of popular culture."[6] It was precisely this play element—its indeterminacy, flexibility, and openness to subjective interpretation—that enabled the circus to tell so many different stories to the consistent satisfaction of its successive state producers. The polyvalence of the show also provided for its popularity among diverse viewers who all appeared to conform to a mythic ideal, even as the circus remained a fun, enchanting, spectacularly amazing entertainment that never lost its appeal to viewers who might not have been so eager to consume any of those stories. The history of the Soviet circus offers unexpected evidence that a popular cultural medium that refused to convey any unambiguous message, narrate any single story, or construct one consistent myth was no less suitable a site for asserting the legitimacy of the Soviet state than were the much less ambiguous forms of culture that are better known by Soviet historians and students of the political uses of popular culture.

By virtue of the political functions that circus productions and the rhetoric surrounding them consistently performed, the entertainment even remained a rarity among the few other forms of popular culture that also managed to escape significant structural change during the Soviet period. For example, Soviet fans consumed spectator sports much like they might have consumed the circus: "in very different, far more playful ways than the state had in mind."[7] Some spectators saw sports not as a demonstration of the benefits of physical fitness that instilled "values of honesty, obedience, discipline, culture, sexual equality and selflessness," as they were meant to, but rather as "an opportunity for pleasure and fun, an arena of unabashedly male bonding, a chance to exhibit the joking cynicism and irony of all sports fans, and a place to idolize heroes of their own, rather than the state's choosing."[8] In this way, "Soviet spectator sports fostered norms of behavior that can be called destabilizing, even counter-hegemonic."[9] Yet unlike spectator sports, whose unruly consumption ultimately served to "undermine the government's quest to obtain the consent of the governed,"[10] the circus potentially both stabilized and destabilized the Soviet government by simultaneously meeting its own demands for ideologically instructive cultural products while also satisfying viewers who demanded cultural products that could be consumed in ways that contradicted the official prescription.

In this sense, the history of the Soviet circus most closely resembles that of mass celebrations in the Stalinist period, which were also characterized by "the multiplicity of meanings" that they made available to their various participants.[11] Soviet and Party leaders organized physical culture parades, celebrations of arctic explorers, and New Year's pageants to establish their authority, assert their legitimacy, and encourage political consent. Yet in doing so, they introduced ideas that "could also be employed to express alternative, unofficial, and subversive viewpoints" as, for example, "when an official harvest festival turned into a drunken, violent melee."[12]

Both Soviet circuses and mass celebrations were surprisingly typical of popular and particularly carnivalesque forms of culture in other contexts, in that they did not function exclusively as modes of resistance to dominant ideologies, nor did they only enforce political compliance and social conformity. Instead, they might have been so vital, enduring, and culturally functional precisely because they always kept these two possibilities in play. The "ideological valency" of the Soviet circus, like Stalin-era celebrations, was one of ambivalence, and in this way both resembled pictorial representations of the circus in nineteenth-century France, in which "carnival was made to serve a variety of political and artistic ends. . . . Its significance was open to debate. That was precisely what made it compelling: it had to be molded to this or that program, . . . its signs had to be won over."[13] The Soviet circus did articulate official ideologies, promote political consent, and encourage social cohesion. Yet its significance remained open to debate, which meant that it could attract even those viewers who might have seen it as an escape from dominant ideologies, an expression of political discontent, or a source of social disorder. This ambivalence is what makes the history of the Soviet circus so surprising, given the plethora of Soviet cultural products that either served the interests of the Soviet state or, alternatively, subverted them.

The Standard Story

The story of the Soviet circus is, in another way, a familiar one. Its history is divided into periods that correspond closely to the succeeding periods in Soviet political history—first there was the revolution and then there was NEP; after the war came the Cold War; following Stalin was de-Stalinization—which are well known to students and scholars of Soviet history. Yet despite its overall adherence to this standard scheme—which itself comes as little surprise, given that Soviet officials deliberately adapted the entertainment to meet their own shifting political imperatives—the history of the circus does introduce some unusual twists into the story of the Soviet Union.

One unexpected pattern that appears in the history of the circus is the closely parallel structure between two periods: the first between 1917 and 1928, the second between 1929 and 1939. Cultural officials began both decades by introducing changes into the circus that they considered revolutionary. They then brought both decades to a close by claiming, not entirely convincingly, that the circus stood as proof that the revolution in Soviet culture had succeeded. While it is true that the means of producing the circus came under state control after 1919 and that significant changes to its administrative structure and personnel were introduced during the period of the first Five-Year Plan, the content of the circus repertoire itself was modified briefly, and incompletely, during both purportedly revolutionary periods. It was actually not until World War II—a period better known for the loosening rather than strengthening of government control over cultural production—that any great transformation of circus performances actually took place. During the war, which emerges as a period of significant innovation in the history of the circus, routines—other than Lazarenko's and a very few others—began to include the kind of ideological content that producers, performers, and official commentators claimed the Soviet state circuses had offered since they were first revolutionized in 1919 and then revolutionized again in 1929.

During World War II, the content of the show, and not only the story that was officially told about it, shifted. Both then shifted again when new ideological demands were placed on the circus in the immediate postwar period, and they then shifted once more after Stalin died. Yet then, unexpectedly, significant innovation in both the circus repertoire and the rhetoric surrounding it stalled. After 1956, the circus began to tell two different stories about, on the one hand, Soviet internationalism and, on the other hand, Soviet individualism, each with unprecedented consistency. The history of the circus between 1956 and 1991 constitutes a single, highly stable period that was unbroken by any significant shift in official ideology, which, as the case of the circus demonstrates, became cemented during these decades.[14] Perhaps the greatest fiction the circus proffered was the story that it, and by implication the larger Soviet collective for which the circus stood, was dynamic and self-renewing—a story that never changed for more than thirty-five years. This failure of ideological innovation after Stalin's death seems to have been a mark of the exhaustion, decline, and eventual demise of the Soviet system.

The Ideal and the Real

Another mark was the failure of the Soviet government to make many of the stories it told come true, at least outside of the circus ring. One of the most significant ideological tasks performed by the circus was to present the ideal Soviet person, and even withstanding the periodic revision to which this figure was subjected, the circus incarnated it consistently. The Soviet circus always told the Soviet people who they were supposed to be, and it always offered proof that at least some ideal Soviet people really did exist already. Whether they were proper proletarians, eager for revolutionary enlightenment; or adherents to socialist labor methods who were capable of achieving impossible feats; or jolly Soviet-born youngsters; or fearless wartime heroes; or members of a multinational family living in comfortable homes and a secure homeland; or lovers of peace, foreigners, and all things universal and humane;

or unique, innovative, optimistic individuals, happily integrated into a self-renewing collective; circus performers really were so many ideal Soviet people. At times, circus viewers might have been too, at least so long as they were seated in the circus, laughing, unafraid, surrounded by their families and all the other unique, idiosyncratic, and apparently ideal Soviets, who together really might have constituted a cohesive community.

In the circus, the ideal was made real, which made it an exceptional product of Soviet culture. Yet precisely because the circus was as exceptional as it was surprising, extraordinary, spectacular, and strange, its claim to represent any reality other than its own might not have been entirely credible. The circus might not have convinced all viewers that everybody outside of the circus really always did perform impossible feats, laugh cheerfully, live in well-appointed homes, or pursue their own interests for the sake of the common good. Some viewers might have known themselves to feel youthful, unafraid, satisfied, secure, and kindly toward foreigners only so long as they remained in the circus. They might have identified more readily with the juggler who dropped her pins, the tumbler who missed his landing, and every one of the clowns, who seemed, at times, to fall far short of the ideal while always claiming to be real Soviet people. For those viewers, circus performers might have been at their most real when they least resembled the ideal. To them, the circus might have offered proof that Soviet reality, outside the space of the circus, was anything but ideal. The story of the circus tells of a fundamental and perhaps fatal dilemma of the Soviet state, which always staked its legitimacy on some ideal that it consistently articulated but could credibly claim to have realized only in such a rare and circumscribed space as the circus. In the end, then, the trouble with the Soviet Union might have been less that it was a circus than that it never really became one.

Notes

Introduction

1. Michael R. Gordon, "Russians Are Left with One Less Reason to Smile," *New York Times*, 27 August 1997, A4.

2. "Russian People Mourn for Celebrated Actor Yuri Nikulin," *Itar-Tass News Agency*, 26 August 1997.

3. Gordon, "Russians Are Left with One Less Reason to Smile," A4.

4. "V poslednii raz na Manezhe," *Rossiiskaia gazeta*, 26 August 1997, 1.

5. Valerii Kichin, "Manezh upustel: Pervyi den' bez Nikulina," *Izvestiia*, 22 August 1997, 1.

6. Daniel Williams, "All of Russia Grieves for Beloved Comic Who Brought Light to Dark Days," *Washington Post*, 23 August 1997, A20.

7. Larisa Smetankina, "Yeltsin, Chernomyrdin Pay Last Respects to Russia's Best Comic," *Itar-Tass News Agency*, 25 August 1997; Igor Veksler, "Chernomyrdin Offers 'Any Help' to Save Actor's Life," *Itar-Tass News Agency*, 13 August, 1997.

8. "Russia's Yuri Nikulin Dies 16 Days after Heart Surgery," *Itar-Tass News Agency*, 21 August, 1997.

9. Robert Serebrennikov, "New Big Diamond Named after Yuri Nikulin," *Itar-Tass News Agency*, 28 August 1997.

10. James Meek, "How to Grin and Bear It," *Manchester Guardian Weekly*, 31 August 1997, 22.

11. Georgii Mrokhovskii, "Chto pomniat ob Artiste cherez dva chasa posle smerti?" *Rossiiskaia gazeta*, 22 August 1997, 3.

12. "Pogasla nepovtorimaia Nikulinskaia ulybka: Velikii artist ushel; Ushel navsegda," *Pravda*, 22–29 August 1997, 1.

13. Kichin, "Manezh upustel," 1.

14. "Pogasla nepovtorimaia Nikulinskaia ulybka," 1.

15. Meek, "How to Grin and Bear It," 22; *Manchester Guardian Weekly*, 31 August 1997, 16.

16. *Liubimyi kloun: Iubileinyi al'manakh* (Moscow: Znanie, 1997), 3.

17. Igor' Kio, *Illiuzii bez illiuzii* (Moscow: Vagrius, 1999), 113.

18. Williams, "All of Russia Grieves for Beloved Comic," A20.

19. Valeria Korchagina, "Moscow Fans Shed Tears for a Clown," *Moscow Times*, 26 August 1997.

20. The English equestrian performer J. Bates was the first to tour Russia in 1764, though he appeared without the other performers featured in Astley's and Hughes's productions. M. Wilson Disher, *Fairs, Circuses and Music Halls* (London: William Collins, 1942); A. H. Saxon, *Enter Foot and Horse: A History of Hippodrama in England and France* (New Haven, CT: Yale University Press, 1968), 10–12; Antony D. Hippisley Coxe, "Equestrian Drama and the Circus," in *Performance and Politics in Popular Drama: Aspects of Popular Entertainment in Theatre, Film, and Television, 1800–1976*, ed. David Bradby, Louis James, and Bernard Sharratt (New York: Cambridge University Press, 1980); George Speaight, *A History of the Circus* (San Diego: A.S. Barnes and Company, 1980), 31–38, 155; Robert Leach, *Revolutionary Theatre* (New York: Routledge, 1994), 4; Helen Stoddart, *Rings of Desire: Circus History and Representation* (Manchester: Manchester University Press, 2000), 15–16; M. E. Shvydkoi, ed., *Tsirkovoe iskusstvo Rossii: Entsiklopediia* (Moscow: Bol'shaia Rossiiskaia entsiklopediia, 2000), 270; Donna Gustafson, "Images from the World Between: The Circus in Twentieth-Century American Art," in *Images from the World Between: The Circus in Twentieth-Century American Art*, ed. Donna Gustafson (Cambridge, MA, and New York: MIT Press and American Federation of Arts, 2001), 11; Marius Kwint, "The Circus and Nature in Late Georgian England," in *Histories of Leisure*, ed. Rudy Koshar (New York: Berg, 2002).

21. Speaight, *A History of the Circus*, 155; Stoddart, *Rings of Desire*, 15–16.

22. Rossiiskii gosudarstvennyi arkhiv literatury i iskusstva (Russian State Archive of Literature and Art) [hereafter RGALI], f. 2607, op. 1, d. 103, l. 68; "Coronation of the Czar," *New York Times*, 5 April 1896, 4.

23. RGALI, f. 2607, op. 1, d. 103, ll. 65–73; Iu. A. Dmitriev, *Russkii Tsirk* (Moscow: Iskusstvo, 1953); Iu. A. Dmitriev, *100 let Moskovskomu ordena Lenina gosudarstvennomu tsirku na Tsvetnom Bul'vare* (Moscow: Vsesoiuznoe biuro propagandy sovetskogo tsirkovogo isksusstva, 1980); Iu. A. Dmitriev, "Samorodki, k 100 letiiu pervogo Russkogo statsionarnogo tsirka," *Sovetskaia estrada i tsirk* 9 (1973): 18–21.

24. Sergei Eisenstein quoted in Leach, *Revolutionary Theatre*, 4.

25. Sergei Iosipovitch Yutkevitch, "Teenage Artists of the Revolution," in *Cinema in Revolution: The Heroic Era of Soviet Film*, ed. Luda Schnitzer, Jean Schnitzer, and Marcel Martin, trans. David Robinson (New York: Hill and Wang, 1973), 29.

26. Aleksandr Benois quoted in Leach, *Revolutionary Theatre*, 5.

27. Aleksandr Kuprin quoted in E. M. Gortinskii, *Tovarishch Tsirk* (Moscow: Sovetskaia Rossiia, 1985), 15.

28. Aleksandr Kuprin, "The White Poodle," in *The Garnet Bracelet and Other Stories*, trans. Stepan Apresyan (Moscow: Foreign Languages Publishing House, 1962), 227–28.

29. Anton Chekhov, "Kashtanka," in *The Essential Tales of Chekhov*, ed. Richard Ford, trans. Constance Garnett (Hopewell, NJ: Ecco Press, 1998).

30. Yuri Olesha, *The Three Fat Men*, trans. Fainna Glagoleva (Moscow: Foreign Languages Publishing House, 1960).

31. Yuri Olesha, *No Day Without a Line: From Notebooks by Yuri Olesha*, ed. and trans. Judson Rosengrant (Evanston, IL: Northwestern University Press, 1998), 71.

32. Ibid., 73.

33. "Dekret ob"edinenii teatral'nogo dela," *Vestnik teatra* 33 (1919): 2; Gosudarstvennyi arkhiv Rossiiskoi Federatsii (State Archive of the Russian Federation) [hereafter GARF], f. 2306, op. 24, d. 79.

34. On the history of the theater department, see Leach, *Revolutionary Theatre*, 25–29.

35. N. Z. M., "2-i Gosudarstvennyi tsirk. Otkrytie sezona," *Vestnik teatra* 36 (1919): 12; "Otkrytie pervogo Gosudarstvennogo tsirka," *Vestnik teatra* 70 (1920): 14.

36. "Tsirki na mestakh," *Vestnik teatra* 78 (1921); Shvydkoi, *Tsirkovoe iskusstvo Rossii*, 400.

37. As Richard Taylor writes, "the Soviet government was . . . faced with more urgent political and economic tasks than the organization of cinema for propaganda purposes and it was not until December 1922 that the industry was centrally organized, first into Goskino and then, two years later, into Sovkino." Richard Taylor, "A 'Cinema for the Millions': Soviet Socialist Realism and the Problem of Film Comedy," *Journal of Contemporary History* 18 (1983): 445.

38. GARF, f. 2306, op. 69, d. 504, l. 2; "Khronologiia gostsirkov," *Tsirk i estrada* 3–4 (1928): 1.

39. M. Khrapchenko, "Dvadtsat' let sovetskogo tsirka," *Pravda*, 23 November 1939, 4.

40. V. Ermans, "Pervaia programma, otkrytie sezona v Moskovskom gostsirke," *Sovetskoe iskusstvo*, 9 October 1939, 4.

41. RGALI, f. 2499, op. 1, d. 23, l. 3.

42. Ibid.; RGALI, f. 2499, op. 1, d. 65, l. 20.

43. Central Statistical Board of the U.S.S.R. Council of Ministers, *Cultural Progress in the U.S.S.R.: Statistical Returns* (Moscow: Foreign Language Publishing House, 1958).

44. RGALI, f. 2499, op. 2, d. 29, l. 5.

45. Laurens van der Post, *Journey into Russia* (Covelo, CA: Island Press, 1964), 38.

46. Ibid.

47. Ibid., 39.

48. RGALI, f. 2499, op. 2, d. 81, l. 11.

49. RGALI, f. 2499, op. 2, d. 13, l. 21.

50. Richard F. Janssen, "The Soviet Circus Has Flash & Style—And Makes Money; For Deeper Meanings, Check Antics of Comrade Clown and Risks of Lion Tamers," *Wall Street Journal*, 1 November 1974, 1; "Ot s"ezda k s"ezdu," *Sovetskaia estrada i tsirk* 2 (1976): 2.

51. "Tol'ko tsifry," *Sovetskaia kul'tura*, 18 September 1979, 4.

52. Iu. Nikulin, "Aplodismentov ne budet," *Pravda*, 24 April 1986, 6.

53. I. I. Zheltov, "O tsirke, nasha anketa," *Tsirk* 3 (1925): 5.

54. "Sovetskii Tsirk v Irane," *Vechernaia moskva*, 12 December 1945, 3; Rossiiskii gosudarstvennyi arkhiv sotsial'no-politicheskoi istorii (Russian State Archive of Social and Political History) [hereafter RGASPI], f. 17, op. 125, d. 371, ll. 179–81; Robert Trumbull, "Soviet Bombards India with Arts," *New York Times*, 5 January 1954, 3.

55. F. G. Bardian, "Zadachi rabotnikov Soiuzgostsirka v svete reshenii XXI s"ezda KPSS," *Sovetskii tsirk* 6 (1959): 13.

56. "Circus Alive Abroad," *Washington Post*, 22 July 1956, H4.

57. Zhorzh Soria, "Eti gastroli nadolgo ostanutsia v pamiat parizhan," *Sovetskaia kul'tura*, 14 April 1956, 4; G. Agadzhanov, "Novye zriteli—novye druz'ia," *Sovetskaia kul'tura*, 21 July 1956, 4.

58. G. Agadzhanov, "Novye zriteli—novye druz'ia," 4; Speaight, *A History of the Circus*, 165–67.

59. Dorothy Kilgallen, "Popvo [sic] has Circus Men Popping Off," *Washington Post*, 13 July 1963, A9.

60. Gustafson, "Images from the World Between," 74; Janet Davis, *The Circus Age: Culture & Society under the American Big Top* (Chapel Hill: University of North Carolina Press, 2002); Marcello Truzzi, "The Decline of the American Circus," in *Sociology and Everyday Life*, ed. Marcello Truzzi (Englewood Cliffs, NJ: Prentice-Hall, 1981).

61. RGALI, f. 2499, op. 2, d. 9, l. 3; Vincent Canby, "Moscow Circus Whirls Into Garden; Horsemen, Clowns and Acrobats Are Delight," *New York Times*, 5 October 1967, 44; "Moscow Circus to Open Tour of Eastern Cities on Nov. 14," *New York Times*, 20 October 1972, 2; Andrew L. Yarrow, "Moscow Circus to Tour America after 10 Years," *New York Times*, 10 March 1988, C26; "Moscow Circus Tour Includes 26 Cities," *New York Times*, 22 August 1989, C6.

62. Richard F. Shepard, "The Ebullient Moscow Circus Arrives, but Apprehensively," *New York Times*, 4 October 1964, 42.

63. In her study of an early twentieth-century circus in Dresden, Marline Otte observes: "Whereas theatrical entertainment increasingly fragmented into a series of class-specific genres, circus audiences came much closer to representing a microcosm of German society at large. For decades, circus shows had attracted members of the court, the nobility and the military, but also men and women of the middle and lower classes (including peasants)." Otte attributes the popularity of circus acts to their "multiple meanings" and concludes that, "for decades, circus acts retained their ambivalent essence because doing so allowed them to speak to highly diverse audiences." Marline Otte, "Sarrasani's Theatre of the World: Monumental Circus Entertainment in Dresden, from Kaiserreich to Third Reich," *German History* 17, no. 4 (1999): 530, 540, 541. Ernest Albrecht similarly explains that in its golden age at the turn of the twentieth century, the circus in the United States "was welcomed by every level of society. For the newly arrived the performances of their countrymen gave them a sense of pride. For second- and third-generation Americans . . . the circus offered nothing more subversive than an irresistible collection of eye-popping oddities. And for fundamentalists who saw entertainment as morally corrupt, the circus's attractions were sold as educational displays." Ernest Albrecht, *The New American Circus* (Gainesville: University of Florida Press, 1995), 2.

64. Ellen Handy refers to the circus as a "theatre of contradictions" in her study of the diversity of photographic representations of the circus. She attributes "the disparate visions of its many visual interpreters" to the properties of the circus itself, which is "a hybrid and episodic entertainment or spectacle evolved from a variety of ancient forms." Ellen Handy, "Photographing 'The splendidest sight that ever was': Cruelty, Alienation, and the Grotesque in the Shadow of the Big Top," in Gustafson, *Images from the World Between*, 92.

65. Stoddart explains that "in political terms, circus as a dramatic form is neither necessarily radical or reactionary; its language of 'show', having absorbed and adapted numerous cultural and historical traditions has proved open to widely differing ideological inflections." She also observes in the circus "latent, and usually highly ambiguous, political implications not only at the level of aesthetics . . . but in their content as well." Stoddart, *Rings of Desire*, 84–85, 97.

66. In 1935 at the All-Soviet Conference of the Stakhanovites, Joseph Stalin declared: "Life has become better, comrades. Life has become more joyous." J. V. Stalin, *Problems of Leninism* (Peking: Foreign Languages Press, 1976), 775–94.

67. Brenda Assael, *The Circus and Victorian Society* (Charlottesville: University of Virginia Press, 2005).

68. Ibid.; Davis, *The Circus Age*; Gregory J. Renoff, *The Big Tent: The Traveling Circus in Georgia, 1820–1930* (Athens: University of Georgia Press, 2008).

69. Various writers attest to the prevalence of this position immediately after the revolution without naming individual adherents to this view, which was not explicitly articulated in the press. A. V. Lunacharskii, "Zadacha obnovlennogo tsirka," *Vestnik teatra* 3 (1919): 5; RGALI, f. 2742, op. 3, d. 93, l. 2; Iu. A. Dmitriev, *Tsirk v Rossii, Ot istokov do 2000 goda* (Moscow: Rossiiskaia politicheskaia entsiklopediia, 2004), 295; Richard Stites, *Russian Popular Culture: Entertainment and Society since 1900* (New York: Cambridge University Press, 1992), 51.

70. V. Ardov, "O tsirke voobshche i pervom gostsirke v chastnosti," *Rabochii Zritel'* 7 (1924): 7; Fedor Bogorodskii, "O tsirke," *Novyi zritel'* 36 (1924): 3–4; B. Aliakritskii, Em. Artem'ev, I. Kovrov, "Diskussiia, polemika o tsirke," *Novyi zritel'* 39 (1924): 24; A. Lunacharskaia, "Na putiakh k novomu zriteliu," *Tsirk* 11 (1927): 1; James Von Geldern, *Bolshevik Festivals, 1917–1920* (Berkeley: University of California Press, 1993), 114; David Lewis Hammarstrom, *Circus Rings Around Russia* (Hamden: Archon Books, 1983), 100–108.

71. Assael, *The Circus and Victorian Society*, 1.

72. Peta Tait, *Circus Bodies: Cultural Identity in Aerial Performance* (New York: Routledge, 2005), 13.

73. Stoddart explains that "the circus . . . plays out these dynamics of human exceptionalism and descent within the range of standard acts which include at one end the gravity-defying grace and strength of the aerialists and high-wire acts and, at the other, the clumsy, pie-flinging, barbarous clowns." Stoddart, *Rings of Desire*, 5.

74. Dankman, "Sovetskii i zapadnyi Tsirk," *Tsirk* 10 (1927): 1.

75. Davis, *The Circus Age*, 12.

76. Peta Tait, "Feminine Free Fall: A Fantasy of Freedom," *Theatre Journal* 48 (1996): 28.

77. Ibid., 29.

78. Ibid., 32.

79. For an interpretation of the circus that posits a "general theory of the circus as a specific language" with a constant cultural function, see Paul Bouissac, *Circus and Culture: A Semiotic Approach* (Bloomington: Indiana University Press, 1976), 10.

80. Choi Chatterjee and Karen Petrone, "Models of Selfhood and Subjectivity: The Soviet Case in Historical Perspective," *Slavic Review* 67 (Winter 2008): 967–86.

81. As Kristin Roth-Ey explains: "Entertainment—or, as it was usually defined in context, *otdykh* (relaxation)—was, along with mobilization and education, a bedrock principle of Soviet culture. . . . When Soviet audiences . . . registered their demands for entertainment, they were operating within, not outside, the ideological framework for Soviet culture." Kristin Roth-Ey, "Mass Media and the Remaking of Soviet Culture, 1950s–1960s" (PhD diss., Princeton University, 2003), 37.

Chapter 1. The Circus Turned Upside Up

1. G. D. Endzinoi, "Narodnyi shut (Al'bom Vitaliia Lazarenko)," in *Vstrechi s proshlym: Sbornik materialov TsGALI*, vol. 1 (Moscow: Sovetskaia Rossiia, 1983), 174. On Lazarenko, see "Gallereia Samorodkov," *Zritel'* 2 (1922): 12–15; *Tridtsatipiatiletnii iubilei Vitaliia Efimovicha Lazarenko* (Moscow: Mosoblit, 1933); Iu. Dmitriev, "Vitalii Lazarenko, k 40-letiiu artisticheskoi deiatel'nosti," *Sovetskoe iskusstvo*, 16 February 1939, 2; Mikh. Dolgopolov, "Sorok let na arene tsirka," *Izvestiia*, 15 February 1939, 4; G. V. Aleksandrov, "Smotr dostizhenii sovetskogo tsirka," *Pravda*, 24 March 1945, 4; A. Argo, "Zhizn' na arene," *Sovetskii tsirk* 2 (1957): 16–18; RGALI, f. 2499, op. 2, d. 297, l. 118; Evgenii Leonov, "Staryi tsirk spravliaet iubilei," *Literaturnaia gazeta*, 12 November 1980, 8; R. Slavskii, *Vitalii Lazarenko* (Moscow: Iskusstvo, 1980); Endzinoi, "Narodnyi shut (Al'bom Vitaliia Lazarenko)"; S. M. Makarov, *Klounada mirovogo tsirka: Istoriia i repertuar* (Moscow: Rosspen, 2001), 65–75.

2. Iu. Dmitriev, *Sovetskii tsirk, ocherk istorii, 1917–1941* (Moscow: Iskusstvo, 1963), 64–65.

3. Ibid., 65.

4. As Richard Stites explains, at the time of the revolution, "a whole array of new symbols and rituals were introduced and infused with anti-capitalism, the collective spirit, atheism, and machine worship. Bolshevik artists and propagandists went to the people with a culture for the people and in doing so they tried to combine the new with the old, self-consciously infusing circus, fair-booth, *lubok*, folk ditties, songs and dances with revolutionary content." Stites, *Russian Popular Culture*, 39. See also Peter Kenez, *The Birth of the Propaganda State: Soviet Methods of Mass Mobilization, 1917–1929* (New York: Cambridge University Press, 1985), 95–118; James Von Geldern, *Bolshevik Festivals, 1917–1920* (Berkeley: University of California Press, 1993); Richard Taylor, *Film Propaganda: Soviet Russia and Nazi Germany* (New York: Harper & Row, 1979), 44–50.

5. The Soviet circus provides a historical example of Stoddart's theoretical claim that circus "goes further than other forms of live art to mobilize physical energies and sensations which fundamentally resist inscription within film and literary language. Not only has it predominantly side-stepped (if only opportunistically) linguistic language for mime, music and physical stunts, it has also traditionally avoided arranging its acts in any kind of narrative form and has favoured restless, itinerant and temporary structures." Stoddart, *Rings of Desire*, 5.

6. Unlike the administrators of the Soviet film industry, who, as Denise Youngblood explains, offered audiences films that were either popular, entertaining, and bourgeois, or unpopular, educational, and revolutionary, circus producers resolved the "entertainment or enlightenment debate" during NEP, by creating popular, entertaining, bourgeois spectacles that they claimed were

educational and revolutionary. As such, the Bolsheviks' production of the circus can also be understood as an attempt to compete with such NEP-era entertainments as American films, whose "success," according to Jeffrey Brooks, "was most of all a result of the Bolsheviks' failure to create a viable alternative. On one level, this was a failure to entertain an audience, but on another, more serious level, it signified the larger tragedy of the revolutionaries' inability to translate their goals into popular imagery and popular language." Denise J. Youngblood, *Movies for the Masses: Popular Cinema and Soviet Society in the 1920s* (Cambridge: Cambridge University Press, 1992), 48; Jeffrey Brooks, "The Press and Its Message: Images of America in the 1920s and 1930s," in *Russia in the Era of NEP: Explorations in Soviet Society and Culture*, ed. Sheila Fitzpatrick, Alexander Rabinowitch, and Richard Stites (Bloomington: Indiana University Press, 1991), 237.

7. Von Geldern, *Bolshevik Festivals*; Stites, *Russian Popular Culture*; Kenez, *The Birth of the Propaganda State*.

8. Stites explains that "the people" were "ready to accept the new plots about revolutionary struggles," but they scorned stylistic novelty or experimentation in favor of linear narrative, positive heroes, and realism." Stites, *Russian Popular Culture*, 42.

9. Otte, "Sarrasani's Theatre of the World," 538–42.

10. "Dekret ob"edinenii teatral'nogo dela," *Vestnik teatra* 33 (1919): 2; Gosudarstvennyi Arkhiv Rossiiskoi Federatsii (State Archive of the Russian Federation) [hereafter GARF], f. 2306, op. 24, d. 79.

11. "Tsirk," *Vestnik teatra* 39 (1919): 13.

12. Ibid.

13. Ibid.; Von Geldern, *Bolshevik Festivals*, 118.

14. S. Konenkov, "V dvadtsatom godu," *Sovetskii tsirk* 2 (1957): 15.

15. A. V. Lunacharskii, "Na novykh putiakh, Konenkov dlia tsirka," *Vestnik teatra* 44 (1919): 6.

16. Ibid.

17. Ibid., 7.

18. Maksimilian Nemchinskii, *Tsirk Rossii naperegonki so vremenem: Modeli tsirkovykh spektaklei, 1920–1990kh godov* (Moscow: GITIS, 2001), 37.

19. Ibid., 39.

20. Ibid., 40–50; "Reorganizatsiia tsirkov," *Vestnik teatra* 63 (1920): 7–8.

21. According to Lazarenko, Maiakovskii solicited his input as he completed drafts of "Championship," which was written specifically for Lazarenko. Vitalii Lazarenko, "Vitalii Lazarenko, Kloun-prygun," in *Sovetskii tsirk, 1918–1938*, ed. Evgenii Kuznetsov (Moscow: Iskusstvo, 1938), 122. For the complete text in translation, see Frantisek Deak and Vladimir Mayakovsky, "The Championship of the Universal Class Struggle," *The Drama Review: TDR* 17, no. 1 (1973): 53–63. For excerpts of the original and a description of the performance, see Dmitriev, *Sovetskii tsirk*, 61–62.

22. Dmitriev, *Sovetskii tsirk*, 62.

23. "Riding Lesson" skits were performed in the circus ring at least as early as the 1890s and remained an occasional feature of the Soviet show through the 1950s. V. E. Ferroni, *200 let na manezhe* (Moscow: Dizain-studiia, 1997), 63.

24. Dmitriev, *Sovetskii tsirk*, 44.

25. Ibid., 45.

26. "Gallereia Samorodkov," 12–15; *Tridtsatipiatiletnii iubilei Vitaliia Efimovicha Lazarenko* (Moscow: Mosoblit, 1933); Dmitriev, "Vitalii Lazarenko," 2; Dolgopolov, "Sorok let na arene tsirka," 4; Aleksandrov, "Smotr dostizhenii sovetskogo tsirka," 4; Argo, "Zhizn' na arene," 16–18; RGALI, f. 2499, op. 2, d. 297, l. 118; Leonov, "Staryi tsirk spravliaet iubilei," 8; Slavskii, *Vitalii Lazarenko*; Endzinoi, "Narodnyi shut (Al'bom Vitaliia Lazarenko)"; Makarov, *Klounada mirovogo tsirka*, 65–75.

27. One of the most influential clowning genres was that of the white-faced clown, whose origins lie in the seventeenth-century *commedia dell'arte*. Following the example of three French farce players who powdered their faces with flour (they are said to have been bakers by trade), actors depicting the *commedia* characters Pedrolino, Gilles, and Pierrot also began to whiten their faces. English pantomime and acrobatic clowns, most famously Joseph Grimaldi, who performed in London's variety theaters at the beginning of the nineteenth century, popularized this practice, which eventually became the mark of a discrete clown type. Although Russian clowns almost certainly imported from the West the whiteface persona, which they called simply *belyi* (white), Russia itself may have been the birthplace of the *ryzhii*—a native clown persona whose appearance predated that of the European august. By the 1870s, the evolution of the *ryzhii* had begun to parallel that of the Western buffoon, and the two personas eventually became indistinguishable, especially after the *ryzhii* began to perform as the comic counterpart of the *belyi* in the Russian ring. For a colorful history of the *commedia dell'arte* including a catalogue of characters and actors who performed them, see Nicoll Allardyce, *Masks, Mimes, and Miracles: Studies in the Popular Theatre* (New York: Cooper Square Publishers, 1963), 214–379; on the pairing of the whiteface clown and the red-headed august, see John H. Towsen, *Clowns* (New York: Hawthorn Books, 1976), 214–23, 310–11.

28. Ibid., 159.

29. Vitalii Lazarenko, "Vitalii Lazarenko, Kloun-prygun," in *Sovetskii tsirk, 1918–1938*, ed. Evgenii Kuznetsov (Moscow, Iskusstvo, 1938), 106.

30. Ibid., 107.

31. Ibid., 117.

32. A. V. Lunacharskii, "Budem smeiat'sia," *Vestnik teatra* 58 (1920): 7–8.

33. A. V. Lunacharskii, "Zadacha obnovlennogo tsirka," *Vestnik teatra* 3 (1919): 5–6.

34. Lazarenko, "Vitalii Lazarenko, Kloun-prygun," 117.

35. Stites, *Russian Popular Culture*, 39, 51–52.

36. Von Geldern, *Bolshevik Festivals*, 119. Von Geldern ends his account in 1921, before the policy of replacing varied circus acts with narrative pantomimes was reversed.

37. Circus performers including Lazarenko, Leon Tanti, and the clown Serzh were temporarily appointed to the Circus Sections' Artistic Council of the Moscow State Circuses, whose members were removed. "V tsirkakh," *Vestnik teatra* 76–77 (1920): 23.

38. Ibid.

39. Nemchinskii, *Tsirk Rossii*, 58.

40. For this and other examples, see Nemchinskii, *Tsirk Rossii*, 332–51, 372–83.

41. GARF, f. 2312, op. 6, d. 6, l. 2.

42. V. Zh-i., "Tsirk. Otkrytie pervogo gostsirka," *Zrelishche* 8 (1922): 25.

43. G. Noks, "Tsirk. Vo vtorom gosudarstvennom," *Zrelishche* 13 (1922): 20.

44. Sergei Sokolov, "Za sovetizatsiiu tsirka," *Tsirk i estrada* 14 (1929): 8.

45. Ibid.

46. K. Finikov, "Tsirk konservativen (golos Rabochego Zritelia)," *Tsirk i estrada* 20–21 (1929): 5.

47. A. V. Lunacharskii, "Piat' let Gosudarstvennykh tsirkov," *Tsirk* 3 (1925): 3.

48. In his study of journalism during the "NEP mass enlightenment project," Matthew Lenoe observes that newspapermen often used the phrase "closer to the masses" as "code" for the task of improving the press and using it "more effectively to influence the masses." Matthew Lenoe, *Closer to the Masses: Stalinist Culture, Social Revolution, and Soviet Newspapers* (Cambridge, MA: Harvard University Press, 2004), 27.

49. Lunacharskii, "Piat' let Gosudarstvennykh Tsirkov," 3.

50. Moris Gorei, "Tsirk Frantsuzkii i Russkii," *Tsirk* 8 (1928): 2.

51. Ibid.

52. Vladimir Durov, "Proekt shkoly tsirka," *Vestnik teatra* 24 (1919): 4.

53. Ibid.

54. V. L. Durov, *My Circus Animals*, trans. John Cournos (New York: Houghton Mifflin, 1936), 73–75.

55. Ibid.

56. Karl Krane, "Sekrety ukrotitelia," *Tsirk* 6 (1926): 11.

57. Ibid.

58. Ibid.

59. A. V. Lunacharskii, "Rebenok i tsirk," *Tsirk* 3 (1925): 10.

60. Ibid.

61. Sotnik, "Tsirk i trud," *Tsirk* 5 (1925): 10.

62. Ibid.

63. V. V. Shvetsov, "Mysli o tsirke," *Tsirk* 6 (1925): 6–7.

64. A. M. Dankman, "To-Ramo," *Tsirk* 1 (1926): 8.

65. To-Ramo in A. M. Dankman, "To-Ramo," 8.

66. Ibid. See also To-Ramo, "Kak Ia pobedil sebia," *Tsirk* 4 (1926): 8; "To-Ramo o svoikh opytakh," *Tsirk* 4 (1926): 8; N. Rukavishnikov, "Vos'moi god Sovetskogo tsirka," *Tsirk* 5 (1926): 1.

67. Izmail Urazov, *Fakiry* (Moscow: Tea-kino-pechat', 1928), 5.

68. Ibid., 8–12.

69. Ibid., 31.

70. "Chrevoveshchateli," *Tsirk* 8 (1927): 11.

71. Ibid.

72. "Tsirk massam—sintez tsirka," *Tsirk* 9 (1925): 6.

73. "Gallereia Samorodkov," 13.

74. Aleksandr Kuprin, "In the Circus," in *Sentimental Romance and Other Stories*, trans. S. E. Berkenblit (New York: Pageant Press, 1969), 71–72.

75. Ibid., 77.

76. "Gallereia Samorodkov," 12–15; B. Eder, "Moi tvorcheskii put'," *Sovetskoe iskusstvo*, 18 November 1939, 3; I. S. Radunskii, *Zapiski starogo klouna*, ed. Iu. A. Dmitriev (Moscow: Iskusstvo, 1954), 23–27; Emil' Kio, *Fokusy i fokusniki*, ed. Iu. A. Dmitriev (Moscow: Iskusstvo, 1958), 23, 66; Zoia Kokh, *Vsia zhizn' v tsirke* (Moscow: Iskusstvo, 1963): 26–29.

77. "Sozdanie Tsirkacha—obshchestvennika," *Tsirk i estrada* 2 (1929): 1.

78. "Zametki na poliakh," *Tsirk i estrada* 2 (1928): 9.

79. Lunacharskii, "Zadacha obnovlennogo tsirka," 5.

80. GARF, f. 2306, op. 24, d. 79, l. 1.

81. Andrei Shibaev, "Nashi tsirki" *Rabochii zritel'* 31 (1924): 13.

82. Zheltov, "O tsirke," 5.

83. E. Magilevich, "O tsirke, nasha anketa," *Tsirk* 7 (1925): 9.

84. On studies of theater viewers, see Lars Kleberg, "The Nature of the Soviet Audience: Theatrical Ideology and Audience Research in the 1920s," in *Russian Theatre in the Age of Modernism*, ed. Robert Russell and Andrew Barratt (New York: St. Martin's Press, 1990); on film reception, see Yuri Tsivian, *Early Cinema in Russia and its Cultural Reception*, ed. Richard Taylor, trans. Alan Bodger (New York: Routledge, 1994); on studies of newspaper readers, see Lenoe, *Closer to the Masses*, 70–100. On the changing composition of American circus audiences, see Mark Irwin West, "A Spectrum of Spectators: Circus Audiences in Nineteenth-Century America," *Journal of Social History* 15, no. 2 (1981): 265–70.

85. A. V. Lunacharskii, "Shkolnaia anketa," *Tsirk* 5 (1925): 5.

86. Ibid.

87. Lunacharskii, "Zadacha obnovlennogo tsirka," 5.

88. Lunacharskii, "Shkolnaia anketa," 5.

89. Ibid.

90. Issledovatel'skaia teatral'naia masterskaia, "Zritel' tsirka," *Sovetskoe iskusstvo*, August 1927, 58.

91. Ibid.

92. Ibid., 59, ellipses in original.
93. Issledovatel'skaia, "Zritel' Tul'skogo tsirka," 54.
94. Ibid.
95. Ibid.
96. Ibid.
97. Ibid., 55.

Chapter 2. The Great Transformation of the Stalin-Era Circus

1. Richard Janssen observed that "the audience applauds tumblers who flub and try again with even more fervor than it applauds those who make it look easy," a phenomenon I have witnessed on two occasions. Janssen, "The Soviet Circus Has Flash & Style," 1.

2. As Douglas Weiner explains, "Many politically active Soviets viewed nature as an obstacle to socialist construction that had to be conquered. . . . Nature was portrayed almost as a consciously antisocialist force which needed to be suppressed. . . . The prescription offered was enticing: nature had to be transformed and bent to human will—from the roots up. Almost imperceptibly, from a multitude of disparate sources in the media and politics, a new slogan became colloquial: 'the great transformation of nature.'" Douglas R. Weiner, *Models of Nature: Ecology, Conservation, and Cultural Revolution in Soviet Russia* (Bloomington: Indiana University Press, 1988), 168–69.

3. Katerina Clark, "Little Heroes and Big Deeds: Literature Responds to the First Five-Year Plan," in *Cultural Revolution in Russia*, ed. Sheila Fitzpatrick (Bloomington: Indiana University Press, 1978).

4. RGALI, f. 2663 op. 1 d. 109, l. 9.

5. RGALI, f. 2663 op. 1 d. 109, ll. 131, emphasis in original.

6. Ibid., 140.

7. For a description of "Makhnovshchina," see Nemchinskii, *Tsirk Rossii*, 63; Dmitriev, *Tsirk v Rossii: Ot istokov do 1917 godov* (Moscow: Iskusstvo, 1977), 403–5.

8. RGALI, f. 335, op. 5, d. 42, l. 3.

9. Dmitriev, *Tsirk v Rossii: Ot istokov do 1917 godov*, 407.

10. I. Urazov, "Moskva Gorit' v tsirke," *Tsirk i estrada* 12 (1930): 6.

11. M. Rafail, "Sotsialisticheskoe vospitanie novogo cheloveka," *Zhizn' iskusstva* 25 (1929): 1.

12. F. G. Bardian, "Proverka khoda sots. sorevnovaniia," *Tsirk i estrada* 8 (1930): 2–3.

13. "Tsirk i Estrada—Udarnye formy zrelishchnogo iskusstva," *Tsirk i estrada* 7 (1930): 1.

14. RGALI, f. 2663, op. 1, d. 1091. 10.

15. RGALI, f. 645, op. 1, d. 31, ll. 6–10.

16. Gorei, "Tsirk Frantsuzkii," 2.

17. RGALI, f. 2663, op. 1, d. 104, ll. 38.

18. RGALI, f. 2742, op. 2, d. 90, l. 19.

19. RGALI, f. 2663, op. 1, d. 109, ll. 59–66.

20. Toby Clark, "The 'New Man's' Body: A Motif in Early Soviet Culture," in *Art of the Soviets: Painting, Sculpture, and Architecture in a One-Party State, 1917–1992*, ed. Matthew Cullerne Brown and Brandon Taylor (Manchester: Manchester University Press, 1993), 40.

21. RGALI, f. 2663, op. 1, d. 109, l. 5.

22. RGALI, f. 2663, op. 1, d. 109, ll. 11–13, 26.

23. Ibid., l. 28.

24. Yury Olesha, "We Are in the Center of Town," in *Complete Short Stories and "Three Fat Men,"* trans. Aimee Anderson (Ann Arbor: Ardis, 1979), 120, 121.

25. Ibid., 121.

26. Kwint, "The Circus and Nature," 56–57.

27. Stoddart, *Rings of Desire*, 35.

28. Otte, "Sarrasani's Theater of the World," 529.

29. RGALI, f. 2607, op. 1, d. 761. 20.

30. Sim. Dreiden, "Tsirk pod vodoi," *Zhizn' iskusstva* 17 (1929): 13.

31. *Tsirk pod vodoi (Chernyi pirat)* (Leningrad: Teakinopechat', 1929), 1–8.

32. Dreiden, "Tsirk pod vodoi," 13.

33. "Tezisnyi doklad upravliaiushchego gostsirkami RSFSR tov. A.M. Dankmana na plenum Ts. K. Vserabisa 25 maia 1930 goda," in *Sostoianie i perspektivy razvitiia tsirkovogo i estradnogo dela v SSSR* (Moscow: Izdanie TsUGTs, 1930), 8–9.

34. M. Nemchinskii, *Raisa Nemchinskaia* (Moscow: Iskusstvo, 1979), 46–47.

35. Ibid.

36. See this book's epigraph for a detailed description of this event.

37. Durov, *My Circus Animals*, 19.

38. RGALI, f. 2499, op. 1 d. 436, l. 2.

39. RGALI, f. 2499, op. 1, d. 436, ll. 6.

40. RGALI, f. 2499, op. 1, d. 436, ll. 4–6.

41. Mikh. Begliarov, "Provintsial'nye bolezni (Golos rabochego zritelia)," *Tsirk i estrada* 74 (1930): 6.

42. "Konferentsiia o Tsirke," *Tsirk i estrada* 12 (1930): 3.

43. B. K., "Bol'she ideinosti, vyshe kachestvo (Konferentsiia rabochego zritelia)," *Sovetskoe iskusstvo*, 21 May 1932, 4.

44. GARF, f. a406, op. 1, d. 1237, ll. 89–90.

45. N. Oruzheinikov, "K chistke apparata GOMETs," *Sovetskoe iskusstvo*, 2 February 1932, 4.

46. "TsUGTs pered Leningradskom oblastnym sovetom po delam iskusstva," *Zhizn' iskusstva* 12 (1929): 4.

47. Oruzheinikov, "K chistke apparata GOMETs," 4.

48. Rabochaia brigada po chistke tsirkovogo upravleniia, "Shest' nomerov na stolakh," *Sovetskoe iskusstvo*, 3 March 1932, 4.

49. "Obezlishennoe upravlenie," *Sovetskoe iskusstvo*, 3 March 1932, 4.

50. "Shest' nomerov," 4.

51. B. K., "Bol'she ideinosti," 4.

52. M. Imas, "Novyi GOMETs, nakanune soveshchaniia rukovoditelei predpriiatii GOMETs," *Sovetskoe iskusstvo*, 3 December 1932, 1.

53. M. Arkh, "Nesostoiavshaiasia rekonstruktsiia, k itogam vsesoiuznoi konferentsii po tsirku," *Sovetskoe iskusstvo*, 2 January 1934, 4.

54. O. Kremnev, "Znakomaia programma," *Sovetskoe iskusstvo*, 5 October 1934, 4.

55. A. Nazarov, "Sovetskii tsirk, Otkrytie sezona v pervom gosudarstvennom tsirke," *Pravda*, 23 September 1936, 4.

56. For a thorough discussion of Soviet triumphalism in this period, see Karen Petrone, *Life Has Become More Joyous, Comrades: Celebrations in the Time of Stalin* (Bloomington: Indiana University Press, 2000).

57. A. Nazarov, "Sovetskii Tsirk," 4.

58. RGALI, f. 2499, op. 1, d. 2, l. 11.

59. "Liubimoe iskusstvo naroda," *Izvestiia*, 22 November 1939, 1.

60. E. Kuznetsov, "Revoliutsiia i tsirk," *Teatr* 1 (1938): 122.

61. Nazarov, "Sovetskii Tsirk," 4.

62. Viktor Ermans, "Tri pokoleniia novaia programma Gostsirka," *Sovetskoe iskusstvo*, 29 January 1937, 6.

63. S. Dikovskii, "Zimnii sezon v tsirke," *Pravda*, 3 October 1937, 4.

64. *Leningradskii Gostsirk, 1937–1938* (Leningrad: Lengorlit, 1937), 1.

65. Al. Al'evich, "Na arene molodezh', Novaia programma v Gostsirke," *Izvestiia*, 2 February 1938, 4.

66. Ibid.

67. Iu. Dmitriev, "Novyi tsirk," *Sovetskoe iskusstvo*, 30 January 1938, 2.

68. "Sovetskii Tsirk," *Sovetskoe iskusstvo*, 6 October 1938, 1.

69. Viktor Ermans, "Na arene molodye talanty, novaia programma v moskovskom tsirke," *Sovetskoe iskusstvo*, 2 February 1938, 4.

70. Al. Morov, "O tsirke," *Pravda*, 6 May 1938, 4.

71. Sheila Fitzpatrick, *The Cultural Front: Power and Culture in Revolutionary Russia* (Ithaca, NY: Cornell University Press, 1992), 11.

72. Ermans, "Na arene molodye talanty," 4.

73. L. Nikulin, "Torzhestvo Sovetskogo tsirka," *Pravda*, 20 November 1939, 2.

74. As Sheila Fitzpatrick explains, some of the *vydvizhentsy* "found themselves abruptly seconded to political and administrative jobs in 1937–1938, replacing Communist bureaucrats and managers who had fallen victim to the Great Purges." Fitzpatrick, *The Cultural Front*, 12.

75. V. Ermans, "Tsirk i Estrada na Vsesoiuznoi s.-kh. Vystavke," *Sovetskoe iskusstvo*, 9 August 1939, 4.

76. Khrapchenko, "Dvadtsat' let Sovetskogo tsirka," 4.

77. Ermans, "Dva pokoleniia," 4.

78. Vitalii Lazarenko, "Bol'shoi i radostnyi prazdnik," *Sovetskoe iskusstvo*, 18 November 1939, 3.

79. A. A. Dorokhov, *Moto-gonki po naklonnomu treku* (Leningrad: Vsesoiuznyi Komitet po delam iskusstv, 1939), 10.

80. Lazarenko, "Vitalii Lazarenko, Kloun-prygun," 118.

81. Dmitriev, "Vitalii Lazarenko," 2.

82. Mikhail N. Rumiantsev, *Karandash, Na arene Sovetskogo tsirka* (Moscow: Iskusstvo, 1977), 19, 20.

83. Ibid., 55.

84. Ibid., 51.

85. Tat'iana Tess, "Aktsent smeshnogo," *Izvestiia*, 22 November 1939, 4.

86. Rumiantsev, *Karandash*, 124.

87. Ibid., 82.

88. N. M. Rumiantseva, *Kloun i Vremia* (Moscow: Iskusstvo, 1989), 13.

89. Iurii Nikulin, *Desiat' trolleibusov klounov*, vol. 1 (Samara: Dom Pechati, 1993), 246.

Chapter 3. Roaring, Laughter

1. G. Aleksandrov, "Iskusstvo lovkosti i sily, Otkrytie sezona v Moskovskom tsirke," *Sovetskoe iskusstvo*, 11 September 1941, 3.

2. Stites, *Russian Popular Culture*, 98–116; Harlow Robinson, "Composing for Victory: Classical Music," in *Culture and Entertainment in Wartime Russia*, ed. Richard Stites (Bloomington: Indiana University Press, 1995), 62–76; Robert A. Rothstein, "Homeland, Home Town, and Battlefield: The Popular Song," in Stites, *Culture and Entertainment in Wartime Russia*, 77–94; Harold B. Segal, "Drama of Struggle: The Wartime Stage Repertoire," in Stites, *Culture and Entertainment in Wartime Russia*, 108–25; Argyrios K. Pisiotis, "Images of Hate in the Art of War," in Stites, *Culture and Entertainment in Wartime Russia*, 141–56; Peter Kenez, "Black and White: The War on Film," in Stites, *Culture and Entertainment in Wartime Russia*, 157–75; Deming Brown, "World War II in Soviet Literature," in *The Impact of World War II on the Soviet Union*, ed. Susan J. Linz (Totowa, NJ: Rowman & Allanheld, 1985), 243–51; Musya Glants, "Images of the War in Painting," in *World War 2 and the Soviet People*, ed. John Garrard and Carol Garrard (New York: St. Martin's Press, 1993), 98–124.

3. Evg. Kuznetsov, "V pervye dni voiny," *Sovetskoe iskusstvo*, 29 June 1941, 4.

4. RGALI, f. 2742, op. 3, d. 3, l. 62.

5. For example, Rosalinde Sartorti describes the 1925 May Day demonstrations that included the "Bolshevik" factory's display of an oversized pair of scissors that cut through the symbol of foreign capital, while the "First Lenin-State Mill" exhibited a windmill that ground up foreign statesmen. Two

years earlier, May Day celebrants encountered a man dressed as a Polish noble-
man, who "made the oddest movements" each time a worker tried to light the
large propane stove beneath the frying pan on which he stood. Sartorti provides further examples of such displays, which, she notes, Piotrovskii referred
to as "industrial metaphor," including a nail factory's hammering a nail into
the coffin of capitalism and a cigarette factory that labeled a gigantic smoldering
cigarette "fascism." Rosalinde Sartorti, "Stalinism and Carnival: Organisation
and Aesthetics of Political Holidays," in *The Culture of the Stalin Period*, ed. Hans
Günther (New York: St. Martin's Press, 1990), 54–55.

6. Oleg Popov, "My Hero," in *The Soviet Circus, A Collection of Articles*, ed.
Alexander Lipovsky, trans. Fainna Glagoleva (Moscow: Progress Publishers,
1967), 45–46.

7. Rumiantsev, *Karandash*, 108.

8. Ibid., 111–12.

9. W. H. Lawrence, "The Circus Moscow Sees," *New York Times*, 30 April
1944, SM 38.

10. I. Fink, "Vladimir Durov i Dem'ian Bednyi," *Sovetskaia estrada i tsirk* 5
(1974): 12–13.

11. Ibid.

12. Pisiotis, "Images of Hate in the Art of War," 143.

13. Fink, "Vladimir Durov i Dem'ian Bednyi," 12–13.

14. RGALI, f. 2499, op. 1, d. 152, ll. 18–25.

15. RGALI, f. 2499, op. 1, d. 152, l. 46.

16. Sartorti, "Stalinism and Carnival," 55–56.

17. Lunacharskii, "Budem smeiat'sia," 7–8.

18. Fink, "Vladimir Durov i Dem'ian Bednyi," 12–13.

19. Aleksandrov, "Iskusstvo lovkost i sily," 3.

20. Vladimir Poliakov, "Iumor na fronte," *Sovetskaia estrada i tsirk* 5 (1975):
6–7.

21. Sergei Makarov, "Eshche raz pro klounadu," *Sovetskaia estrada i tsirk* 2
(1975): 18.

22. Leon Harris, *The Moscow Circus School* (New York: Atheneum, 1970), 31.

23. Ol'ga Pozdneva, "Ukrotitel' leopardov, repetitsiia na arena," *Moskovskii
bol'shevik*, 2 February 1945, 4.

24. N. Strel'tsov, "Novoe v iskusstve tsirka," *Sovetskoe iskusstvo*, 8 March
1945, 3.

25. Ibid.

26. D. Rudnev, "Krug Smelosti, novaia programma v Leningradskom gosudarstvennom tsirke," *Pravda*, 4 February 1941, 6.

27. P. Venskii, "Zveri ukrotitelia Klichisa," *Vechernaia Moskva*, 19 July 1945, 4.

28. Dmitriev, "Novyi tsirk," 2.

29. D. Zaslavskii, "Tvorcheskii smotr v Moskovskom tsirke," *Trud*, 5 March
1946, 4.

30. Boris Eder, *Jungle Acrobats of the Russian Circus, Trained Animals in the Soviet Union*, trans. O. Gorchakov (New York: Robert McBride Co., 1958), 100–101.

31. Zaslavskii, "Tvorcheskii smotr v Moskovskom tsirke," 4.

32. "Prazdnik sovetskogo tsirka," *Moskovskii Bol'shevik*, 8 March 1946, 3.

33. RGALI, f. 2499, op. 1, d. 439, ll. 9–10.

34. RGALI, f. 2499, op. 1, d. 437, l. 101.

35. RGALI, f. 2499, op. 1, d. 437, ll. 43–45.

36. A. Roslavlev, "Na manezhe tsirka," *Vechernaia Moskva*, 17 March 1945, 3.

Chapter 4. Home Front

1. Elena Zubkova, *Russia After the War, Hopes, Illusions, and Disappointments, 1945–1957*, trans. Hugh Ragsdale (New York: M.E. Sharpe, 1998), 22; Margaret K. Stolee, "Homeless Children in the USSR, 1917–1957," *Soviet Studies* 40 (1988): 64–83; Donald Filtzer, "The Standard of Living of Soviet Industrial Workers in the Immediate Postwar Period, 1945–1948," *Europe-Asia Studies* 51 (1999): 1013–38.

2. As Sheila Fitzpatrick explains, "The members of the new Soviet elite of the 1930s strove for a 'cultured' way of life, were attentive to domestic comfort and consumer goods, and were concerned about social protocol and propriety." Although in the 1930s material rewards were "as yet available only to the few," the state promised that "when the building of socialism is completed, there will be abundance for all to share." Fitzpatrick, *The Cultural Front*, 217, 227. See also Jukka Gronow, *Caviar with Champagne: Common Luxury and the Ideals of the Good Life in Stalin's Russia* (New York: Berg, 2003).

3. Vera Dunham writes that in postwar fiction, "slowly, the paragon of the forward-striding communist took on a new form. Someone resembling a middleclass careerist replaced the revolutionary saint of the twenties and the party vigilante of the thirties. He appeared now in the form of a vigorous manager. He progressed rapidly in his career. He was content in his family life. He aspired to a private house and, perhaps, to a dacha. He drove his own private car." Vera Dunham, *In Stalin's Time: Middleclass Values in Soviet Fiction* (Durham, NC: Duke University Press, 1990), 18.

4. Vladimir Poliakov, *All Evening in the Ring . . .* (Moscow: Vneshtorgizdat, 1971), 15.

5. Harrison E. Salisbury, "Soviet Clowns Poke Fun at U.S. by Adding Wit to Kremlin's Line," *New York Times*, 20 April 1949, 1.

6. RGALI, f. 962, op. 23, d. 4, l. 68.

7. RGALI, f. 2499, op. 1, d. 44, ll. 20–21.

8. RGALI, f. 962, op. 23, d. 4, l. 74.

9. RGALI, f. 2499, op. 1, d. 447, ll. 81–87.

10. RGALI, f. 962, op. 23, d. 4, ll. 62–64.

11. RGALI, f. 2499, op. 1, d. 449, ll. 69–70.

12. RGALI, f. 2499, op. 1, d. 441, ll. 99–100.

13. Zubkova, *Russia After the War*, 43–44.

14. RGALI, f. 2499, op. 1, d. 446, ll. 32–33.

15. A. Viktorov, *S perom u Karandasha* (Moscow: Molodaia gvardiia, 1971), 87.

16. Salisbury, "Soviet Clowns Poke Fun at U.S.," 1.

17. RGALI, f. 962, op. 23, d. 4, ll. 30–32; Rumiantsev, *Karandash*, 111–12.

18. RGALI, f. 962, op. 23, d. 4, l. 64.

19. Salisbury, "Soviet Clowns Poke Fun at U.S.," 1.

20. RGALI, f. 962, op. 23, d. 4, ll. 30–32.

21. RGALI, f. 962, op. 23, d. 4, ll. 69–73.

22. RGALI, f. 2499, op. 1, d. 50, ll. 99–101.

23. Although Reid is concerned with the post-Stalin period, her conclusion can be applied to the earlier postwar period, since she posits the gendering of legitimacy claims during the Khrushchev period not as a change but as a continuation of past practices. Susan E. Reid, "Masters of the Earth: Gender and De-Stalinisation in Soviet Reformist Painting of the Khrushchev Thaw," *Gender & History* 11 (1999): 276–312.

24. Susan E. Reid, "Cold War in the Kitchen: Gender and the De-Stalinization of Consumer Taste in the Soviet Union under Khrushchev," *Slavic Review* 61 (2002): 221.

25. RGALI, f. 962, op. 23, d. 4, l. 16.

26. RGALI, f. 2499, op. 1, d. 440, l. 102.

27. RGALI, f. 2499, op. 1, d. 447, ll. 119–120.

28. As Lisa Kirschenbaum argues, the categories of family and nation were deliberately conflated in the wartime press and popular imagery in order to encourage the Soviet population's emotional attachment to the "motherland." Karen Petrone first dates the "gendering of the Soviet land as the 'motherland'" to the mid-1930s, when the Stalinist government revived nationalist and filial sentiments, both of which the concept of the motherland evoked, in an effort to engender popular loyalty to the Soviet state. During the Cold War, the Soviet Union was again figured as a feminine domain deserving of popular allegiance, in this case the home—a metaphor that articulated an appeal to popular loyalty that would be convincing only if the home remained an identifiably feminine domain. Lisa A. Kirschenbaum, "'Our City, Our Hearths, Our Families': Local Loyalties and Private Life in Soviet World War II Propaganda," *Slavic Review* 59 (2002): 825–47; Karen Petrone, *Life Has Become More Joyous*, 53–55.

29. Kirschenbaum, "'Our City, Our Hearths, Our Families.'"

30. RGALI, f. 2499, op. 1, d. 438, l. 78.

31. RGALI, f. 2499, op. 1, d. 438, l. 26.

32. RGALI, f. 2499 op. 1 d. 438, l. 90.

33. RGALI, f. 2499, op. 1, d. 448, ll. 95–96.

34. Lynne Attwood, *Creating the New Soviet Woman: Women's Magazines as Engineers of Female Identity, 1922–1953* (New York: St. Martin's Press, 1999), 13.

35. RGALI, f. 2499, op. 1, d. 439, 12.

36. V. Ermans, "Shkola smelosti," *Sovetskoe iskusstvo*, 6 April 1941, 4.

37. Zaslavskii, "Tvorcheskii smotr v Moskovskom tsirke," 4.

38. *Laureaty 1-go mezhdunarodnogo festivalia tsirkov 1956 g. i uchastniki gastrolei Sovetskogo tsirka v Bel'gii, Frantsii, Anglii, Vengrii, Germanii, i Pol'she* (Moscow: Izdanie Moskovskogo ob"edineniia Teatral'no-zrelishchnykh kass, 1957), 20.

39. Iu. Dmitriev, introduction to *Vsia zhizn' v tsirke*, by Zoia Kokh, 3–6.

40. "Primite moi komplimenty," *Sovetskaia estrada i tsirk* 10 (1970): 22–23.

41. N. Krivenko, *Talant [sic], Daring, Beauty, The Soviet Circus* (Moscow: Izdatel'stvo Agenstva pechati Novosti, 1968), 148.

42. M. Tartakovskii, "Na arene tsirka," *Sovetskii sport*, 23 October 1958, 4.

43. N. Lagina, "Muzhestvennaia i obaiatel'naia," *Sovetskaia estrada i tsirk* 3 (1970): 4–6.

44. RGALI, f. 2499, op. 2, d. 1238, ll. 361–63.

45. Dmitriev, introduction to Kokh's *Vsia zhizn' v tsirke*, 6.

46. Peta Tait, *Converging Realities: Feminism in Australian Theatre* (Sydney: Currency Press, 1994), 108.

47. Natalia Rumiantseva, "Sovremennost' i chudesa na arene," *Sovetskaia estrada i tsirk* 2 (1974): 8–9.

48. RGALI, f. 2499, op. 1, d. 30, l. 17.

49. Moskovskii tsirk, "'Nashi Gosti' (artisty tsirkov bratskikh respublik, Nov.–Dec. 1948, Jan. 1949)," 20–22.

50. RGALI, f. 2499, op. 1, d. 447, l. 307.

Chapter 5. In Defense of Offensive Peace

1. Irina Bugrimova, "Gastroli chekhoslavatskogo tsirka," *Pravda*, 30 August 1954, 3.

2. Vladimir Durov, "Talant i masterstvo: Gastroli artistov tsirka Germanskoi Demokraticheskoi Respubliki v Moskve," *Trud*, 18 August 1955, 4.

3. "Circus Alive Abroad," *Washington Post*, 22 July 1956, H4.

4. Zhorzh Soria, "Eti gastroli nadolgo ostanutsia v pamiat parizhan," *Sovetskaia kul'tura*, 14 April 1956, 4; G. Agadzhanov, "Novye zriteli—novye druz'ia," *Sovetskaia kul'tura*, 21 July 1956, 4.

5. Agadzhanov, "Novye zriteli—novye druz'ia," 4; Speaight, *A History of the Circus*, 165–67.

6. Soria, "Eti gastroli nadolgo ostanutsia," 4.

7. V. Filatov, "Na manezhakh zapadnoi evropy," *Sovetskaia kul'tura*, 21 July 1956, 4.

8. Ali-Bek Kantemirov quoted in B. Fedorov, *Dzhigit Osetii* (Ordzhonikidze: Severo-osetinskoe knizhnoe izdatel'stvo, 1960), 30.

9. Kennett Love, "Mission from Moscow: Three Bears and a Goose Captivate London," *New York Times*, 23 May 1956, 33.

10. "My raportuem partii svoei . . . ," *Sovetskii tsirk* 9 (1961): 1.

11. B. Galich, "Tsirk na ulitsakh stolitsy," *Sovetskii tsirk* 1 (1957): 6–8.

12. Poliakov, *All Evening in the Ring . . .* , 26.

13. Ibid.

14. RGALI, f. 2499, op. 1, d. 90, l. 5.

15. Evg. Gerushin, "Frantsuzkii tsirk v SSSR," *Sovetskii tsirk* 1 (1961): 18–19.

16. E. Semenov, "Druzhba," *Sovetskii tsirk* 9 (1961): 14–15.

17. I. Tumanov, "Arena Druzhby," *Sovetskii tsirk* 3 (1957): 1–4.

18. Viktor Ermans, "Mastera zarubezhnogo i sovetskogo tsirka v Moskve," *Sovetskaia kul'tura*, 26 November 1957, 4.

19. Tumanov, "Arena Druzhby," 1–4.

20. A. Gryaznov, "In the Circuses of Europe," in *The Soviet Circus: A Collection of Articles*, ed. Alexander Lipovsky, trans. Fainna Glagoleva (Moscow: Progress Publishers, 1967), 25–26.

21. Vladimir Durov, "Malen'kie Londontsy—malen'kim Moskivicham," *Sovetskii tsirk* 10 (1961): 27–28.

22. Iu. Dmitriev, "O Russkom tsirke," *Izvestiia*, 15 September 1957, 4.

23. Iu. Dmitriev, "Put' Sovetskogo tsirka," *Sovetskii tsirk* 2 (1957): 9.

24. P. Maiatskii, "Proshlo dva goda," *Sovetskii tsirk* 6 (1958): 5–6.

25. Iu. A. Dmitriev, *Tsirk v Rossii: Ot istokov do 2000 goda* (Moscow: Rossiiskaia politicheskaia entsiklopediia, 2004), 523.

26. Fedorov, *Ali-Bek Kantemirov: Dzhigit Osetii*, 11.

27. Ibid., 12.

28. Ibid., 31–32, 5.

29. Moskovskii tsirk, "'Nashi Gosti,'" 20–22.

30. Valentin Filatov, "Po zakonu velikogo bratstva," *Sovetskaia estrada i tsirk* 12 (1972): 6–8.

31. Moskovskii tsirk, "'Nashi Gosti,'" 20–22.

32. RGALI, f. 2499, op. 2, d. 228, ll. 38–42.

33. Gordon R. Trembath, *The Great Moscow Circus, 1968* (Melbourne: Michael C. Edgley, 1968).

34. Nikolai Krivenko, *The Magic Bowl* (Moscow: Soiuzgostsirk, 1969), 31.

35. RGALI, f. 2499, op. 2, d. 228, l. 90.

36. RGALI, f. 2499, op. 1, d. 21, l. 12.

37. RGALI, f. 2499, op. 1, d. 30, l. 34.

38. RGALI, f. 2499, op. 1, d. 54, ll. 183, 185.

39. Iu. Dmitriev, "Na arene Moskovskogo tsirka," *Moskovskaia pravda*, 18 April 1954, 4.

40. Iurii Blagov, *Chudesa na manezhe* (Moscow: Iskusstvo, 1984), 60.

41. RGALI, f. 2499, op. 2, d. 1238, ll. 138–44.

42. "Navstrechu XXII s"ezdu KPSS," *Sovetskii tsirk* 5 (1961): 3.

43. S. Zinin, "Zinaida Tarasova i mrachnyi volshebnik," *Moskovskii komsomolets*, 14 September 1963, 3.

44. *Chudesa bez chudes* (Moscow: Soiuzgostsirk, 1971), 11.

45. Oleg Sokol quoted in "Kommentarii k aplodismentam," *Sovetskaia estrada i tsirk* 1 (1976): 3.

46. "Greatest Show Off Earth Is a Soviet Circus Joke," *New York Times*, 6 November 1957, 12.

47. P. Chernega and S. Razumov, "Artisty berut slovo," *Sovetskii tsirk* 4 (1961): 2–3.

48. V. Lisin quoted in "Slava bogatyriam kosmosa!" *Sovetskii tsirk* 9 (1962): 2.

49. Ku. Shtraus, "U 'Dedushki' Russkoi Aviatsii," *Sovetskii tsirk* 10 (1962): 10–11.

50. Adriian Nikolaev and Pavel Popovich, "Masteram Sovetskogo tsirka," *Sovetskii tsirk* 11 (1962): 1.

51. V. Filatov, "Bear Circus," in *The Soviet Circus: A Collection of Articles*, ed. Alexander Lipovsky, trans. Fainna Glagoleva (Moscow: Progress Publishers, 1967), 7.

52. Janssen, "The Soviet Circus has Flash & Style," 1.

53. RGALI, f. 2499, op. 2, d. 81, l. 14.

54. RGALI, f. 2499, op. 2, d. 85, l. 4.

55. Nikolai Krivenko, *Sovetskii Tsirk, 1971–1975* (Moscow: Soiuzgostsirk, 1975), 6.

56. Nina Velekhova, "Strasti krugloi areny," *Sovetskaia estrada i tsirk* 9 (1972): 12–13.

57. Iu. Dmitriev, "Istinnoe sovershenstvo," *Sovetskaia kul'tura*, 14 July 1978, 5.

58. RGALI, f. 2499, op. 2, d. 1481, ll. 1–5.

59. Fedorov, *Ali-Bek Kantemirov: Dzhigit Osetii*, 19.

60. RGALI, f. 2499, op. 2, d. 30, l. 1.

61. "Partiinomu s"ezdu—dostoinuiu vstrechu," *Sovetskaia estrada i tsirk* 11 (1970): 1.

62. The circus was only one of many institutions that made this case during the Cold War. As Margot Light explains, "Once [the concept of peaceful coexistence] was expanded beyond the simple idea of the absence of war and the encouragement of international economic relations . . . it became apparent that there were contradictions between peaceful coexistence (which defined state relations) and proletarian internationalism (which defined class relations) that were extremely difficult to reconcile. . . . Soviet scholars expended a great deal of effort on showing that peaceful coexistence was consonant with international revolution and that the Soviet Union could be both the standard bearer of peace and a force for radical change within other societies." Margot Light, *The Soviet Theory of International Relations* (New York: St. Martin's Press, 1988), 46.

63. Richard F. Shepard, "One-Ring Moscow State Circus Begins Engagement at Garden," *New York Times*, September 25, 1963, 38.

Chapter 6. Courting Jesters

1. In 1966, F. G. Bardian claimed that part of the reason foreign audiences loved the Soviet circus was "because it is always searching for the new." F. G. Bardian, "Tsirk, dostoiny kosmosa," *Sovetskaia kul'tura*, 29 March 1966, 4. Two years later, a glossy history of the circus published in both English and Russian explained that "the new and the original, a driving urge to pioneer—this is part of the very nature of Soviet circus art!" Krivenko, *Talant* [*sic*], *Daring, Beauty*, 65. In 1970, Valentin Filatov wrote that "the most characteristic feature of Soviet circus art is the inextinguishable spirit of creative searching, the striving to widen the boundaries of genres, of opening in each of them new fresh pages." Valentin Filatov, "Orden na Znameni," *Sovetskaia estrada i tsirk* 4 (1970): 9.

2. Viktor Ermans, "Iskusstvo besstrashnykh," *Sovetskaia kul'tura*, 2 February 1957, 3. Similarly, in a 1968 interview, the aerial gymnast Liuba Pisarenkova explained that she never grew bored performing the same routine every night because each time she performed it, she saw it "anew." She added that she hoped that on different days, viewers' impressions of the routine were not the same. R. Iur'ev, "Liubite li vy tsirk," *Literaturnaia gazeta*, 1 January 1969, 1.

3. A. Shirai, "Novaia stranitsa v zhanre," *Sovetskaia estrada i tsirk* 1 (1970): 15; T. Chebotarevskaia, "Muzhestvo," *Sovetskaia estrada i tsirk* 3 (1971): 20–21.

4. Aleksandr Marianov, "V ozhidanii chuda," *Sovetskaia kul'tura*, 14 January 1986, 8. In 1958, Iurii Dmitriev praised Emil' Teodorovich himself for "continuing in the best traditions of his predecessors" while he "openly revolted against the legacy of the various magi and fakirs." Iu. Dmitriev, "Kio and his Predecessors," in *The Soviet Circus: A Collection of Articles*, ed. Alexander Lipovsky, trans. Fainna Glagoleva (Moscow: Progress Publishers, 1967), 79.

5. RGALI, f. 2499, op. 1, d. 295, ll. 72, 67.

6. RGALI, f. 2499, op. 2, d. 85, ll. 28, 37.

7. Mikhail Zarin, "Gde traditsii, a gde shtampy . . . ," *Sovetskaia kul'tura*, 3 September 1968, 3.

8. Nikolai Krivenko, "Prelest' novizny," *Sovetskaia kul'tura*, 14 October 1977, 5.

9. Mikhail Rumiantsev, "Voevat' smekhom," *Trud*, 16 September 1979, 4.

10. Oleg Popov, "Tvorit' dlia naroda," *Sovetskii tsirk* 2 (1957): 3.

11. Oleg Popov, *Russian Clown*, trans. Marion Koenig (London: Macdonald & Co., 1970), 103.

12. Iu. Nikulin, "Kogda smeetsia zritel', razmyshlenia o klounade," *Literaturnaia gazeta*, 12 November 1969, 8.

13. V. Shvarts, "Iunost' otpravliaetsia v put'," *Sovetskaia kul'tura*, 5 July 1983, 4.

14. V. Il'in, "Manezh sobiraet 'zvezd,' *Sovetskaia kul'tura*, 27 September 1988, 4.

15. Far more performers received individual attention in the years before Stalin's death, though a number were frequently singled out for praise in the earlier period.

16. "K novym tvorcheskim uspekham," *Sovetskaia estrada i tsirk* 8 (1974): 5.

17. Iu. Dmitriev, "Pust' zazhigaiutsia zvezdy," *Sovetskaia kul'tura*, 30 September 1975, 4.

18. Evgenii Milaev, "Parad-alle na glavnoi arene," *Sovetskaia kul'tura*, 18 September 1979, 4.

19. Vladimir Shakhidzhanian, "V tsirke rabotat' trudno," *Sovetskaia kul'tura*, 13 November 1986, 5.

20. V. Il'in, "Manezh sobiraet 'zvezd,'" 4.

21. Like the circus repertoire, Soviet literature was also concerned with the relationship of the individual to the collective. As Katerina Clark explains, "The main thrust of early fifties prose was . . . one of reaction against High Stalinist values. . . . Directly or indirectly, the main target of writers, critics, and even policy-makers was that backbone of High Stalinist political culture, namely, hierarchy and privilege, and the cult of the titanic hero that went with them. . . . The fifties saw a growing cult, not of the 'little man' as a 'cog' or 'bolt' in society's great 'machine,' but rather of the ordinary person as an individual. This cult was reflected in several ways: in campaigns to reintroduce 'sincerity' and 'the lyric' in literature (read: individual expression, debunking of unrealistic characterization, and paying more attention to love and other feelings) and in concern for the right of individuals to a full and unhindered private life." Katerina Clark, *The Soviet Novel: History as Ritual*, 3rd ed. (Bloomington: Indiana University Press, 2000), 215–16.

22. "Navstrechu velikoi date," 1.

23. Mstislav Zapashnyi, "Peregruzki na . . . Konveiere," *Sovetskaia kul'tura*, 4 January 1977, 4.

24. A. Kolevatov, "Veselye ogni," *Pravda*, 27 August 1979, 3.

25. Viktor Shklovskii, "The Clown, Comedy and Tragedy," in *The Soviet Circus: A Collection of Articles*, ed. Alexander Lipovsky, trans. Fainna Glagoleva (Moscow: Progress Publishers, 1967), 37.

26. "Kommunism nachinaetsia segodnia!" *Sovetskii tsirk* 10 (1961): 1–2.

27. A. Barten, "Diametr—vsegda trinadtsat' metrov," *Literatura i zhizn'*, 7 September 1960, 2.

28. Iurii Olesha, "K otkrytiiu sezona," *Trud*, 23 September 1947, 4.

29. RGALI, f. 2499, op. 1, d. 58, l. 22.

30. Mikhail Dolgopolov, "Novoe v tsirke," *Izvestiia*, 11 April 1951, 3.

31. RGALI, f. 2499, op. 2, d. 85, l. 6; A. Viktorov, "Internatsional'naia programma," *Sovetskaia kul'tura*, 21 September 1973, 3.

32. Iurii Dmitriev, "Vecher v parizhskom tsirke," *Literaturnaia gazeta*, 3 January 1961, 2.

33. F. G. Bardian quoted in E. Mikhailov, "Torzhestvo krasoty chelovecheskoi," *Sovetskaia kul'tura*, 9 September 1969, 2.

34. V. Ardov, "Mysli o sovetskoi klounade," *Sovetskii tsirk* 1 (1980): 8.

35. See also Iu. Dmitriev, "Zvuchit slova na manezhe," *Sovetskaia kul'tura*, 5 July 1983, 4; Shvarts, "Iunost' otpravliaetsia v put'," 4.

36. V. Gorokhov, "I pliusy, i minusy: Novyi spektakl' Moskovskogo tsirka na Tsvetnom bul'vare," *Sovetskaia kul'tura*, 24 May 1984, 5.

37. "Liubimoe zrelishche naroda."

38. B. Kalmanovskii, "Neskol'ko Zamechanii," *Sovetskii tsirk* 7 (1961): 13.

39. L. Losev, "'Zdravstvui, stolitsa!' Na arene Moskovskogo tsirka," *Moskovskaia pravda*, November 1953, 3.

40. P. Massal'skii, "Vpechatlenie prekrasnoe," *Sovetskaia kul'tura*, 18 January 1977, 5.

41. Irina Bugrimova, "Smelye liudi i dobrye zveri," *Sovetskaia kul'tura*, 16 October 1981, 5.

42. V. Filatov, "Medvezhii tsirk," *Moskovskii komsomolets*, 29 January 1956, 4.

43. L. Nikiforova, "Molodezh' na arene," *Moskovskii komsomolets*, 8 March 1956, 3.

44. E. Durova, "Polosatye zvezdy areny," *Sovetskaia estrada i tsirk* 10 (1976): 20–21.

45. Eder, *Jungle Acrobats of the Russian Circus*, 13.

46. Krivenko, *Talant* [sic], *Daring, Beauty*, 92.

47. Iu. Dmitriev, "The Durovs," in *The Soviet Circus: A Collection of Articles*, ed. Alexander Lipovsky, trans. Fainna Glagoleva (Moscow: Progress Publishers, 1967), 16.

48. Boris Eder, "Svet Areny," *Trud*, 28 September 1969, 4.

49. Eder, "Four-Legged Performers," 105.

50. V. Vakhramov, "I gamadrila mozhon obuchit," *Sovetskaia kul'tura*, 15 February 1983, 4.

51. RGALI, f. 2499, op. 1, d. 54, l. 15.

52. P. Bernatskii, "Arena druzhby," *Sovetskii tsirk* 11 (1961): 5.

53. Viktorov, *S Perom u Karandasha*, 54.

54. For example, materials collected for the 1933 GOMETs annual plan included a proposal for the formation of small circus collectives "that would combine all elements of circus art, that would be connected by a defined thematic line, and that would be saturated with a definite artistic-political content." RGALI, f. 2663, op. 1, d. 104, l. 110. See also RGALI, f. 2499, op. 1, d. 2, l. 1; I. M. Imas, *Sostoianie i Perspektivy Tsirkovogo dela, materialy k dokladu direktora GOMETsa t. M.I. Imasa na IV pleneume TsK RABIS* (Moscow: Izdanie GOMETs, 1933), 5.

55. Iurii Nikulin, "Tsirk—moi rodnoi dom," *Sovetskaia kul'tura*, 18 September 1973, 5.

56. RGALI, f. 2499, op. 1, d. 56, l. 63.

57. N. El'shevskii, "O narodnosti iskusstva tsirka," *Sovetskii tsirk* 6 (1959): 7.

58. Oleg Popov, "Ulybka liudiam tak nuzhna," *Sovetskaia kul'tura*, 17 May 1977, 5.

59. Ibid., 39.

60. Ibid., 105.

61. A. Viktorov, "Neishcherpaemye vozmozhnosti," *Sovetskaia kul'tura*, 2 February 1961, 3.

62. Iurii Nikulin, *Pochti ser'ezno* . . . (Moscow: Iskusstvo, 1987), 19. All future citations are from the 1989 edition of Nikulin's memoirs: Nikulin, *Desiat' trolleibusov klounov*.

63. Ibid., 134.

64. V. Ivashkovskii, "Volshebnik iz mar'inoi roshchi," *Sovetskaia kul'tura*, 18 April 1985, 4.

65. N. Khalatov, "Anatolii Marchevskii—kloun bez maski," *Sovetskaia estrada i tsirk* 6 (1975): 22.

66. Viktor Ardov, "Put' k samomu sebe," *Sovetskaia estrada i tsirk* 5 (1970): 24–26.

67. Viktorov, *S Perom u Karandasha*, 55.

68. Iu. Dmitriev, "Pamiati Leonida Engibarova," *Sovetskaia estrada i tsirk* 11 (1972): 20.

69. Ivashkovskii, "Volshebnik iz mar'inoi roshchi," 4.

70. Poliakov, *All Evening in the Ring*, 59.

71. Iurii Blagov, *Nashi klouny* (Moscow: Iskusstvo, 1977), 35.

72. Khalatov, "Anatolii Marchevskii," 22–23.

73. Nikulin, *Desiat' trolleibusov klounov*, 2:34–41.

74. Christopher Wren, "In Russia, the Circus Is an Art Form," *New York Times*, 14 December 1975, D5.

75. R. Slavskii, *Leonid Engibarov* (Moscow: Iskusstvo, 1972), 65.

76. RGALI, f. 2499, op. 1, d. 98, l. 6.

77. B. Eder, "Razgovor o tsirke, nekotorye voprosy razvitiia tsirkovogo iskusstva," *Izvestiia*, 5 September 1956, 3.

78. RGALI, f. 2499 op. 2 d. 39a, l. 7.

79. RGALI, f. 2499, op. 2, d. 35, l. 1.

80. Jack Raymond, "Circus Retains Lure in Moscow, It Attracts Big Crowds with Its Animals and Acrobats and Slapstick Skits," *New York Times*, 19 March 1956, 15.

81. Ibid.

82. Ibid., 71.

83. RGALI, f. 2499, op. 2, d. 228, ll. 13–15.

84. RGALI, f. 2499, op. 2, d. 303, l. 31.

85. Iu. Dmitriev, "Tsirk—v puti," *Literatura i zhizn'*, 6 April 1962, 4.

86. Nikulin, *Desiat' trolleibusov klounov*, 2:166.

87. Max Frankel, "What Makes Ivan Laugh," *New York Times*, 31 January 1960, SM12.

88. I. Mart'ianov, "Reprizy na mestnye temy (zametki zritelia)," *Sovetskii tsirk* 1 (1961): 19.

89. Nikulin, *Desiat' trolleibusov klounov*, 1:142.

90. Van der Post, *Journey into Russia*, 42.

91. Poliakov, *All Evening in the Ring* . . . , 68.
92. Van der Post, *Journey into Russia*, 43.
93. Schechter, *The Congress of Clowns*, 90.

Conclusion

1. Stites, *Russian Popular Culture*, 5. Stites also observes that the revolution was "the main agent of destruction" of Russian popular culture. See also Fitzpatrick, *The Cultural Front*, 5, 21.
2. Stites, *Russian Popular Culture*, 41.
3. Fitzpatrick, *The Cultural Front*, 5. Fitzpatrick later observes that "all Marxist intellectuals agreed, without even thinking about it, that proletarian culture had little or nothing to do with observable popular lower-class habits and cultural tastes. 'Vulgar,' 'tasteless,' or 'trivial' culture was obviously not proletarian; and if workers liked it, obviously they had been infected with petty-bourgeois attitudes" (21). Here she cites Jeffrey Brooks, who writes, "the popularity of the pre-revolutionary popular culture was a feature of the market economy, and in this respect it was something Soviet leaders were not able or willing to replicate." Jeffrey Brooks, "Competing Modes of Popular Discourse, Individualism and Class Consciousness in the Russian Print Media, 1880–1928," in *Culture et Révolution*, ed. Marc Ferro and Sheila Fitzpatrick (Paris: École des Hautes Études en Sciences Sociales, 1989), 72.
4. Von Geldern, *Bolshevik Festivals, 1917–1921*, 133.
5. Stites, *Russian Popular Culture*, 39.
6. Von Geldern explains that the new responsibilities given to popular entertainments and objects "could be met only at the price of structural changes. The play element that had been the essence of popular culture could not always bear the messages thrust on it by the Revolution." Von Geldern, *Bolshevik Festivals, 1917–1921*, 133.
7. Robert Edelman, *Serious Fun: A History of Spectator Sports in the USSR* (New York: Oxford University Press, 1992), 17.
8. Ibid., 6.
9. Ibid., 15.
10. Ibid., 245.
11. Petrone, *Life Has Become More Joyous*, 20.
12. Ibid., 2–3, 9.
13. Marcus Verhagen, "Whipstrokes," *Representations* 58 (1997): 118.
14. This development is consistent with Aleksei Yurchak's observation that Soviet ideology became formalized after Stalin's death, with the result that its forms were reproduced so frequently that they were emptied of any ideological meaning and made available for reinvestment with new meanings. According to Yurchak, this discursive shift explains how the Soviet system created the

conditions for its own collapse, while simultaneously rendering those conditions invisible, and the circus stands as yet another example of an official cultural product that confirms his interpretation. Alexei Yurchak, *Everything Was Forever, Until It Was No More: The Last Soviet Generation* (Princeton, NJ: Princeton University Press, 2006).

Bibliography

Archives

Russian State Archive of Literature and Art (RGALI)
    f. 336 Vladimir Vladimirovich Maiakovskii (*lichnyi fond*)
    f. 645 Glavnoe upravlenie po delam khudozhestvennoi literatury i iskusstva
        (Glaviskusstvo) i sektor iskusstva i literatury Narkromprosa
    f. 656 Glavnoe upravlenie po kontrol'iu za repertuarom pri komitete po
        delam iskusstv pri SNK SSSR
    f. 962 Komitet po delam iskusstv pri SM SSSR
    f. 2499 Vsesoiuznyoe ob"edinenie gosudarstvennykh tsirkov (Soiuzgostsirk)
    f. 2607 Nikitin, Akim Aleksandrovich, Petr Aleksandrovich, Dmitrii
        Aleksandrovich
    f. 2663 Mark Izrailevich Imas (*lichnyi fond*)
    f. 2742 Evgenii Mikhailovich Kuznetsov (*lichnyi fond*)
Russian State Archive of Social and Political History (RGASPI)
    f. 17 Tsentral'nyi Komitet KPSS
    op. 60 Otdel agitatsii i propagandy TsK
    op. 125 Upravlenie propagandy i agitatsii TsK
State Archive of the Russian Federation (GARF)
    f. 2306 Narodnyi komissariat po prosveshcheniiu RSFSR
    f. 2312 Glavnyi politiko-prosvetitel'nyi komitet RSFSR
    f. 406 Narodnyi komissariat raboche-krest'ianskoi inspektsii RSFSR

Books and Articles

"1-i gosudarstvennyi tsirk." *Vestnik teatra* 42 (1919): 10.

Abramov, Aleksandr. "Tsirk slyshish'?" *Novyi zritel'* 2 (1924): 3–4.

Agadzhanov, G. "Novye zriteli—novye druz'ia." *Sovetskaia kul'tura*, 21 July 1956, 4.

Albrecht, Ernest. *The New American Circus*. Gainesville: University of Florida Press, 1995.

Aleksandrov, G. V. "Iskusstvo lovkosti i sily, Otkrytie sezona v Moskovskom tsirke." *Sovetskoe iskusstvo*, 11 September 1941, 3.

———. "Smotr dostizhenii sovetskogo tsirka." *Pravda*, 24 March 1945, 4.

Al'evich, Al. "Na arene molodezh', Novaia programma v Gostsirke." *Izvestiia*, 2 February 1938, 4.

Aliakritskii, B., Em. Artem'ev, and I Kovrov. "Diskussiia, polemika o tsirke." *Novyi zritel'* 39 (1924): 24.

Allardyce, Nicoll. *Masks, Mimes, and Miracles: Studies in the Popular Theatre*. New York: Cooper Square Publishers, 1963.

Angarskii, V., and L. Victorov. *Oleg Popov*. Moscow: Iskusstvo, 1964.

Ardov, V. "Mysli o sovetskoi klounade." *Sovetskii tsirk* 1 (1980): 8.

———. "O tsirke voobshche i pervom gostsirke v chastnosti." *Rabochii Zritel'* 7 (1924): 7.

———. "Put' k samomu sebe." *Sovetskaia estrada i tsirk* 5 (1970): 24–26.

Argo, A. "Zhizn' na arene." *Sovetskii tsirk* 2 (1957): 16–18.

Assael, Brenda. *The Circus and Victorian Society*. Charlottesville: University of Virginia Press, 2005.

Attwood, Lynne. *Creating the New Soviet Woman: Women's Magazines as Engineers of Female Identity, 1922–1953*. New York: St. Martin's Press, 1999.

B. K. "Bol'she ideinosti, vyshe kachestvo (Konferentsiia rabochego zritelia)." *Sovetskoe iskusstvo*, 21 May 1932, 4.

Bardian, F. G. "Proverka khoda sots. sorevnovaniia." *Tsirk i estrada* 8 (1930): 2–3.

———. "Tsirk, dostoiny kosmosa." *Sovetskaia kul'tura*, 29 March 1966, 4.

———. "Zadachi rabotnikov Soiuzgostsirka v svete reshenii XXI s"ezda KPSS." *Sovetskii tsirk* 6 (1959): 13.

Barten, A. "Diametr—vsegda trinadtsat' metrov." *Literatura i zhizn'*, 7 September 1960, 2.

Begliarov, Mikh. "Provintsial'nye bolezni (Golos rabochego zritelia)." *Tsirk i estrada* 74 (1930): 6.

Beller, V. P. "22 milliona zritelei." *Sovetskoe iskusstvo*, 18 November 1939, 3.

Bernatskii, P. "Arena druzhby." *Sovetskii tsirk* 11 (1961): 5.

Blagov, Iurii. *Chudesa na manezhe*. Moscow: Iskusstvo, 1984.

———. *Kha-kha-kha! Sbornik klounad*. Moscow: Iskusstvo, 1971.

———. *Nashi klouny*. Moscow: Iskusstvo, 1977.

Bogorodskii, Fedor. "O tsirke." *Novyi zritel'* 36 (1924): 3–4

Bouissac, Paul. *Circus and Culture: A Semiotic Approach*. Lanham, MD: University Press of America, 1985.

Brandist, Craig. *Carnival Culture in the Soviet Modernist Novel*. New York: St. Martin's Press, 1996.

Brooks, Jeffrey. "Competing Modes of Popular Discourse, Individualism and Class Consciousness in the Russian Print Media, 1880–1928." In *Culture et Révolution*, edited by Marc Ferro and Sheila Fitzpatrick, 71–82. Paris: École des Hautes Études en Sciences Sociales, 1989.

———. "The Press and Its Message: Images of America in the 1920s and 1930s." In *Russia in the Era of NEP: Explorations in Soviet Society and Culture*, edited by Sheila Fitzpatrick, Alexander Rabinowitch, and Richard Stites, 231–52. Bloomington: Indiana University Press, 1991.

Brown, Deming. "World War II in Soviet Literature." In *The Impact of World War II on the Soviet Union*, edited by Susan J. Linz, 243–52. Totowa, NJ: Rowman & Allanheld, 1985.

Bugrimova, Irina. "Gastroli chekhoslavatskogo tsirka." *Pravda*, 30 August 1954, 3.

———. "Smelye liudi i dobrye zveri." *Sovetskaia kul'tura*, 16 October 1981, 5.

Canby, Vincent. "Moscow Circus Whirls Into Garden; Horsemen, Clowns and Acrobats Are Delight." *New York Times*, 5 October 1967, 44.

Central Statistical Board of the U.S.S.R. Council of Ministers. *Cultural Progress in the U.S.S.R.: Statistical Returns*. Moscow: Foreign Language Publishing House, 1958.

Chatterjee, Choi, and Karen Petrone. "Models of Selfhood and Subjectivity: The Soviet Case in Historical Perspective." *Slavic Review* 67 (Winter 2008): 967–86.

Chebotarevskaia, T. "Muzhestvo." *Sovetskaia estrada i tsirk* 3 (1971): 20–21.

Chekhov, Anton. "Kashtanka." In *The Essential Tales of Chekhov*, edited by Richard Ford, 67–84. Translated by Constance Garnett. Hopewell, NJ: Ecco Press, 1998.

Chernega, P., and S. Razumov. "Artisty berut slovo." *Sovetskii tsirk* 4 (1961): 2–3.

Chernenko, I. *Zdravstvui, Tsirk!* Moscow: Molodaia gvardiia, 1968.

"Chrevoveshchateli." *Tsirk* 8 (1927): 11.

Chudesa bez chudes. Moscow: Soiuzgostsirk, 1971.

"Circus Alive Abroad." *Washington Post*, 22 July 1956, H4.

Clark, Katerina. "Little Heroes and Big Deeds: Literature Responds to the First Five-Year Plan." In *Cultural Revolution in Russia*, edited by Sheila Fitzpatrick, 189–206. Bloomington: Indiana University Press, 1978.

———. *Petersburg, Crucible of Cultural Revolution*. Cambridge, MA: Harvard University Press, 1995.

———. *The Soviet Novel: History as Ritual*. 3rd ed. Bloomington: Indiana University Press, 2000.

------. "The Quiet Revolution in Intellectual Life." In *Russia in the Era of NEP: Explorations in Soviet Society and Culture*, edited by Sheila Fitzpatrick, Alexander Rabinowitch, and Richard Stites, 210–30. Bloomington: Indiana University Press, 1991.

Clark, Toby. "The 'New Man's' Body: A Motif in Early Soviet Culture." In *Art of the Soviets: Painting, Sculpture, and Architecture in a One-Party State, 1917–1992*, edited by Matthew Cullerne Brown and Brandon Taylor, 33–50. Manchester: Manchester University Press, 1993.

"Coronation of the Czar." *New York Times*, 5 April 1896, 4.

Croft-Cooke, Rupert, and Peter Cotes. *Circus*. London: Elek, 1976.

Curtis, J. A. E. "Down with the Foxtrot! Concepts of Satire in the Soviet Theatre of the 1920s." In *Russian Theatre in the Age of Modernism*, edited by Robert Russell and Andrew Barratt, 219–35. New York: St. Martin's Press, 1990.

Dankman, A. M. "Gostsirki." *Novyi zritel'* 45 (1925): 14.

------. "Problemy sovremennogo tsirka." *Tsirk* 8 (1927): 1.

------. *Raport GOMETs 8-mu vsesoiuznomu s"ezdu rabotnikov iskusstv*. Moscow: Izdanie GOMETs, 1932.

------. *Sostoianie i perspektivy razvitiia tsirkovogo i estradnogo dela v SSSR*. Moscow: Izdanie TsUGTs, 1930.

------. "Sovetskii i zapadnyi Tsirk." *Tsirk* 10 (1927): 1.

------. "To-Ramo." *Tsirk* 1 (1926): 8

Dats-Fore. "Griadushchii tsirk." *Vestnik teatra* 78 (1921): 2.

Davis, Janet. *The Circus Age: Culture & Society under the American Big Top*. Chapel Hill: University of North Carolina Press, 2002.

"Dekret ob"edinenii teatral'nogo dela." *Vestnik Teatra* 33 (1919): 2.

Dikovskii, S. "Zimnii sezon v tsirke." *Pravda*, 3 October 1937, 4.

Disher, Wilson M. *Fairs, Circuses and Music Halls*. London: William Collins, 1942.

Dmitriev, Iu. *100 let Moskovskomu ordena Lenina gosudarstvennomu tsirku na Tsvetnom Bul'vare*. Moscow: Vsesoiuznoe biuro propagandy sovetskogo tsirkovogo iksusstva, 1980.

------. "The Durovs." In *The Soviet Circus: A Collection of Articles*, edited by Alexander Lipovsky, 9–18. Translated by Fainna Glagoleva. Moscow: Progress Publishers, 1967.

------. "Istinnoe sovershenstvo." *Sovetskaia kul'tura*, 14 July 1978, 5.

------. *Istoriia sovetskogo tsirka v samom kratkom ocherke*. Moscow: Iskusstvo, 1980.

------. "Kio and His Predecessors." In *The Soviet Circus: A Collection of Articles*, edited by Alexander Lipovsky, 71–84. Translated by Fainna Glagoleva. Moscow: Progress Publishers, 1967.

------. "Na arene Moskovskogo tsirka." *Moskovskaia pravda*, 18 April 1954, 4.

------. "Novyi tsirk." *Sovetskoe iskusstvo*, 30 January, 1938, 2.

------. "O Russkom tsirke." *Izvestiia*, 15 September 1957, 4.

————. "Pamiati Leonida Engibarova." *Sovetskaia estrada i tsirk* 11 (1972): 20.

————. "Pust' zazhigaiutsia zvezdy." *Sovetskaia kul'tura*, 30 September 1975, 4.

————. "Put' Sovetskogo tsirka." *Sovetskii tsirk* 2 (1957): 9.

————. *Russkii Tsirk*. Moscow: Iskusstvo, 1953.

————. "Samorodki, k 100 letiiu pervogo Russkogo statsionarnogo tsirka." *Sovetskaia estrada i tsirk* 9 (1973): 18–21.

————. *Sovetskii tsirk, ocherk istorii, 1917–1941*. Moscow: Iskusstvo, 1963.

————. "Tsirk—v puti." *Literatura i zhizn'*, 6 April 1962, 4.

————. *Tsirk v Rossii: Ot istokov do 1917 godov*. Moscow: Iskusstvo, 1977.

————. *Tsirk v Rossii: Ot istokov do 2000 goda*. Moscow: Rossiiskaia politicheskaia entsiklopediia, 2004.

————. "Vecher v parizhskom tsirke." *Literaturnaia gazeta*, 3 January 1961, 2.

————. "Vitalii Lazarenko, k 40-letiiu artisticheskoi deiatel'nosti." *Sovetskoe iskusstvo*, 16 February 1939, 2.

————. "Zvuchit slova na manezhe." *Sovetskaia kul'tura*, 5 July 1983, 4.

Dobrenko, Evgeny. *The Making of the State Writer: Social and Aesthetic Origins of Soviet Literary Culture*. Translated by Jesse M. Savage. Stanford, CA: Stanford University Press, 2001.

Dolgopolov, Mikh. "Novoe v tsirke." *Izvestiia*, 11 April 1951, 3.

————. "Sorok let na arene tsirka." *Izvestiia*, 15 February 1939, 4.

Dorokhov, A. A. *Moto-gonki po naklonnomu treku*. Leningrad: Vsesoiuznyi Komitet po delam iskusstv, 1939.

Dreiden, Sim. "Tsirk pod vodoi." *Zhizn' iskusstva* 17 (1929): 13.

————. "V tsirke." *Zhizn' iskusstva* 17 (1928): 13.

Dunham, Vera. *In Stalin's Time: Middleclass Values in Soviet Fiction*. Durham, NC: Duke University Press, 1990.

During, Simon. *Modern Enchantments: The Cultural Power of Secular Magic*. Cambridge, MA: Harvard University Press, 2002.

Durov, V. L. *My Circus Animals*. Translated by John Cournos. New York: Houghton Mifflin, 1936.

————. "Proekt shkoly tsirka." *Vestnik teatra* 24 (1919): 4.

Durov, Vladimir. "Malen'kie Londontsy—malen'kim Moskivicham." *Sovetskii tsirk* 10 (1961): 27–28.

————. "Talant i masterstvo, Gastroli artistov tsirka Germanskoi Demokraticheskoi Respubliki v Moskve." *Trud*, 18 August 1955, 4.

Durova, E. "Polosatye zvezdy areny." *Sovetskaia estrada i tsirk* 10 (1976): 20–21.

Edelman, Robert. *Serious Fun: A History of Spectator Sports in the USSR*. New York: Oxford University Press, 1993.

Eder, Boris. "Four-Legged Performers." In *The Soviet Circus: A Collection of Articles*, edited by Alexander Lipovsky, 99–112. Translated by Fainna Glagoleva. Moscow: Progress Publishers, 1967.

————. *Jungle Acrobats of the Russian Circus: Trained Animals in the Soviet Union*. Translated by O. Gorchakov. New York: Robert McBride Co., 1958.

———. "Moi tvorcheskii put'." *Sovetskoe iskusstvo*, 18 November 1939, 3.

———. "Razgovor o tsirke, nekotorye voprosy razvitiia tsirkovogo iskusstva." *Izvestiia*, 5 September 1956, 3.

———. "Svet Areny." *Trud*, 28 September 1969, 4.

El'shevskii, N. "O narodnosti iskusstva tsirka." *Sovetskii tsirk* 6 (1959): 7.

Endzinoi, G. D. "Narodnyi shut (Al'bom Vitaliia Lazarenko)." In *Vstrechi s proshlym: Sbornik materialov TsGALI*, vol. 1, 174. Moscow: Sovetskaia Rossiia, 1983.

Engibarov, Leonid, ed. *Liubimyi Tsirk*. Moscow: 1974.

Ermans. V. "Dva pokoleniia, novaia programma v Moskovskom gostsirke." *Sovetskoe iskusstvo*, 14 December 1938, 4.

———. "Iskusstvo besstrashnykh." *Sovetskaia kul'tura*, 2 February 1957, 3.

———. "Mastera zarubezhnogo i sovetskogo tsirka v Moskve." *Sovetskaia kul'tura*, 26 November 1957, 4.

———. "Pervaia programma, otkrytie sezona v Moskovskom gostsirke." *Sovetskoe iskusstvo*, 9 October 1939, 4.

———. "Shkola smelosti." *Sovetskoe iskusstvo*, 6 April 1941, 4.

———. "Tri pokoleniia novaia programma Gostsirka." *Sovetskoe iskusstvo*, 29 January 1937, 6.

———. "Tsirk i Estrada na Vsesoiuznoi s.-kh. Vystavke." *Sovetskoe iskusstvo*, 9 August 1939, 4.

Fandor. "Otkrytie gostsirka." *Novyi Zritel'* 39 (1925): 13.

Fedorov, B. *Ali-Bek Kantemirov: Dzhigit Osetii*. Ordzhonikidze: Severo-osetinskoe knizhnoe izdatel'stvo, 1960.

Ferroni, V.E. *200 let na manezhe*. Moscow: Dizain-studiia, 1997.

Field, Deborah A. "Irreconcilable Differences: Divorce and Conceptions of Private Life in the Khrushchev Era." *Russian Review* 57 (1998): 599–613.

Filatov, V. "Bear Circus." In *The Soviet Circus: A Collection of Articles*, edited by Alexander Lipovsky, 139–152. Translated by Fainna Glagoleva. Moscow: Progress Publishers, 1967.

———. "Medvezhii tsirk." *Moskovskii komsomolets*, 29 January 1956, 4.

———. "Na manezhakh zapadnoi evropy." *Sovetskaia kul'tura*, 21 July 1956, 4.

———. "Orden na Znameni." *Sovetskaia estrada i tsirk* 4 (1970): 9.

———. "Po zakonu velikogo bratstva." *Sovetskaia estrada i tsirk* 12 (1972): 6–8.

Filtzer, Donald. "The Standard of Living of Soviet Industrial Workers in the Immediate Postwar Period, 1945–1948." *Europe-Asia Studies* 51 (1999): 1013–38.

Finikov, K. "Tsirk konservativen (golos Rabochego Zritelia)." *Tsirk i estrada* 20–21 (1929): 5.

Fink, I. "Vladimir Durov i Dem'ian Bednyi." *Sovetskaia estrada i tsirk* 5 (1974): 12–13.

Fitzpatrick, Sheila. *The Cultural Front: Power and Culture in Revolutionary Russia*. Ithaca, NY: Cornell University Press, 1992.

———. "The Emergence of Glaviskusstvo: Class War on the Cultural Front, 1928–29." *Soviet Studies* 2 (1971): 236–53.

———. *Everyday Stalinism: Ordinary Life in Extraordinary Times.* New York: Oxford University Press, 1999.

Foregger. "Kadr tsirkachei." *Tsirk* 1 (1926): 3.

Frankel, Max. "What Makes Ivan Laugh." *New York Times*, 31 January 1960, SM12.

Galich, B. "Tsirk na ulitsakh stolitsy." *Sovetskii tsirk* 1 (1957): 6–8.

"Gallereia Samorodkov." *Zritel'* 2 (1922): 12–15.

Gerushin, Evg. "Frantsuzkii tsirk v SSSR." *Sovetskii tsirk* 1 (1961): 18–19.

Glants, Musya. "Images of the War in Painting." In *World War 2 and the Soviet People*, edited by John Garrard and Carol Garrard, 98–124. New York: St. Martin's Press, 1993.

Gordon, Michael R. "Russians Are Left with One Less Reason to Smile." *New York Times*, 27 August 1997, A4.

Gorei, Moris."Tsirk Frantsuzkii i Russkii." *Tsirk* 8 (1928): 2.

Gorokhov, V. "I pliusy, i minusy: Novyi spektakl' Moskovskogo tsirka na Tsvetnom bul'vare." *Sovetskaia kul'tura*, 24 May 1984, 5.

Gortinskii, E. M. *Tovarishch Tsirk.* Moscow: Sovetskaia Rossiia, 1985.

"Greatest Show Off Earth Is a Soviet Circus Joke." *New York Times*, 6 November 1957, 12.

Gronow, Jukka. *Caviar with Champagne: Common Luxury and the Ideals of the Good Life in Stalin's Russia.* New York: Berg, 2003.

Gryaznov, A. "In the Circuses of Europe." In *The Soviet Circus: A Collection of Articles*, edited by Alexander Lipovsky, 19–28. Translated by Fainna Glagoleva. Moscow: Progress Publishers, 1967.

Guldber, Jørn. "Socialist Realism as Institutional Practice: Observations on the Interpretation of the Works of Art of the Stalin Period." In *The Culture of the Stalin Period*, edited by Hans Günther, 149–77. New York: St. Martin's Press, 1990.

Gustafson, Donna. "Images from the World Between: The Circus in Twentieth-Century American Art." In *Images from the World Between: The Circus in Twentieth-Century American Art*, edited by Donna Gustafson, 9–84. Cambridge, MA, and New York: MIT Press and American Federation of Arts, 2001.

Handy, Ellen. "Photographing 'The splendidest sight that ever was': Cruelty, Alienation, and the Grotesque in the Shadow of the Big Top." In *Images from the World Between: The Circus in Twentieth-Century American Art*, edited by Donna Gustafson, 105–28. Cambridge, MA, and New York: MIT Press and American Federation of Arts, 2001.

Hammarstrom, David Lewis. *Circus Rings Around Russia.* Hamden: Archon Books, 1983.

Harris, Leon. *The Moscow Circus School.* New York: Atheneum, 1970.

Hippisley Coxe, Anthony D. "Equestrian Drama and the Circus." In *Perform-
ance and Politics in Popular Drama: Aspects of Popular Entertainment in Theatre,
Film, and Television, 1800–1976*, edited by David Bradby, Louis James, and
Bernard Sharratt, 109–18. New York: Cambridge University Press, 1980.

Ivashkovskii, V. "Volshebnik iz mar'inoi roshchi." *Sovetskaia kul'tura*, 18 April
1985, 4.

Ilin, V. "Manezh sobiraet 'zvezd.'" *Sovetskaia kul'tura*, 27 September 1988, 4.

Imas, M. I. *Sostoianie i Perspektivy Tsirkovogo dela, materialy k dokladu direktora
GOMETsa t. M.I. Imasa na IV pleneume TsK RABIS*. Moscow: Izdanie GOMETs,
1933.

———. "Novyi GOMETs, nakanune soveshchaniia rukovoditelei predpriiatii
GOMETs." *Sovetskoe iskusstvo*, 3 December 1932, 1.

Issledovatel'skaia teatral'naia masterskaia. "Zritel' tsirka." *Sovetskoe iskusstvo*,
August 1927, 58–59.

———. "Zritel' Tul'skogo tsirka." *Sovetskoe iskusstvo*, February 1928, 53–55.

Iur'ev, R. "Liubite li vy tsirk." *Literaturnaia gazeta*, 1 January 1969, 1.

Ivashkovskii, V. "Volshebnik iz mar'inoi roshchi." *Sovetskaia kul'tura*, 18 April
1985.

Janssen, Richard F. "The Soviet Circus Has Flash & Style—And Makes Money:
For Deeper Meanings, Check Antics of Comrade Clown and Risks of Lion
Tamers." *Wall Street Journal*, 1 November 1974, 1.

Jenkins, Ron. *Acrobats of the Soul: Comedy and Virtuosity in Contemporary American
Theatre*. New York: Theatre Communications Group, 1988.

Kalmanovskii, B. "Neskol'ko Zamechanii." *Sovetskii tsirk* 7 (1961): 13.

Karandash. *Nad chem smeetsia kloun?* Moscow: Iskusstvo, 1987.

Kenez, Peter. "Black and White: The War on Film." In *Culture and Entertainment
in Wartime Russia*, edited by Richard Stites, 157–75. Bloomington: Indiana
University Press, 1995.

———. *The Birth of the Propaganda State: Soviet Methods of Mass Mobilization,
1917–1929*. New York: Cambridge University Press, 1985.

Kenez, Peter, and David Shepherd. "'Revolutionary' Models of High Literature: Resisting Poetics." In *Russian Cultural Studies*, edited by Catriona Kelly
and David Shepherd, 21–55. New York: Oxford University Press, 1998.

Khalatov, N. "Anatolii Marchevskii—kloun bez maski." *Sovetskaia estrada i tsirk*
6 (1975): 22.

Khrapchenko, M. "Dvadtsat' let sovetskogo tsirka." *Pravda*, 23 November 1939, 4.

"Khronologiia gostsirkov." *Tsirk i estrada* 3–4 (1928): 1.

Kichin, Valerii. "Manezh upustel: Pervyi den' bez Nikulina." *Izvestiia*, 22 August
1997, 1.

Kilgallen, Dorothy. "Popvo [sic] has Circus Men Popping Off." *Washington Post*,
13 July 1963, A9.

Kio, Emil'. *Fokusy i fokusniki*. Edited by Iu. A. Dmitriev. Moscow: Iskusstvo,
1958.

Kio, Igor'. *Illiuzii bez illiuzii*. Moscow: Vagrius, 1999.

Kirschenbaum, Lisa A. "'Our City, Our Hearths, Our Families': Local Loyalties and Private Life in Soviet World War II Propaganda." *Slavic Review* 59 (2002): 825–47.

Kleberg, Lars. "The Nature of the Soviet Audience: Theatrical Ideology and Audience Research in the 1920s." In *Russian Theatre in the Age of Modernism*, edited by Robert Russell and Andrew Barratt, 172–195. New York: St. Martin's Press, 1990.

"K novym tvorcheskim uspekham." *Sovetskaia estrada i tsirk* 8 (1974): 5.

Kokh, Zoia. *Vsia zhizn' v tsirke*. Moscow: Iskusstvo, 1963.

Kolevatov, A. "Veselye ogni," *Pravda*, 27 August 1979, 3.

"Kommentarii k aplodismentam." *Sovetskaia estrada i tsirk* 1 (1976): 3.

"Kommunism nachinaetsia segodnia!" *Sovetskii tsirk* 10 (1961): 1–2.

Konenkov, S. T. *Moi Vek: Vospominaniia*. Moscow: Politizdat, 1988.

———. "V dvadtsatom godu." *Sovetskii tsirk* 2 (1957): 15.

"Konferentsiia o Tsirke." *Tsirk i estrada* 12 (1930): 3.

Korchagina, Valeria. "Moscow Fans Shed Tears for a Clown." *Moscow Times*, 26 August 1997.

Krane, Karl. "Sekrety ukrotitelia." *Tsirk* 6 (1926): 11.

Krasnianskii, E. *Vstrechi v puti: Stranitsy vospominanii—Teatr, Estrada, Tsirk*. Edited by S. Valerin. Moscow: Vserossiiskoe teatral'noe obshchestvo, 1967.

Krivenko, N. *The Magic Bowl*. Moscow: Soiuzgostsirk, 1969.

———. "Prelest' novizny." *Sovetskaia kul'tura*, 14 October 1977, 5.

———. *Sovetskii Tsirk, 1971–1975*. Moscow: Soiuzgostsirk, 1975.

———. *Talant [sic], Daring, Beauty: The Soviet Circus*. Moscow: Izdatel'stvo Agenstva pechati Novosti, 1968.

Kuprin, Alexander. "In the Circus." In *Sentimental Romance and Other Stories*, 43–77. Translated by S. E. Berkenblit. New York: Pageant Press, 1969.

———. "The White Poodle." In *The Garnet Bracelet and Other Stories*, 204–39. Translated by Stepan Apresyan. Moscow: Foreign Languages Publishing House, 1962.

Kuznetsov, Evgenii Mikhailovich. "Revoliutsiia i tsirk." *Teatr* 1 (1938): 122.

———. *Tsirk, Proiskhozhdenie, razvitie, perspektivy*. Moscow: Iskusstvo, 1971.

———. "V pervye dni voiny." *Sovetskoe iskusstvo*, 29 June 1941, 4.

Kwint, Marius. "The Circus and Nature in Late Georgian England." In *Histories of Leisure*, edited by Rudy Koshar, 45–60. New York: Berg, 2002.

Lagina, N. "Muzhestvennaia i obaiatel'naia." *Sovetskaia estrada i tsirk* 3 (1970): 4–6.

Lahusen, Thomas. "From Laughter 'Out of Sync' to Post-Synchronized Comedy: How the Stalinist Film Musical Caught Up with Hollywood and Overtook It." In *Socialist Cultures East and West: A Post-Cold War Reassessment*, edited by Dubravka Juraga and M. Keith Booker, 31–42. Westport: Praeger, 2002.

————. *How Life Writes the Book: Real Socialism and Socialist Realism in Stalin's Russia*. Ithaca, NY: Cornell University Press, 1997.

Lapido, A. V. "Novogo klouna." *Tsirk* 5 (1925): 11.

Laureaty 1-go mezhdunarodnogo festivalia tsirkov 1956 g. i uchastniki gastrolei Sovetskogo tsirka v Bel'gii, Frantsii, Anglii, Vengrii, Germanii, i Pol'she. Moscow: Izdanie Moskovskogo ob"edineniia Teatral'no-zrelishchnykh kass, 1957.

Lawrence, H. W. "The Circus Moscow Sees." *New York Times*, 30 April 1944, SM 38.

Lazarenko, Vitalii [Efimovich]. "Vitalii Lazarenko, Kloun-prygun." In *Sovetskii tsirk, 1918–1938*, edited by Evgenii Kuznetsov, 105–28. Moscow: Iskusstvo, 1938.

Lazarenko, Vitalii [Vitalevich]. "Bol'shoi i radostnyi prazdnik." *Sovetskoe iskusstvo*, 18 November 1939, 3.

Leach, Robert. *Revolutionary Theatre*. New York: Routledge, 1994.

Leningradskii Gostsirk, 1937–1938. Leningrad: Lengorlit, 1937.

Lenoe, Matthew. *Closer to the Masses: Stalinist Culture, Social Revolution, and Soviet Newspapers*. Cambridge, MA: Harvard University Press, 2004.

Leonov, Evgenii. "Staryi tsirk spravliaet iubilei." *Literaturnaia gazeta*, 12 November 1980, 8.

Light, Margot. *The Soviet Theory of International Relations*. New York: St. Martin's Press, 1988.

"Liubimoe zrelishche naroda." *Sovetskaia kul'tura*, 28 August 1954.

Liubimyi kloun: Iubileinyi al'manakh. Moscow: Znanie, 1997.

Losev, L. "'Zdravstvui, stolitsa!' Na arene Moskovskogo tsirka." *Moskovskaia pravda*, November 1953, 3.

Love, Kennett. "Mission from Moscow: Three Bears and a Goose Captivate London." *New York Times*, 23 May 1956, 33.

Lunacharskaia, A. "Na putiakh k novomu zriteliu." *Tsirk* 11 (1927): 1.

————. "Natsionalizm v tsirke." *Tsirk* 2 (1926): 1.

Lunacharskii, A. V. "Budem smeiat'sia." *Vestnik teatra* 58 (1920): 7–8.

————. "Na novykh putiakh, Konenkov dlia tsirka." *Vestnik teatra* 44 (1919): 6–7.

————. "Piat' let Gosudarstvennykh Tsirkov." *Tsirk* 3 (1925): 3.

————. "Rebenok i tsirk." *Tsirk* 3 (1925): 10.

————. "Shkolnaia anketa." *Tsirk* 5 (1925): 5.

————. "Tsirkach i sovremennaia zhizn'." *Tsirk* 10 (1926): 3–4.

————. "Zadacha obnovlennogo tsirka." *Vestnik teatra* 3 (1919): 5.

M., N. Z. "2-i Gosudarstvennyi tsirk: Otkrytie sezona." *Vestnik teatra* 36 (1919): 12.

Magilevich, E. "O tsirke, nasha anketa." *Tsirk* 7 (1925): 9.

Maiatskii, P. "Proshlo dva goda." *Sovetskii tsirk* 6 (1958): 5–6.

Makarov, S. M. "Eshche raz pro klounadu." *Sovetskaia estrada i tsirk* 2 (1975): 18.

————. *Klounada mirovogo tsirka: Istoriia i repertuar*. Moscow: Rosspen, 2001.

Manser, Rodney N. *Circus: The Development and Significance of the Circus, Past, Present, and Future.* Blackburn, UK: Richford, 1987.

Marianov, Aleksandr. "V ozhidanii chuda." *Sovetskaia kul'tura,* 14 January 1986, 8.

Mar'ianovskii, Viktor. *Kio, Otets i synov'ia.* Moscow: Iskusstvo, 1984.

Mart'ianov, I. "Reprizy na mestnye temy (zametki zritelia)." *Sovetskii tsirk* 1 (1961): 19.

Martin, Terry. *The Affirmative Action Empire: Nations and Nationalism in the Soviet Union, 1923–1939.* Ithaca, NY: Cornell University Press, 2001.

Massal'skii, P. "Vpechatlenie prekrasnoe." *Sovetskaia kul'tura,* 18 January 1977, 5.

McKechnie, Samuel. *Popular Entertainments through the Ages.* New York: Benjamin Bloom, 1969.

McReynolds, Louise. *Russia at Play: Leisure Activities at the End of the Tsarist Era.* Ithaca, NY: Cornell University Press, 2003.

Meek, James. "How To Grin and Bear It." *Manchester Guardian Weekly,* 31 August 1997, 22.

Mestechkin, M. *Nevydumannyi tsirk.* Moscow: Iskusstvo, 1978.

Mikhailov, E. "Torzhestvo krasoty chelovecheskoi." *Sovetskaia kul'tura,* 9 September 1969, 2.

Milaev, Evgenii. "Parad-alle na glavnoi arene." *Sovetskaia kul'tura,* 18 September 1979, 4.

Morov, Al. "O tsirke." *Pravda,* 6 May 1938, 4.

"Moscow Circus to Open Tour of Eastern Cities on Nov. 14." *New York Times,* 20 October 1972, 2.

"Moscow Circus Tour Includes 26 Cities." *New York Times,* 22 August 1989, C6.

Moskovskii tsirk. "'Nashi gosti' (artisty tsirkov bratskikh respublik, Nov.–Dec. 1948, Jan. 1949)." Program, Moscow Circus, 1948.

Mrokhovskii, Georgii. "Chto pomniat ob Artiste cherez dva chasa posle smerti?" *Rossiiskaia gazeta,* 22 August 1997, 3.

"My raportuem partii svoei . . ." *Sovetskii tsirk* 9 (1961): 1.

"Navstrechu XXII s"ezdu KPSS." *Sovetskii tsirk* 5 (1961): 3.

"Navstrechu velikoi date." *Sovetskaia estrada i tsirk* 3 (1969): 1.

Nazarov, A. "Sovetskii Tsirk, Otkrytie sezona v pervom gosudarstvennom tsirke." *Pravda,* 23 September 1936, 4.

Nemchinskii, Maksimilian. *Raisa Nemchinskaia.* Moscow: Iskusstvo, 1979.

———. *Tsirk Rossii naperegonki so vremenem: Modeli tsirkovykh spektaklei, 1920–1990kh godov.* Moscow: GITIS, 2001.

———. *Tsirk v zerkale stseny.* Moscow: Sov. Rossiia, 1983.

Nikiforova, L. "Molodezh' na arene." *Moskovskii komsomolets,* 8 March 1956, 3.

Nikitin, A. "Tsirk i estrada." *Rabochii zritel'* 27 (1924): 18.

Nikolaev, Adriian, and Pavel Popovich. "Masteram Sovetskogo tsirka." *Sovetskii tsirk* 11 (1962): 1.

Nikulin, Iu. "Aplodismentov ne budet." *Pravda*, 24 April 1986, 6.

———. *Desiat' trolleibusov klounov*. 2 vols. Samara: Dom Pechati, 1993.

———. "Kogda smeetsia zritel', razmyshlenia o klounade." *Literaturnaia gazeta*, 12 November 1969, 8.

———. *Pochti ser'ezno* . . . Moscow: Iskusstvo, 1987.

———. "Tsirk—moi rodnoi dom." *Sovetskaia kul'tura*, 18 September 1973, 5.

Nikulin, L. "Novoe v tsirke." *Novyi zritel'* 7 (1924): 3.

———. "Torzhestvo Sovetskogo tsirka." *Pravda*, 20 November 1939, 2

Noks, G. "Tsirk: Vo vtorom gosudarstvennom." *Zrelishche* 13 (1922): 20.

"Obezlishennoe upravlenie." *Sovetskoe iskusstvo*, 3 March 1932, 4.

Olesha, Iurii. "K otkrytiiu sezona." *Trud*, 23 September 1947, 4.

———. *No Day Without a Line: From Notebooks by Yuri Olesha*. Edited and translated by Judson Rosengrant. Evanston, IL: Northwestern University Press, 1998.

———. "Spectacles." In *Complete Short Stories and "Three Fat Men,"* 112–15. Translated by Aimee Anderson. Ann Arbor: Ardis, 1979.

———. *The Three Fat Men*. Translated by Fainna Glagoleva. Moscow: Foreign Languages Publishing House, 1960.

———. "We Are in the Center of Town." In *Complete Short Stories and Three Fat Men,"* 116–121. Translated by Aimee Anderson. Ann Arbor: Ardis, 1979.

Oruzheinikov, N. "K chistke apparata GOMETs." *Sovetskoe iskusstvo*, 2 February 1932, 4.

"Otkrytie pervogo Gosudarstvennogo tsirka." *Vestnik teatra* 70 (1920): 14.

"Ot s"ezda k s"ezdu." *Sovetskaia estrada i tsirk* 2 (1976): 2.

Otte, Marline. "Sarrasani's Theater of the World: Monumental Circus Entertainment in Dresden, from Kaiserreich to Third Reich." *German History* 17, no. 4 (1999): 527–42.

Oznobishin, N. *Illiuziony (Fokusniki i charodei)*. Moscow: Teakinopechat', 1929.

P. Ts. "O Samikh Sebe, tsirkachi o tsirke." *Sovetskoe iskusstvo*, 9 December 1932, 4.

"Partiinomu s"ezdu—dostoinuiu vstrechu." *Sovetskaia estrada i tsirk* 11 (1970): 1.

"Pervye derevenskie tsirki." *Tsirk i estrada* 11 (1928): 1.

Petrone, Karen. *Life Has Become More Joyous, Comrades: Celebrations in the Time of Stalin*. Bloomington: Indiana University Press, 2000.

Pisiotis, Argyrios K. "Images of Hate in the Art of War." In *Culture and Entertainment in Wartime Russia*, edited by Richard Stites, 141–56. Bloomington: Indiana University Press, 1995.

"Pogasla nepovtorimaia Nikulinskaia ulybka: Velikii artist ushel; Ushel navsegda." *Pravda*, 22–29 August 1997, 1.

Poliakov, Vladimir. *All Evening in the Ring* . . . Moscow: Vneshtorgizdat, 1971.

———. "Iumor na fronte." *Sovetskaia estrada i tsirk* 5 (1975): 6–7.

Popov, Oleg. "My Hero." In *The Soviet Circus: A Collection of Articles*, edited by Alexander Lipovsky, 39–59. Translated by Fainna Glagoleva. Moscow: Progress Publishers, 1967.

———. *Russian Clown*. Translated by Marion Koenig. London: Macdonald & Co., 1970.

———. "Tvorit' dlia naroda." *Sovetskii tsirk* 2 (1957): 3.

———. "Ulybka liudiam tak nuzhna." *Sovetskaia kul'tura*, 17 May 1977, 5.

Pozdneva, Ol'ga. "Ukrotitel' leopardov, repetitsiia na arena." *Moskovskii bol'shevik*, 2 February 1945, 4.

"Prazdnik sovetskogo tsirka." *Moskovskii bol'shevik*, 8 March 1946, 3.

"Primite moi komplimenty." *Sovetskaia estrada i tsirk* 10 (1970): 22–23.

Rabochaia brigada po chistke tsirkovogo upravleniia. "Shest' nomerov na stolakh." *Sovetskoe iskusstvo*, 3 March 1932, 4.

Radunskii, I. S. *Zapiski starogo klouna*. Edited by Iu. A. Dmitriev. Moscow: Iskusstvo, 1954.

Rafail, M. "Sotsialisticheskoe vospitanie novogo cheloveka." *Zhizn' iskusstva* 25 (1929): 1.

Raymond, Jack. "Circus Retains Lure in Moscow, It Attracts Big Crowds with Its Animals and Acrobats and Slapstick Skits." *New York Times*, 19 March 1956, 15.

Reid, Susan. E. "Cold War in the Kitchen: Gender and the De-Stalinization of Consumer Taste in the Soviet Union under Khrushchev." *Slavic Review* 61 (2002): 211–52.

———. "Masters of the Earth: Gender and Destalinisation in Soviet Reformist Painting of the Khrushchev Thaw." *Gender & History* 11 (1999): 276–312.

Renoff, Gregory J. *The Big Tent: The Traveling Circus in Georgia, 1820–1930*. Athens: University of Georgia Press, 2008.

"Reorganizatsiia tsirkov." *Vestnik teatra* 63 (1920): 7–8.

Riordan, James. *Sport in Soviet Society: Development of Sport and Physical Education in Russia and the USSR*. New York: Cambridge University Press, 1977.

Robin, Regine. "Popular Literature of the 1920s." In *Russia in the Era of NEP: Explorations in Soviet Society and Culture*, edited by Sheila Fitzpatrick, Alexander Rabinowitch, and Richard Stites, 253–67. Bloomington: Indiana University Press, 1991.

———. *Socialist Realism: An Impossible Aesthetic*. Translated by Catherine Porter. Stanford, CA: Stanford University Press, 1992.

Robinson, Harlow. "Composing for Victory: Classical Music." In *Culture and Entertainment in Wartime Russia*, edited by Richard Stites, 62–76. Bloomington: Indiana University Press, 1995.

Roslavlev, A. "Na manezhe tsirka." *Vechernaia Moskva*, 17 March 1945, 3.

Roth-Ey, Kristin. "Mass Media and the Remaking of Soviet Culture, 1950s–1960s." PhD diss., Princeton University, 2003.

Rothstein, Robert A. "Homeland, Home Town, and Battlefield: The Popular Song." In *Culture and Entertainment in Wartime Russia*, edited by Richard Stites, 77–94. Bloomington: Indiana University Press, 1995.

Rudnev, D. "Krug Smelosti, novaia programma v Leningradskom gosudarstvennom tsirke." *Pravda*, 4 February 1941, 6.

Rukavishnikov, N. "Vos'moi god Sovetskogo tsirka." *Tsirk* 5 (1926): 1.

Rumiantsev, Mikhail N. *Karandash: Na arene Sovetskogo tsirka*. Moscow: Iskusstvo, 1977.

———. "Voevat' smekhom." *Trud*, 16 September 1979, 4.

Rumiantseva, N. M. *Kloun i Vremia*. Moscow: Iskusstvo, 1989.

———. "Sovremennost' i chudesa na arene." *Sovetskaia estrada i tsirk* 2 (1974): 8–9.

"Russian People Mourn for Celebrated Actor Yuri Nikulin." *Itar-Tass News Agency*, 26 August 1997.

"Russia's Yuri Nikulin Dies 16 Days after Heart Surgery." *Itar-Tass News Agency*, 21 August 1997.

Salisbury, Harrison E. "Soviet Clowns Poke Fun at U.S. by Adding Wit to Kremlin's Line." *New York Times*, 20 April 1949, 1.

Sartorti, Rosalinde. "Stalinism and Carnival: Organisation and Aesthetics of Political Holidays." In *The Culture of the Stalin Period*, edited by Hans Günther, 41–77. New York: St. Martin's Press, 1990.

Saxon, A. H. *Enter Foot and Horse: A History of Hippodrama in England and France*. New Haven, CT: Yale University Press, 1968.

Schechter, Joel. *The Congress of Clowns and Other Russian Circus Acts*. San Francisco: Kropotkin Club of San Francisco, 1998.

Segal, Harold B. "Drama of Struggle: The Wartime Stage Repertoire." In *Culture and Entertainment in Wartime Russia*, edited by Richard Stites, 108–25. Bloomington: Indiana University Press, 1995.

Semenov, E. "Druzhba." *Sovetskii tsirk* 9 (1961): 14–15.

Serebrennikov, Robert. "New Big Diamond Named after Yuri Nikulin." *Itar-Tass News Agency*, 28 August 1997.

Shakhidzhanian, Vladimir. "V tsirke rabotat' trudno." *Sovetskaia kul'tura*, 13 November 1986.

Shepard, Richard F. "The Ebullient Moscow Circus Arrives, but Apprehensively." *New York Times*, 4 October 1964, 42.

———. "One-Ring Moscow State Circus Begins Engagement at Garden." *New York Times*, 25 September 1963, 38.

Shershenevich, Vadim. "Tsirk: Neobkhodimo meshatel'stvo." *Zrelishche* 2 (1922): 15.

"Shest' nomerov na stolakh." *Sovetskoe iskusstvo*, 3 March 1932, 4.

Shibaev, Andrei."Nashi tsirki." *Rabochii zritel'* 31 (1924): 13.

Shirai, A. "Novaia stranitsa v zhanre." *Sovetskaia estrada i tsirk* 1 (1970): 15.

Shklovskii, Viktor. "The Clown, Comedy and Tragedy." In *The Soviet Circus: A Collection of Articles*, edited by Alexander Lipovsky, 33–38. Translated by Fainna Glagoleva. Moscow: Progress Publishers, 1967.

Shtraus, K. "U 'Dedushki' Russkoi Aviatsii." *Sovetskii tsirk* 10 (1962): 10–11.

Shvarts, V. "Iunost' otrpavliaetsia v put'." *Sovetskaia kul'tura*, 5 July 1983, 4.

Shvetsov, V. V. "Mysli o tsirke." *Tsirk* 6 (1925): 6–7.

Shvydkoi, M. E., ed. *Tsirkovoe iskusstvo Rossii, entsiklopediia*. Moscow: Bol'shaia Rossiiskaia entsiklopediia, 2000.

"Slava bogatyriam kosmosa!" *Sovetskii tsirk* 9 (1962): 2.

Slavskii, R. *Leonid Engibarov*. Moscow: Iskusstvo, 1972.

———. *Sovetskii tsirk v gody velikoi otechestvennoi voiny*. Moscow: Moskovskii izdatel'sko-poligraficheskii tekhnikum imeni russkogo pervopechatnika Ivana Fedorova, 1975.

———. *Vitalii Lazarenko*. Moscow: Iskusstvo, 1980.

Smetankina, Larisa. "Yeltsin, Chernomyrdin Pay Last Respects to Russia's Best Comic." *Itar-Tass News Agency*, 25 August 1997.

Sokolov, Ippolit. "Teilor-Aktor." *Tsirk* 4 (1925): 11.

Sokolov, Sergei. "Za sovetizatsiiu tsirka." *Tsirk i estrada* 14 (1929): 8.

Soria, Zhorzh. "Eti gastroli nadolgo ostanutsia v pamiat parizhan." *Sovetskaia kul'tura*, 14 April 1956, 4.

Sotnik. "Tsirk i trud." *Tsirk* 5 (1925): 10.

"Sovetskii Tsirk." *Sovetskoe iskusstvo*, 6 October 1938, 1.

"Sovetskii Tsirk v Irane." *Vechernaia Moskva*, 12 December 1945, 3.

"Sozdanie Tsirkacha—obshchestvennika." *Tsirk i estrada* 2 (1929): 1.

Speaight, George. *A History of the Circus*. San Diego: A.S. Barnes and Company, 1980.

Stites, Richard. *Culture and Entertainment in Wartime Russia*. Bloomington: Indiana University Press, 1995.

———. *Russian Popular Culture: Entertainment and Society since 1900*. New York: Cambridge University Press, 1992.

Stoddart, Helen. *Rings of Desire: Circus History and Representation*. Manchester: Manchester University Press, 2000.

Stolee, Margaret K. "Homeless Children in the USSR, 1917–1957." *Soviet Studies* 40 (1988): 64–83.

Strel'tsov, N. "Novoe v iskusstve tsirka." *Sovetskoe iskusstvo*, 8 March 1945, 3.

Tait, Peta. *Circus Bodies: Cultural Identity in Aerial Performance*. New York: Routledge, 2005.

———. *Converging Realities: Feminism in Australian Theatre*. Sydney: Currency Press, 1994.

———. "Danger Delights: Texts of Gender and Race in Aerial Performance." *New Theatre Quarterly* 12 (1996): 43–49.

———. "Feminine Free Fall: A Fantasy of Freedom." *Theatre Journal* 48 (1996): 27–34.

Tartakovskii, M. "Na arene tsirka." *Sovetskii Sport*, 23 October 1958, 4.

Taylor, Richard. "A 'Cinema for the Millions'—Soviet Socialist Realism and the Problem of Film Comedy." *Journal of Contemporary History* 18 (1983): 439–61.

———. *Film Propaganda: Soviet Russia and Nazi Germany*. New York: Harper & Row, 1979.

Tess, Tat'iana. "Aktsent smeshnogo." *Izvestiia*, 22 November 1939, 4.

"Tol'ko tsifry." *Sovetskaia kul'tura*, 18 September 1979, 4.

To-Ramo. "Kak Ia pobedil sebia." *Tsirk* 4 (1926): 8.

"To-Ramo o svoikh opytakh." *Tsirk* 4 (1926): 8.

Towsen, John H. *Clowns*. New York: Hawthorn Books, 1976.

Trembath, Gordon R. *The Great Moscow Circus 1968*. Melbourne: Michael C. Edgley, 1968.

Tridtsatipiatiletnii iubilei Vitaliia Efimovicha Lazarenko. Moscow: Mosoblit, 1933.

Trumbull, Robert. "Soviet Bombards India with Arts." *New York Times*, 5 January 1954, 3.

Truzzi, Marcello. "The Decline of the American Circus." In *Sociology and Everyday Life*, edited by Marcello Truzzi, 314–22. Englewood Cliffs, NJ: Prentice-Hall, 1981.

"Tsirk." *Vestnik teatra* 39 (1919): 13.

"Tsirk i Estrada—Udarnye formy zrelishchnogo iskusstva." *Tsirk i estrada* 7 (1930): 1.

"Tsirk massam—sintez tsirka." *Tsirk* 9 (1925): 6.

Tsirk pod vodoi (Chernyi pirat). Leningrad: Teakinopechat', 1929.

"Tsirki na mestakh." *Vestnik teatra* 78 (1921): 24.

Tsivian, Yuri. *Early Cinema in Russia and its Cultural Reception*. Edited by Richard Taylor. Translated by Alan Bodger. New York: Routledge, 1994.

"TsUGTs pered Leningradskim oblastnym sovetom po delam iskusstva." *Zhizn' iskusstva* 12 (1929): 4.

Tumanov, I. "Arena Druzhby." *Sovetskii tsirk* 3 (1957): 1–4.

Urazov, Izmail. *Fakiry*. Moscow: Tea-kino-pechat', 1928.

——. "Moskva Gorit' v tsirke." *Tsirk i estrada* 12 (1930): 6.

Vakhramov, V. "I gamadrila mozhon obuchit." *Sovetskaia kul'tura*, 15 February 1983, 4.

Van der Post, Laurens. *Journey into Russia*. Covelo, CA: Island Press, 1964.

Veksler, Igor. "Chernomyrdin Offers 'Any Help' to Save Actor's Life." *Itar-Tass News Agency*, 13 August 1997.

Velekhova, Nina. "Strasti krugloi areny." *Sovetskaia estrada i tsirk* 9 (1972): 12–13.

Venskii, P. "Zveri ukrotitelia Klichisa." *Vechernaia Moskva*, 19 July 1945, 4.

Verhagen, Marcus. "Re-figurations of Carnival: The Comic Performer in Fin-de-siècle Parisian Art." PhD diss., University of California, Berkeley, 1994.

——. "Whipstrokes." *Representations* 58 (1997): 115–40.

Vichevsky, Anatoly. *Soviet Literary Culture in the 1970s: The Politics of Irony with an Anthology of Ironic Prose*. Translated by Michael Biggins and Anatoly Vishevsky. Gainesville: University Press of Florida, 1993.

Viktorov, A. "Internatsional'naia programma." *Sovetskaia kul'tura*, 21 September 1973, 3.

——. "Neischerpaemye vozmozhnosti." *Sovetskaia kul'tura*, 2 February 1961, 3.

———. *S perom u Karandasha*. Moscow: Molodaia gvardiia, 1971.

Von Geldern, James. *Bolshevik Festivals, 1917–1920*. Berkeley: University of California Press, 1993.

Von Wiegand, Sharmion. "In the Soviet Circus, Fun Goes Serious, the Many New Shows Mix with Amusement, and the Clown Uses Satire for Social Ends." *New York Times*, 26 November 1933, SM10.

Voprosy planirovaniia iskusstva, materialy vsesoiuznogo soveshchaniia po planirovaniiu iskusstva pri gosplane SSSR 10–12/VI 1930 g. Moscow: Gosudarstvennoe Planovo-khoziaistvennoe izdatel'stvo, 1930.

"V poslednii raz na Manezhe." *Rossiiskaia gazeta*, 26 August 1997, 1.

"V tsirkakh." *Vestnik teatra* 76–77 (1920): 23.

Warner, Elizabeth A. *Folk Theatre and Dramatic Entertainments in Russia*. Cambridge: Chadwyck-Healey, 1987.

———. *The Russian Folk Theatre*. The Hague: Mouton, 1977.

Weiner, Douglas R. *Models of Nature: Ecology, Conservation, and Cultural Revolution in Soviet Russia*. Bloomington: Indiana University Press, 1988.

Williams, Daniel. "All of Russia Grieves for Beloved Comic Who Brought Light to Dark Days." *Washington Post*, 23 August 1997, A20.

Wren, Christopher. "In Russia, the Circus Is an Art Form." *New York Times*, 14 December 1975, D5.

Yarrow, Andrew L. "Moscow Circus to Tour America after 10 Years." *New York Times*, 10 March 1988, C26.

Youngblood, Denise. *Movies for the Masses: Popular Cinema and Soviet Society in the 1920s*. Cambridge: Cambridge University Press, 1992.

Yurchak, Alexei. *Everything Was Forever, Until It Was No More: The Last Soviet Generation*. Princeton, NJ: Princeton University Press, 2006.

Yutkevitch, Sergei Iosipovitch Yutkevitch. "Teenage Artists of the Revolution." Translated by David Robinson. In *Cinema in Revolution: The Heroic Era of Soviet Film*, edited by Luda Schnitzer, Jean Schnitzer, and Marcel Martin, 11–42. New York: Hill and Wang, 1973.

"Zametki na poliakh." *Tsirk i estrada* 2 (1928): 9.

Zapashnyi, Mstislav."Peregruzki na . . . Konveiere." *Sovetskaia kul'tura*, 4 January 1977, 4.

Zapashnyi, Valter Mikhailovich. *Risk, bor'ba, liubov'*. Moscow: Vagrius, 2002.

Zarin, Mikhail. "Gde traditsii, a gde shtampy . . ." *Sovetskaia kul'tura*, 3 September 1968, 3.

Zashkovoi. "O tsirke, nasha anketa." *Tsirk* 2 (1925): 8.

Zaslavskii, D. "Tvorcheskii smotr v Moskovskom tsirke." *Trud*, 5 March 1946, 4.

Zh-i., V. "Tsirk: Otkrytie pervogo gostsirka." *Zrelishche* 8 (1922): 25.

Zheltov, I. I. "O tsirke, nasha anketa." *Tsirk* 3 (1925): 5.

Zhukov, I. "Razrushim bar'er mezhdu nami, diskussionaia." *Tsirk* 11 (1926): 6.

Zguta, Russell. *Russian Minstrels: A History of the Skomorokhi*. Philadelphia: University of Pennsylvania Press, 1978.

Zinin, S. "Zinaida Tarasova i mrachnyi volshebnik." *Moskovskii komsomolets*, 14 September 1963, 3.

Zubkova, Elena. *Russia After the War: Hopes, Illusions, and Disappointments, 1945–1957*. Translated by Hugh Ragsdale. New York: M.E. Sharpe, 1998.

Index

Page numbers in italics indicate illustrations.

Taylorism and, 51; value of hard work and, 45
eggs, 128, 130–31, 133–34, 136
Ehrenburg, Il'ia, 33
Eilik, 108–9
Eisenstein, Sergei, 7
Eizhen, 39
elephants, 11, 18, 44–45, 197
elitism, 41, 57, 129, 239n2
El'shevskii, N., 200
Engibarov, Leonid, *125*, 201–2, 205–6
England, 12, 24, 68; Cold War era and, 130, 138–39, 144; as imperialistic, 130; offensive peace and, 165–66, 169–70; Wembley Stadium and, 169–70
Entente, 35–36
entrepreneurs, 6, 14, 20–21, 30, 49, 52–55
Erdman, Boris, 33
Ermans, B., 82–83
Ermans, Viktor, 79–81, 153, 169, 186, 244n2
escapism, 8, 14, 26, 68, 91, 218–19
Estonia, 10

factories, 43, 59, 63, 76, 81, 131, 145, 237n5
Fadeeva, O., 150–53, 158–59
fakirs, 18, 46–47, 50, 244n4
farmers, 13, 28
fascism, 94–96, 152, 237n5
"Fashions" (performance), 143
Fatima, 196
fear: animal trainers and, 102–6, 108; of fear, 106–10; national security and, 16, 130, 136, 143, 150, 159; William Tell routines and, 106–10
February Revolution, 40
Fedorov, B., 172
Filatov, Valentin: bears and, 178, 195–96; offensive peace and, 165–66; pictures of, *123*, *124*; science and, 178
Finikov, A. K., 43
Fink, Il'ia, 147
fire breathers, 51
First International Circus Festival, 153–54
First State Circus, 9, 33–34, 43, 74
Fisher and Wolf, 69
Fitzpatrick, Sheila, 236n74, 239n2, 248n3

Five-Year Plan for Industrialization and Socialist Construction, 59–60, 63–64, 75, 77, 80, 145, 219
"Flight of an Airplane around the Eiffel Tower" (performance), 71
flips, 14–15, 18, 35–36, 49, 59, 111, 187
food: animal acts and, 98; clown skits on, 130, 133–34; eggs, 128, 130–31, 133–34, 136; harvest failures and, 137; privations and, 16, 48–49, 128, 137; socialism and, 128, 130, 132–33, 137
Foregger, N. M., 33
France, 7, 38, 139, 165–66, 168, 170, 193, 204, 218
Frankel, Max, 210
Friar, 36
friendships: "Arena of Friendship" and, 167, 169–70; international, 164–70; multinational, 170–75; offensive peace and, 163–75
Fritz, 81, 98–99

"Galactica" (performance), 180
Galich, B., 167–68
Ganetskii, I. S., 76
gangsters, 5, 13, 28
geese, 8, 96–97
George, Lloyd, 36
Georgia, 10, 167, 172
Georgiev, A., 171
German Democratic Republic (GDR), 164–65, 167–68
Gismatulin, M., 157
Glavkurupr, 54
Goebbels, Joseph, 95, 134, 140
Gogol, Nikolai, 4
Goleizovskii, Kas'ian, 33
Golubtseva, 143–44
Gordon, Michael R., vii
Gorei, Moris, 44, 65
Gorkii, Maksim, 33–34
Gorkomkhoz, 210
Gorky Park, 168
Gorokhov, V., 194
Great Transformation, 15–16, 60, 64, 90, 219, 234n2
Greece, 133, 141

White Army, 36
"The White Poodle" (Kuprin), 8
Wild West acts, 32
Williams, Daniel, 5
William Tell routines, 106–10
Wilson, Woodrow, 36
women: acrobats and, 23, 153–55; aerialists and, 13, 19, 23–24, 153–54, 180; animal trainers and, 23, 153, 155; Antonescu routine and, 96; beauty and, 23, 147, 152–56, 177; breaking laws of nature and, 15–16; circus themes and, 193; clowns and, 109, 209, 213; Cold War era and, 145–57; costumes of, 156–57; cunning, 34; double burden of, 24, 129; equestrian, 111, 156; eroticization of, 23–24; First International Circus Festival and, 153–54; Five-Year Plan and, 63; greater population of, 128; Great Transformation and, 90; gymnastics and, 153–54, 244n2; happiness and, 24, 129, 145–51, 154; of high birth, 6; household duties of, 130, 147–52; infantile bourgeois, 35; intellectual, 55; juggling and, 153; late Soviet circus and, 193; laws of nature and, 72; as master of ceremonies, 153; material prosperity and, 145–57; 153; maternal instincts of, 23, 150, 153, 159; middle and lower classes and, 227n63; military and, 147; Mother Moscow and, 146–47; narratives on, 147–52; national security and, 159; offensive peace and, 165, 167, 172–73, 177; population demographics of, 128; rhetoric on, 23; socialism and, 24; "Someone Else's Mother" and, 147–49; Soviet ideal and, 15–16, 19, 23–24, 60, 63–64, 66, 72, 75, 90, 145–61; unwed mothers and, 128; virtues of, 153, 155–56; Vladimirskii paper and, 66; World War II era and, 23–24

Wordsworth, William, 68
"Workers Creating a City" (performance), 35
Workers' Leader, 36
World Festival of Youth and Students, 188
World War I era, 32
World War II era, 10, 16, 21, 91, 182, 219–20, acrobats and, 104, 111; air raids and, 101; audiences and, 93–94, 100–101, 106, 108–10; black-outs and, 92; clowns and, 93–98, 102, 106–11; deaths during, 128; gymnastics and, 111; Hitler and, 97–100, 138–40, 144; industry and, 94; labor and, 94; laughter and, 93–102, 110; Moscow Circus and, 92, 102; Nazis and, 93, 96–100, 138–40; rhetoric and, 16, 104; women and, 23–24
Wrangel, Petr, 36
Wren, Christopher, 205
wrestlers, 33, 36–37, 49–50

Yankees, 12, 36
Yeltsin, Boris, 3
Youngblood, Denise, 229n6
Young Kirgizia, 172
Yurchak, Aleksei, 248n14
Yusupov, Akram, 211

Zagoskin, M. N., 7
Zapashnyi, Maritsa, 155–56
Zapashnyi, Mstislav, 179, 191
Zapashnyi, Val'ter, 155–56
Zaporozh'e, 11
Zarin, Michael, 187
Zaslavskii, D., 105–6
Zhak, 107, 137
Zheltov, I. I., 11, 53
Zhizn' iskusstva journal, 70
Zinin, S., 177
Ziskind, E., 155–56
Zubkova, Elena, 128, 137–38